FROM

GRUNTS
TO
GIGABYTES

COMMUNICATIONS AND SOCIETY

DAN LACY

University of Illinois Press   Urbana and Chicago

P
91
L 313
1996

This book is printed on acid-free paper.

An earlier version of chapter 11 appeared in *Publishing Research
Quarterly* 9 (Summer 1993): 3–15.

Library of Congress Cataloging-in-Publication Data

Lacy, Dan Mabry, 1914–
    From grunts to gigabytes : communications and society / Dan Lacy.
    p.   cm.
    Includes bibliographical references and index.
    ISBN 0-252-02228-9 (cloth). — ISBN 0-252-06531-X (pbk.)
    1. Communication—History. 2. Communication—Technological
innovations. 3. Communication—Social aspects. 4 Communication
policy—History. I. Title.
P91.L313 1996
302.2'09—dc20   95-32512
                                                              CIP

For Hope, once more, with love

Introduction

Human beings have communicated with each other since the hominid genus emerged, beginning no doubt with grunts and gestures and employing now an almost incredible array of technologies that can convey across the face of the globe living, moving images and that can store, arrange, manipulate, and transmit billions of bytes of data with the instant speed of light. Their enlarged ability to communicate more elaborate bodies of information more quickly and to broader audiences has been achieved in part by the development of new skills, such as speaking and writing, and in increasing part by the invention of new technology, from pen and paper to television and the computer.

The patterns of skills and technologies with which humans have been able to communicate have profoundly affected the societies in which they have lived. Their capacity for speech itself, indeed, may be said to have defined them as modern humans, as Homo sapiens sapiens.

One of the results of developing more effective modes of communication has been the creation of power. Hominids who could talk in full sentences had great advantages over those who could only grunt and gesture and over all other animals lacking even that ability, and the modern language-competent form of Homo sapiens prevailed over its contemporaries and predecessors. The Egyptians and Chinese and Greeks and Romans, who could write, erected empires over the illiterate barbarians. The little European peninsula, which first made effective use of print, swept out over the world, mastering societies with limited or no use of the press. The industrial societies of the late nineteenth century combined techniques of producing paper from wood pulp, mechanical typesetting, and high-speed rotary presses to make print abundantly available for almost everyone. In part in consequence of this achievement they were able to divide and control the rest of the world. And in the late twentieth century the countries of Western Europe and

North America that had integrated the computer into their economies were able clearly to dominate those societies that had failed to do so.

The developing techniques of communication helped to convey power in two ways. The first is by enlarging and speeding the flow of current communication. It might be the capacity of the chief of a hunting band to lay out plans and signal attacks, or the ability that writing gave a Roman emperor to convey instructions to and receive report from distant commanders and governors, or the opportunity of a nineteenth-century general to use the telegraph to stay in instant contact with his troops, or the capacity of a contemporary corporate executive to use the computer to keep current track of operational details throughout a global company. Whatever the case, power is invested in the society that can send messages fastest and farthest.

But communications systems also convey power in another and perhaps even more important way. Different methods of communication provide different ways of storing, preserving, and providing access to a society's accumulated knowledge. In the chapters that follow, this accumulated lore of a society is referred to as its "public compendium": all the knowledge that a society has stored and can make available to its members. In preliterate eras this compendium could exist only in the flickering domains of human memory. The lore of any tribe existed only in the minds of its elders, handed down orally to oncoming generations. It was subject to erosion or loss as memory faded or sages died. Merely to maintain a society's precious store of knowledge required unending effort; its increase could be achieved only with the slow accretion of centuries, and any really complex accumulation of knowledge would press against the capacity of human memory to contain it.

Writing for the first time made it possible to maintain knowledge outside the frail grasp of memory and to accumulate bodies of knowledge beyond the capacity of the human mind to retain. After print was invented, it could preserve the public compendium more assuredly than could scarce manuscripts and could make it available to a far wider public. Photography, with its extension to motion picture films and videotapes, has made it possible to add visual images to the verbal descriptions in the public compendium.

From the invention of writing onward the public compendium was created by embodying information in artifacts (books and later records or pictures or films), duplicating them in numerous copies, and preserving the copies in collections. For the first time, the computer made it possible to incorporate information in the public compendium without these constraints. By strokes on a keyboard, information could be embodied in discs from which it could be drawn by any appropriately equipped and connected user. The cost threshold of incorporating information into the compendium was thus radically lowered, with one act of recording taking the place of making, distributing, and housing thousands of duplicates. Enormously increased bodies of information can now be assembled and used, from philosophical texts to the myriads of records of transactions on which the conduct of affairs is based. Through computerized catalogs and indexes the computer has also vastly facilitated access to the public compendium, not only as it is stored in computer accessible databases but also as it exists in print. This capacity to accumulate information, to organize it and make it available, and to preserve it for future use has grown with giant and rapidly accelerating leaps as the technology of communication has moved from writing through print and audiovisual records to the computer. It has made possible the advance of civilization by the progressive accumulation of knowledge until today humankind can have access to an almost infinite store that is the source of society's almost dangerously unlimited power.

The communications system of a society not only helps to determine its aggregate power but also goes far to determine the distribution of power within the society. The sharing of power tends to correspond to the sharing of access to information. In preliterate societies, all can speak and all can hear; there is rough equality of communication and, in most societies, of economic status. Subsequent developments in communication have required the learning of special skills, such as reading, writing, and computer use. And increasingly they have required the use of expensive equipment such as printing presses, motion picture studios, broadcasting facilities, and computer set-ups. This has imposed some limits on who can receive communications and even severer limits on who can control their dissemination. Even more important, the new technologies have required the creation of large organizations for their management: publishing houses, motion picture producers and distributors, and broadcasting networks, thus concentrating power in their directors.

Thus the newer communications technologies have thrust ambiguously in opposite directions. They have greatly enlarged the audience for communication so that the whole body of the public is served by mass circulation newspapers and magazines and by broadcasts. On the other hand, they have narrowed control over the input of information into these massive systems and vested it in the large corporations, or in some cases government agencies, that own the requisite facilities. The mass democracies that emerged in the industrialized countries over the last century and a half would hardly have been possible without mass print and later without broadcasting; yet the very developments that drew the whole population into the sharing of political power opened the possibility of their manipulation.

The increasingly close relationship of means of communication to power has invited, indeed, has seemed to demand, the intervention of governments to exercise control. This control from the early days of printing has included measures intended to prevent the dissemination of information or ideas that might challenge or weaken established authority, religious or political. With the rise of popular government came a conviction that the power of the people required limits on the power of officeholders to determine what could and what could not be made available to the public to read. "Freedom of the press" became a dogma of the democracies and in the United States was incorporated in the Constitution. With the increasing role of large-scale organizations in the corporate control of new communications technologies, however, came the realization that freedom of communication needed to be protected not only *from* the government but also *by* the government. In consequence, there have been important, and controversial, actions by government to limit monopoly or oligopoly power over communication and to regulate the licensees entrusted with the operation of telegraph and telephone companies and the conduct of broadcasting, as well as measures to provide the literacy and other skills needed to share in the flow of information.

In general the effect of any new technology, whether it be writing or printing or broadcasting or computers, has been to create a small privileged class that has had the requisite skills and facilities to use the new technology. In the early days of literacy only rulers and their scribes and priestly hierarchies could use the new powers; in the early days of computers only very large corporations and government agencies were similarly empowered. As each new communication system matured, the ability to use it broadened. Today literacy is generally assumed for almost everyone in industrialized countries, and school children are made familiar with computers from an early age. Nevertheless, differences remain, and even in advanced societies the difference between those who are and those who are not effectively literate in a full sense is one of the principal determinants of who are and who are not able to participate fully in the economy and the polity.

The differing modes of communication affect the structure of society as well as the residence of power. When communication is only oral, social units are necessarily small, villages or tribes, within face-to-face contact or the range of messengers. Writing made possible empires as the range of communication broadened. But with literacy limited and writing confined to manuscripts, communication still had to flow through personal contact, with commands filtering down from kings and popes and reports moving upward through feudal and ecclesiastical hierarchies. Each successive development in communications— print, mass printing of the late nineteenth century, and broadcasting— made possible direct communication from a central source to larger and larger bodies of individual recipients without the necessity of passing through a hierarchical chain. Print made possible the Protestant Reformation by enabling Luther, Calvin, and other leaders to reach their audiences directly without the intervention of the established priesthood. Within the Catholic church itself the ability of the papacy to make its written decrees and encyclicals available directly to parish priests and to the faithful lessened the power of territorial bishops and archbishops. Similarly, print enabled laws and royal commands to be disseminated directly to the public, empowering the central governments of the newly emerging states at the expense of the feudal baronies. In our own day we have seen evangelists enabled by television to reach enormous audiences directly, independent of the structure of established churches. Candidates for office similarly appeal to voters and raise funds directly by the use of television, diminishing the role of party organizations.

Different means of communication also affect our internal perceptions of reality. In more traditional societies, before the audiovisual revolution, when travel was rare and the impact even of print was smaller, the family and the local community were a matrix within which concepts and values were formed. Those concepts and values were likely to be relatively uniform and compelling within the community and relatively stable from generation to generation. The ubiquity of print and even more of television in our present society provides a much broader and more diffuse matrix for character formation, enhancing opportunities for independence and change but weakening coherence and stability.

When we react to conditions or events beyond our immediate perception, we are responding not to reality itself but to the pictures of reality in our minds, to use an expression of Walter Lippmann. Those pictures are shaped by the messages that flow through our systems of communication. Those systems by virtue of their technology and structure affect, in turn, the form and content of those messages. What is novel, dramatic, and lending itself to vivid imagery may predominate in those media whose technology and economy press them to seek mass audiences. The ownership of media by large corporations may dispose them toward the conveyance of conservative messages sustaining the status quo; a technology that permits messages to be conveyed without large investments, like cassette recordings, mimeographing, and desktop publishing, conversely may allow for the dissemination of dissident views. Examples are the clandestine distribution of cassettes of Khomeini's sermons in prerevolutionary Iran or the *samizdat* publishing by typewriter and carbon paper in the Soviet Union.

But the shaping of images of reality by the means of communication does not depend entirely on the control of those means; in part it is inherent in their own character. The very use of words themselves splits the all-surrounding envelopment of reality and seizes hold of and brings to attention selected aspects of that reality, like a spotlight playing on individual objects within an indeterminate mist. Words make possible the creation in the mind of a usable picture of the environment in which we are immersed, stripped of irrelevancies.

The nature of the pictures in our minds tends to be projected on our concepts of reality. The mental pictures within an oral society are likely to be fluctuant and impermanent, embodied only in the changeable flows of human memory. Hence in such societies reality itself was conceived as fluctuant and impermanent. The gods were envisioned as many and changing in their forms and character; mythical creatures abounded; geography was vague and shifting.

With the coming of writing, texts became fixed and unaltering, stretching in orderly line after line. The pictures in the mind in turn became stable, and in time a literate mentality emerged, shaped by the pattern of written texts, that saw the universe as orderly and governed by uniform rules. Broadcasting in our day has restored some of the characteristics of oral mentality; the computer has reinforced those of the highly literate culture.

All these manifold consequences of our changing systems of communication are determined by three factors: the inherent technology of the method of communication, which imposes certain patterns and limitations on what is conveyed and whom it reaches; the pattern of organization and control, which becomes increasingly important as the systems of communication require increasing investment in an ever more complex and expensive technology; and, finally, the public policy that society follows in encouraging, limiting, and shaping the systems of communication. Insofar as communications help to determine the patterns and evolution of our society, public communications policy is our instrument to help shape our own future.

It will be the purpose of this book to examine various systems of communication that society has evolved, from human speech to the computer and the satellite, to consider the effects of each on our society,

and to give thought to appropriate public policy. Geographically, attention will narrow from humankind in considering language, to Western
Europe with respect to print, and to the industrialized West, particularly the United States, in discussion of the newer media. The treatment
will necessarily be brief and suggestive rather than detailed or defini-
tive, but perhaps it may be useful in opening areas for discussion.

From Grunts to Gigabytes

—1—

Words

In the beginning was the word.
—John 1:1 (RSV)

So out of the ground the Lord God formed every beast of the field and every bird of the air, and brought them to the man to see what he would call them; and whatever the man called every living creature, that was its name.
—Genesis 2:19–20 (RSV)

Then they said, "Come let us build ourselves a city, and a tower with its top in the heavens, and let us make a name for ourselves, lest we be scattered abroad upon the face of the whole earth." And the Lord came down to see the city and the tower, which the sons of men had built. And the Lord said, "Behold, they are one people, and they have all one language; and this is only the beginning of what they will do; and nothing they propose to do will now be impossible for them. Come, let us go down, and there confuse their language, that they may not understand one another's speech." So the Lord scattered them abroad from there over the face of all the earth, and they left off building the city.
—Genesis 11:4–8 (RSV)

Perhaps we cheat a little in the quotation above from the Gospel according to St. John. Although "logos" in the Greek original was used as a term for what we call a "word," its meaning, especially as St. John used it, was far broader. He meant something like a conceived ideal, an ideal that had existed forever in the mind of God, and, indeed, in a sense *was* God and was translated ("became flesh") in the person of Christ.

And yet we are not too far from the mark, for the whole concept of an idea, a logos, existing in the mind and related to, but independent of, tangible reality is one made possible only by words, our very instrument of conception. And thus, truly, the word *was* present at the beginning, certainly at the beginning of humanness.

The authors of Genesis conceived of speech as the first power God gave to man, at the very beginning, even before He had created woman. It was the means by which God gave man dominion over the beasts of the field and the birds of the air. By naming them, he could hold them in his mind and become their master.

And in this story there is a deep truth, for it was the achievement of speech that separated the relatively weak, clawless, and fangless humans from their fellow hominids and from all other animals and made them specifically human, endowed with such a power that ultimately, in the words of Genesis, "nothing that they propose to do will now be impossible for them."

Nobody knows when speech began. Biological evolution had proceeded over tens of millions of years from the first appearance of mammals to the appearance of the hominid lines, and the genus *Homo* emerged perhaps two million years ago. We can only guess at the potentialities of speech from the size and pattern of brains as determined from the interior surface of fossil skulls and from the structure of the pharynx. The ability to produce a considerable variety of humanlike sounds may have existed in the earliest members of the genus, but even the simplest speech probably does not antedate Neanderthals, beginning 250,000 to 300,000 years ago. And the language ability even of Neanderthals may have been quite limited. A reasonable guess would be that although archaic humans, including Neanderthals and other species and subspecies, may have had limited vocabularies, they almost certainly lacked the extensive vocabulary and, even more important, the complex grammar and syntax that enable modern individuals to form sentences and construct a verbally embodied image of reality.

The achievement of this much more powerful capacity probably began with the emergence of biologically modern people in Africa one to two hundred thousand years ago. In Western Europe the humans of the Aurignacian period, beginning thirty-five to forty thousand years ago, suddenly—at least in an evolutionary time scale—developed a complex set of tools, made not only of stone but of bone and ivory as well, of differentiated types made for a variety of purposes. At the same time, beautiful images were painted on cave walls, and beads and other forms of personal adornment were made. Clearly, this new breed of humans, differing physically from the Neanderthals, had achieved a rich set of conceptual patterns and images. Their paintings appear to have been related to shamanistic rituals. Settlements became more dense, necessarily involving more complex social relations. So elaborate a cultural repertoire could hardly have been achieved without a full and complex language.

Modern humanity, so empowered, spread rapidly across the world, eliminating all other hominid species. Every tribe of every race and every environment, from the most "primitive" to the most advanced, has a rich and fluent language with an abundant vocabulary and a structured syntax—a language capable of addressing all the needs of its life. A human could be defined as the animal that talks.

It was speech that made Homo sapiens sapient, that provided a competitive advantage as a hunter and an organizer of social life, that separated human beings from all other animals, even from other primates. It provided the capacity to communicate among the members of a hunting band or war party, to convey knowledge, to issue commands, to report the presence of game or of camping grounds, and to deal competently with the demands of Stone Age life.

But the power of words was, and is, vastly greater than the achievement of functional communication. All words are abstractions. They reach into the continuing chaos surrounding every individual and enable the word-user to single out a thing or quality or event that needs attention, to withdraw it from the encompassing totality, and to hold it in mind. He or she can deal then with the concept, not with the reality itself. With the use of words one can create categories: "Man" or "stone" or "tree" need not symbolize a particular man or stone or tree, but the whole class to which it belongs. Even the name of a particular person refers not only to his or her manifestation at the moment but also to all of his or her existence, past and future as well. Words can be combined into sentences, creating a flow of events or a scene existing in the mind or setting forth a general rule: "A clay pot heated by fire becomes hard and strong."

These capacities of words enable humans to create in their minds a picture of selected parts of reality, paralleling the reality itself but simplified, clarified, and rearranged by the use of word-symbols. With words, humans can wrest from the otherwise incomprehensible flood of sensation enveloping them a usable universe existing in symbols within their minds, from which they can reach forth again into the encompassing reality to impress their will upon it. Abstraction from reality through the use of words becomes the means of mastering reality.

Words bring into being a whole new group of cognitive essences. "Meaning" is born of words, as the relation of a worded statement to an underlying reality; "truth" as well, as a measure of the quality of that relationship; and "comprehension," as the successful symbolizing of an aspect of reality in a pattern of words. Consciousness, too, as the knowing that we know, is made possible by the words with which we express our knowing. A web of words enables us to reach out into the dark reality about us and draw forth into the light of our minds that conceived universe in which we live our conscious lives.

But living words are not merely abstractions that draw conception from reality. They are metaphors as well, whose meaning is created from human experience. When we say that a girl's eyes are "blue," we are not making the abstract statement that light refracted from her pupils has a wave-length of approximately 475 nanometers; we are saying that her eyes seem like the clear sky or the sea in certain lights or near the hue of violets. We cannot use the word "yellow" without the sentence being haunted with cowardice and gold and sunlight and buttercups. Every word not only abstracts meaning from reality but also adds a human and poetic investment of meaning from the memory of past experience. Meaning is not an invariant and dyadic relation between a word and its referent. It is a triadic relation in which the experience and qualities of the knower flow into the meaning.

The austere demands of mastery force us toward the use of new kinds of terms cleansed of these connotative and metaphorical additions in order to achieve an abstract and invariant correspondence between symbol and fact. Biological taxonomy retreats to Latin, and the white oak becomes *Quercus alba* to clear the mind of sturdiness and endurance and the oak-hulled ships of the line; "lepidopteran" blots out the shimmering image of "butterfly." Numbers seek to escape the net of words entirely, so that "2" represents not "two" or "zwei" or "deux" or "dos" but the bare concept of twoness itself. Systems uncomfortable with names that represent an individual in all his or her diversity—wife, mother, executive, dancer, lover, tennis-player, father, son—substitute account numbers, stripped of all meaning except the faceless, genderless, ageless depositor or debtor or credit-card holder.

But at the same time that the drive toward mastery thrusts us into more and more abstract language, withdrawn from the fluid reality of life, spoken words draw us back into that reality. The speaking of words is not only the creation of an abstract conception paralleling reality but also an act within reality. When a soldier cries "Charge!" or a man says "I love you!" he is not creating an imagined or recounted world; he is acting in a real one. It is a distinction Justice Oliver Wendell Holmes was to make between one who expounds an ideology and one who cries "Fire!" in a crowded theater. Even after the invention of writing, even within the varied media of the late twentieth century, spoken words retain their special force as actions. The president at his inauguration, the witness at a trial, swears an oath aloud; bride and groom pledge their vows in speech, and in speech the minister "pronounces" them man and wife; the actual saying of "hoc est corpus" is necessary to the transformation of the bread into flesh. The spoken word lives both in the mind and in the world; rooted in both, it flows back and forth between them.

So long as the word existed only as a pattern of sound waves pressing on the ears of listeners or held for a time in memory, its potential was limited. In our time all humans, whether or not they can or do read, live in a culture shaped by writing. Except in the most remote tribes, whatever language we speak is largely formed to be written and read. It is almost impossible to imagine life in an oral society untouched by literacy. But something can be recaptured from folktales and epics written down before the qualities of their oral origins were entirely obscured and from contemporary observations of oral societies early in their contacts with literacy.

The accumulated knowledge of an oral society, its public compendium of knowledge, existed only in the memory of living men and women. It could be drawn on only by personal contact with those in whose memory it was stored. To preserve it from the erasure of time and forgetfulness and death was a constant struggle. Practical wisdom was pressed into rhymed and easily remembered proverbs. Genealogies recited over and over and passed from generation to generation provided some framework for history. Epic poems with memorable rhythms and formulaic mnemonic devices attempted to hold the memories of a culture together in a coherent form. Knowledge was concrete, specific, and ungeneralized, because orality is not a medium for the elaboration of generalized theories. Syllogisms were incomprehensible in oral societies. Technology may have been ingenious, but science in the form of theorems and verified hypotheses did not exist.

Because the struggle merely to preserve knowledge was so difficult, its accumulation from generation to generation was painfully slow. A neolithic culture could pass unchanged through millennia and millennia, content to have preserved its hoarded knowledge from one generation to another. Progress did come, however, slowly and sporadically. The domestication of plants and animals, the development of agriculture, the ability to tan leather, work wood, weave cloth, shape and fire pottery, make and use fire, and the beginning of urban life were all achievements of preliterate societies, and they are the underpinning of later technology. But progress, even when once gained, was tenuously held. Many high neolithic cultures, like the Mississippian in what is now the United States and the Mayan, which had even acquired a kind of writing and had achieved a very high level of architecture and astronomy, simply slid back into a primitive state in the absence of a means of fixing their knowledge in a more permanent form than ephemeral speech and decaying memory.

Because of the almost desperate concern of oral societies to preserve the knowledge they held, change was feared as the bringer of loss, not sought as the path to gain. The idea of "progress" as the normal flow of history did not exist; indeed, history itself was not seen as a flow but as at best a circling stasis. A deep-rooted conservatism characterized all oral communities.

Lacking the means to communicate with distant places or times, each oral community lived in a little island of the here and now. It knew the past beyond two or three generations only in legend; beyond a few days' journey lay only an unknown world of mystery. Images of the past and of lands beyond the nearby were unfixed, fluctuant, and mist-enveloped; the gods themselves were numerous, polymorphic, and transformed into one another. Conceptions of reality beyond the concrete immediacy of daily life were embraced in the flowing forms of myth.

Most oral communities were small—a band, a tribe, or a village—in which every member was in daily contact with most other members in face-to-face communication using a common language. All members, untroubled except in times of warfare or forced migration by variant ideas from outside, shared a uniform culture. Some members might be more skilled hunters or arrow-makers or potters or weavers than others, but the painfully handed down technologies of the tribe were open to all. Although sachems might be committed to the memorizing and passing on of legends and rituals, and although there might be sacred mysteries known only to a few, all members lived out their lives bathed in a common and enclosed culture with rarely an intrusion of alien ideas that could provoke questioning or stimulate individuality. The noetic reality lay in the community, not the individual.

Although some preliterate cultures, such as the Polynesian, were highly structured and had a powerful ruling class and subordinate classes that were essentially slaves, simpler oral cultures were generally egalitarian. No large body of specialized knowledge or communication skills empowered their holders to dominate the society. By and large, the technology and the body of knowledge and ideas of the tribe or band or village were shared; they were sated together or starved together and moved in consensus.

Nor were oral societies usually able to assert power over large groups beyond the range of oral contact. Without the means to keep accounts, to record decrees, to issue orders, or to receive reports except face-to-face, they lacked the instruments of power. There could be temporary confederacies, such as Powhatan had created in the lower James River and Chesapeake area at the time of first European settlement, but hardly permanent governments. Early empires in the valleys of the Nile, the Euphrates, and the Indus and in Meso-America came with the rudiments of writing as a necessary instrument. Even the apparent exception, the preliterate Inca Empire, had a mnemonic device, the *quipo* or knotted rope, that served some of the communication and recording functions of writing. Political organization among preliterate societies generally remained small, fluid, unstructured, and egalitarian.

"Literature" as the aggregation of lettered texts of course did not exist in oral cultures. What did exist were *performances:* of tales or proto-dramas or of poetry having no rigidly fixed form, drawn from the performer's memory, and responding in each rendition to the character and mood of performer and audience. We can capture this evanescent "literature" only at the margins between orality and literacy, when orally formed works like the Homeric epics or the Genesis tales are first captured in, and transformed by, writing or, in modern times, when the tellers of folktales, already touched by literate culture, speak into the microphone and tape recorder of another world.

But in these works the stamp of orality is still present. An oral work, even a complex epic like the *Iliad* or the *Odyssey,* is never an interwoven whole but a collection of more or less independent scenes or episodes that can be strung together, rearranged, added to, or omitted. The work is filled with mnemonic clues to aid the reciter's memory. Clichés repeat themselves: Hera is always ox-eyed; dawn is always rosy-fingered. Formulaic language is repeated time and again. Rhythm and, in some languages, rhyme aid memory. Architecturally structured sentences with relative clauses and qualifying phrases hardly exist. As in a child's tale today, one simple statement follows another, connected essentially by "ands" not by "therefores" or "because ofs" or "whiches" or "whens." But with this simplicity there is a vivid charm of words springing from life itself, a charm that has made the *Iliad* and the *Odyssey,* the Sanskrit epics, the folktales, myths, and legends of many cultures, enduring treasures.

The oral use of words, the transcendentally important invention of our ancient ancestors, remains the identifying stamp of our humanity even in the midst of the flood of high-technology communication of our own time. The day-to-day conduct of our lives is carried on in speech, with our comrades and fellow workers, with those with whom we deal in business, and with those we love. Our lives are shaped by the words we hear from infancy, and we shape the life about us by those we use.

Words formed in speech underlie all our later forms of communication, as they are written down, printed, recorded, broadcast, and transformed into the computer's binary bits. All the technologies of communication we have developed over the millennia since humans learned to talk are simply further empowerments of the word.

Thus empowered, words enable us to capture in their net the universe, whose billions of galaxies each hold billions of stars greater than our sun and whose vast distances the instant leap of light can traverse only in billions of years. Words enable us to penetrate that which is infinitely small, beyond the atom itself to particles and waves, half energy and half matter, at the innermost fringes of being. In words flow forth the deepest emotions that possess us; through words we enter the minds and hearts of others, perhaps long dead or far distant. And all this infinite variety of the boundless universe, the unending sweep of time, the rich bounty of emotion, and the complex interplay of thought are conceived and held in our minds through the glory of words. Indeed, as God, beholding the Tower of Babel, forebodingly said of word-possessing mankind, "This is only the beginning of what they will do; and nothing they propose to do will now be impossible for them."

—2—

Letters

In the earliest dawn of history, perhaps as early as humans could talk, they were able to draw. In almost every place that people have been, pictures painted on the walls of caves or carved into the sides of cliffs, often tens of thousands of years old, leave a record of human perceptions. Pictures were made to create a record, to send a message, and to work a magic spell—perhaps, like a poem, only to express a feeling. Pictures served many of the functions of writing but were not themselves writing, at least at first. They represented not words but things in themselves. They were a separate way of symbolizing reality, parallel to but quite independent of speech, just as today the stick drawing of a skirted figure used in airports to identify women's restrooms does not stand for any word—not for "women" or "ladies" or "damen" or "femmes" or "señoras"—but only for the fact itself of the gender-specific facility.

But as the millennia passed, the two symbol systems tended to coalesce. It is difficult to draw a picture of an abstract idea or a proper name, although both are readily symbolized in spoken words. The creator of a drawn or painted record hence had to find a way in which a drawing could represent not the idea or person directly, but rather the spoken words that in turn named the idea or individual. We still do that in the drawing of rebuses and the enactment of charades. If one sought to represent pictorially the proper name "Bowman," one might draw not a picture of the person so named but a picture of a bow and of a man. The drawing leads us to its object not directly but by suggesting the sounds of the spoken words that represent the object.

In ancient times the most developed of this form of what we now call writing was perhaps the Egyptian system of hieroglyphs. On the temple walls and monuments of the pharaohs pictures that represent the thing depicted, like a drawing of the sun, are found interspersed with pictures that had come to represent not objects but sounds, perhaps the sound of the spoken word for the thing depicted, perhaps merely the sound of the first syllable or the first consonant of that word. This pictographic character has been retained in such written languages as Chinese, in which tens of thousands of characters are highly stylized forms of pictures that by direct representation or oblique reference signify an enormous range of things or actions or ideas. Such a system is only partially linked to spoken words. The same character may signify one spoken word to a user of Mandarin, another to a Cantonese, and a third to a Japanese and yet have the same meaning for all.

Among the speakers of Semitic languages in the Near East, the use of drawings to represent things and ideas followed a different path. Instead of developing thousands of characters to represent concepts directly, the Semites moved toward the representation of sounds and formed a relatively few characters, each representing a consonant or group of consonants. Their languages were such that the differentiation of vowels was usually not essential to the identification of words, and the consonantal alphabets of Phoenician, Hebrew, and similar languages served reasonably well to represent spoken words. True writing emerged, in which the visual symbols represented only the sounds of spoken words, which in turn symbolized the things or actions or ideas to be recorded or conveyed.

The Greeks perfected alphabetic writing in the first millennium B.C.E. Because vowel differences were important in spoken Greek, vowel symbols were added to modified Semitic symbols for consonants. A marvelously flexible and efficient instrument resulted. By the use of only some two dozen signs, any word in the Greek language could be represented. Any literate Greek, seeing the signs, could pronounce the word they represented, whether or not that person had heard it before or knew its meaning. And the signs that represented any word could be written, even if the person writing it had never before seen it inscribed. Merely by learning twenty-odd signs and the sound represented by each, one could acquire a whole new, almost miraculous, power. Speech could now be captured from the air, fixed in material form, and preserved for future times or sent to distant places. The world changed.

Indeed, it had begun to change many centuries before the invention of the Greek alphabet, when the civilizations of the Nile, Euphrates, and Indus valleys and the river basins of China began to use pictographic, cuneiform, and hieroglyphic writing. Even these early prealphabetic systems made it possible to keep records and to send messages, two essential skills in the administration of large-scale enterprises. Contracts could be made definite; inventories could be recorded; records of taxes could be maintained; royal decrees and established laws could be promulgated; instructions could be sent from a center of power to distant subordinates; and reports could be received in return. Enormous powers were aggregated to those societies whose rulers commanded the new skills of writing. For the first time it became possible to organize large governments capable of predicting and responding to the annual floods of the Nile and managing the irrigation systems of the Euphrates, Tigris, and Indus rivers. Large treasuries could be accumulated, with records of receipts and expenditures. Standing armies could be organized and paid, and their commanders could receive written orders and prepare written reports. Empire, as Harold Innis pointed out many years ago in *Empire and Communications,* was made possible by writing.

It would be untrue, however, to say that writing *caused* the aggregation of imperial power. It was the emergence of governing authorities required to manage the flooding and irrigation problems and the growing volume and complexity of trade that created an urgent need for an ability to make records and convey messages, which in turn evoked the development of writing. As would be the case in many later "revolutions" in communication, changes in modes of communication and in the social, political, and economic environment went hand in hand, each needing the other for its fulfillment, each stimulating and reinforcing the other. But although writing did not *create* imperial power, without it imperial power could not have been achieved and maintained.

Writing not only brought power to the societies that used it, but it also dramatically altered the distribution of power within those societies. For the first time in human history there was a communications skill not shared substantially equally by all members of society. All could speak and hear; only a very few could write and read. And to those few, or to those who commanded their services, accrued the enormous power the new skills made possible. Writing not only gave Egypt and similar early empires vast power but it also concentrated that power in the hands of an absolute ruler and that person's immediate court, which were served by a corps of uniquely skilled scribes. In some ways the situation resembled that of the early days of the computer, when only powerful governmental agencies or very large corporations could afford the monster machines whose operation required the services of a small corps of computer experts with a then rare and mysterious skill.

The long history of the association of power with access to new communications technologies had begun.

The early forms of writing involved incising symbols on stone or on wet clay subsequently dried or baked into flat bricks. The absence of a light, relatively inexpensive, and abundant writing surface was a limitation. Only a powerful court or a very wealthy enterprise could make effective use of the new skill, and even that use was limited by the clumsy restrictions imposed by stone and clay.

A change came with the use of papyrus, beginning about 2000 B.C.E. This writing surface is made from a reed common on the lower Nile. The reed had to be harvested and split and its hard outer covering removed. Its fibrous inner layer, after having been soaked, was placed in two cross-wise layers and thoroughly pounded. When it had been dried, it made a strong, light surface that could easily take ink. The necessarily small strips of papyrus could be sewn together to make a scroll of almost any desired length. Although it was a slow and tedious job to prepare papyrus and it was still very expensive, it was far more available and usable than any prior medium.

For the first time, the tiny corps of expert scribes around the pharaoh could be expanded. The number of clerks could rise to the thousands in the later dynasties, and the amount of written material increased accordingly. Bureaucracies could grow, which both extended the power of the ruler and diluted its absolute character. In Egypt, a writing-skilled priesthood became a partially independent possessor of power and able to constrain the pharaoh's authority. Subordinate rulers, now able to employ writing and writers themselves, were able to create something of a feudal structure.

A modern role for writing matured about the fifth century B.C.E. in Greek city states. It was easy to learn and use the new alphabet, and at the height of Greek power probably as many as 20 to 30 percent of the adult male citizens of such cities as Athens were literate. Universal literacy for free men was a frequently discussed ideal, and schools to teach youths to read and write were common. In a few cities they were even supported or subsidized with charitable or public funds so that poor boys could attend. There was never mass literacy in the modern sense. Very few women were taught to read, nor were slaves, except for the occasional servant trained to do clerical work for his master; in rural areas literate workers were rare indeed. But male members of the leading classes of Greece were almost uniformly literate. And even those who could not read lived their lives enveloped in a literate culture. The plays they saw, the poems they heard read, and the general intellectual content of their society were all shaped by writing. They were governed by written laws, and their economic activities were recorded in written contracts, inventories, and bills of sale. They voted by writing words on bits of pottery, even if someone else had to write the words for them. For the first time in the history of the world, writing, although still the skill of a minority, shaped a civilization.

Essentially the same conditions prevailed later in Rome in its most splendid period. Again, perhaps 20 to 30 percent of the free men in Rome itself and in the other principal cities of its empire were literate. Its culture, as in Greece, was a literate culture. Large corps of clerks carried on, in writing, the day-to-day business of the empire. Writing was even more central to government in Rome than in Greece, for the administration of its territories straddling the known world required a constant flow of instructions and reports, the maintenance of complex accounts, the recording and promulgation of laws and regulations, and other extensive uses of written documents.

In what ways did writing affect these first two societies to be based on its extensive use? Clearly, to an even greater degree than had been the case in the nations of the Nile, the Euphrates, and the Indus, writing underlay and made possible the power of empire. Without writing, Greek fleets could not have defeated the Persians, nor could Alexander's troops have conquered the fabled cities of Asia. The Roman Empire's vast domain, from the border lands of Scotland and the Atlantic shores of Portugal to the upper Nile and the banks of the Euphrates, was organized and controlled by a flow of documents: laws, orders, inventories, tax returns, accounts, and imperial rescripts.

And the spread of writing went hand in hand with the spread of power within those states. We have seen that in Pharaonic Egypt, when writing had been the rare skill of the king's scribes, power was unitary and vested in the crown. It had become shared with a priestly caste and a quasi-feudal nobility only as writing spread to those classes and their servants. Similarly, in the principal cities of Greece and the Roman Empire the spread of literacy to embrace rather broadly the upper levels of male society corresponded to a like spreading of power. In fifth-century Athens and in Republican Rome the electorate, most of whom were literate, embraced a considerable proportion of adult males and had a real share of political power. Even under the principate, when Rome could no longer pretend to even a limited democracy, real power was widely shared. The emperor's authority might be asserted as absolute, but in practice he governed with the participation and tacit consent of a large landed aristocracy and a far larger military and civil bureaucracy. The literate skill of this bureaucracy was indispensable to the imperial service. Hence, it enabled the bureaucrats to share significantly in the conduct of empire. The military bureaucracy was powerful enough to overthrow, install, and restrain emperors. The writing-skilled, power-wielding elite of Greece and Rome was still a small part of the total population and was confined to urban males of propertied classes, but it represented a major broadening of both literacy and power from the structures of the preclassical empires such as Egypt.

A second important consequence of the broadening literacy was the possibility of a steady accumulation of knowledge. Merely preserving the little hoard of knowing was an endless and often unsuccessful struggle in preliterate societies. The effort of society was not to gain new knowledge but to pass on to new generations the fragile memories that embodied all society's lore. Writing provided a ward against time's erasure. Complex bodies of knowledge, too large for any one person's immediate memory, could be accumulated. The history of Herodotus and Thucydides, the philosophy of Plato and Aristotle, the science of Archimedes and Hippocrates, and the mathematics of Euclid and Pythagoras could be assembled, preserved, added to, and transmitted.

The public compendium of knowledge could now exist as an entity independent of individual memory. Its content was scant, and the scattered paucity of copies severely limited access to it. Nevertheless, the existence and availability, however limited, of this compendium changed history. For the first time, society formed an idea of the possibility of progress. Its hoard of knowledge could be subject not to a persistently feared erosion but to a regular and confidently built augmentation. This was a fundamental psychological change, helping to produce the pride and buoyant optimism of Greece and Rome in their primes.

But writing did more than record and transmit words already embodied in speech. It was not the mere amanuensis of orality. Writing made possible a different kind of language, and because it did it changed the content as well as the form of word-embodied knowledge and ideas. We have seen that word-formed concepts in a oral society were fluid, existing only at the moment of expression and changing with each expression. They were simple, fitted to easy retention in memory. Each saying was a transaction between speaker and hearer, shaped to the particular purposes of each. But with writing the statement becomes not a transaction but a "text," fixed in form and, once created, having its own existence independent of the original author and the indeterminate many who may then or later read it. Freed from dependence on memory and recitation, each statement could be far more extensive and complex than was possible in an oral society. Writing became a kind of scaffolding or armature on which could be constructed elaborate sentences, paragraphs, and treatises, embodying concepts of causal and temporal relations beyond the capacity of an oral society to erect.

It was thus not only that knowledge could be preserved and transmitted but also that a different kind of knowledge could be constructed. A treatise as elaborate as Thucydides' history could now for the first time be brought together, preserved, duplicated, and circulated among an extensive body of readers. But it is perhaps even more important that it was a different *kind* of history: documented facts, set forth *as* facts, not as legends and myths, and fixed upon the page. The systematic, structured thought of Euclid, proof linked to proof, step by step, that was made possible by writing was an entirely different *kind* of thought from that possible to oral cultures.

Knowledge was no longer fluid and evanescent, flowing from memory to memory, from speaker to listener, and changing in form and content with each repetition. It became fixed, uniform from copy to copy and from one reading to another, acquiring the authority of permanence. And it could be shared across generations and great distances. A papyrus with the poetry of Ovid might be among the possessions of a Roman officer stationed on the Nubian frontier of upper Egypt; Virgil might be read by a campfire along Hadrian's wall on the Scottish border. Knowledge was not only made fixed and surer but also shared among a wide community and vastly broadened in scope. The frontiers of time and space were pushed back. Where the mists of legend had surrounded each living oral community, concealing the past beyond a few generations and the surrounding lands beyond a few days' journey, there was now a known geography stretching from Land's End to India and a known history stretching back for centuries. There was a fixed concept of natural law that governed the circling of the planets and the processes of the earth. Plato had conceived the fixity of truths, existing in words and disembodied from the imperfect and changing world of the senses. In sum, there was a new domain of ideas and concepts, fixed in and peculiar to writing and quite different in kind from the fluid lore of oral society.

Now that people could form and preserve ordered and stable concepts, they projected back upon the conceived universe the clarity and orderliness of those concepts. The polymorphous and myth-embodied world of oral societies was reconceived as orderly and obedient to fixed laws: The sun and stars and planets revolved in their unchanging spheres; the shapes and patterns of space were set in Euclidean concepts; relations of cause and effect were defined as formal or material or efficient or final; and logic was arrayed in syllogisms. Reality was conceived as arranged in permanent and meaningful patterns like the written theorems evolved to describe it. The basis for science was laid.

Law, too, took new forms. In oral societies a flexible and customary sense of right governed the making of judgments. A judge, or more likely a group representing the community, made decisions between parties based on a sense of what was equitable as to those particular parties in the specific circumstances of that case. There was no abstract and impersonal law, equally applicable to all parties whatever their individual natures and in all cases, whatever the particular circumstances. Such a concept came only with the existence of written laws, abstracted from individual circumstances and universally applicable. Codes, whether of Hammurabi, or handed down at Sinai to the Hebrews, or decreed by Justinian, came only with writing. This was true not only of the actual content of such codes but also of the very idea of law itself as an abstract concept, transcending time and individual circumstances.

The same kind of transformation affected religious concepts. The images of the gods in oral societies as superhumans with quasi-human presences and all too human passions of lust and anger and jealousy, polymorphous beings who were changeable in their presence and powers, reflected the fluid character of oral concepts. As societies became literate, the abstract patterns of writing, enduring in fixed form and independent of specific times and circumstances of utterance, began to affect conceptions of divinity as those concepts found expression in writing. "God" tended to become a more abstract and spiritual concept, lifted, like writing, out of the circumstances of time and place or of particular manifestations in perceptible forms, replacing the many individual "gods" conceived in oral expression. Monotheistic conceptions of God as, in St. John's words, a "logos" unbound by time or place, came only with writing. The pagan culture inherited from oral days was, of course, not forgotten by Greeks and Romans; it was simply no longer believed in by the highly literate, existing rather as a romantic and nostalgic set of symbols to enrich their literature.

"Literature" names itself as a product of literacy. Long before there was writing there were poems and dramas, fixed in more or less definite form in memory, that performed the function of mediation between reality and conception that we call literature. Such early-recorded works as the Homeric epics and the Genesis tales remain as evidence of their superb qualities, which can also be heard today in the taped folktales of preliterate cultures. But those creations were subject to memory-bound limitations. Writing opened whole new possibilities. Now that works no longer had to be retained in memory in order to be preserved, they could be long, more complex and abstract, and freed from dependence on mnemonic cues. They could be in prose rather than necessarily in more easily remembered verse. Authorship became independent of performance; works were fixed as the author's creation, not repeatedly recreated in recitation. Authorship hence became individual and self-conscious, with works deliberately created, revised and edited, and placed in permanent form.

In oral societies only a few works could be so frequently performed, like those of Homer, as to acquire a more or less stable and recognized identity. It would be difficult to conceive of an extensive *body* of separate, individually recognized works in an oral culture. Writing made possible the existence of many hundreds, even thousands, of identifiable works, fixed in form, usually of identifiable authorship, and self-consciously created in recognized genres. For the first time, we can speak of a "body" of Greek or Roman literature.

Also for the first time we can speak of cultures aware of themselves as cultures. It has been suggested (notably by Leslie Dewart in *Evolution and Consciousness*) that the self-consciousness of individuals evolved only in the matrix of speech-using communities. Somewhat similarly, cultures became aware of themselves *as* coherent and distinct cultures only when they shared a common writing-embodied set of ideas and knowledge transcending immediate limitations of time and place. Greece and Rome were more than geographical territories or governments; they were civilizations, each sharing and aware that it shared, a body of knowledge, beliefs, traditions, and cultural values expressed in a body of writings. Indeed, if people became human when they could talk, they became civilized when they could write.

But it should be remembered that even at the peak of Greek and later of Roman literacy the culture expressed and recorded in writing embraced only a minority. Literacy remained a rare skill among women and the working classes and in the rural areas where most of the subjects of those empires lived. Writing might shape the governments over them, it might organize the armies in which they were compelled to serve, it might facilitate the commerce that gathered in the products of their labor, and it might record the theology of the new Christian religion that reached them through oral sermons. But the day-to-day life of early Europeans and Middle Easterners, even within the bounds of the Greek or Roman empires, was little affected, especially in its mental content. Life flowed on evenly, as it had from neolithic times, with the same techniques of farming and husbandry, spinning and weaving, carpentry and metalworking, and the same superstitions and folk wisdom.

The two streams of society, literate and oral, have continued to flow side by side through history. Writing-based perceptions of reality have underlain the technological, scientific, commercial, and governmental achievements of society. Day-to-day life, in its personal and working contexts and in its emotional meaning, has continued in the domain of orality. An adequate mastery of the resources of writing—which involves far more than the bare ability to read and write—has been a principal marker of the wavering boundary line between the gentry who dominate society and the population at large.

This is true of society as well as of individuals. It is the solidly literate societies of Western Europe, North America, and the Pacific Rim that have affluent power. Societies in which the mass of the people is inadequately literate, and in which a writing-based perception and mastery of reality has not been generally internalized, are those that are torn by poverty and weakness.

Efforts to reduce the poverty of individuals or of nations have often had as a high priority the reduction of illiteracy, and indeed this is an important and necessary step. But the achievement of bare literacy, of the ability to pronounce the words represented by letters upon a page, is but the opening of a door. To enter the literate world, to perceive reality in the ordered and rational patterns in which writing arrays it, and to learn how to use the enormous power of the written compendium of knowledge requires vastly more. For societies as for individuals, it is a challenge never completely met.

The literate culture cast only pools of light in the larger cities and smaller ones in scattered provincial cities, reflected only dimly across most of the land and not penetrating the darkness of Northern and Western Europe beyond the legions' reach. And it was at best a flickering and inconstant light. Although preserved within the shelter of the Roman and later Byzantine empires, Greek literacy waned as the wealth and cultural elan of Greece diminished. And in the West there was a precipitous decline in writing as Rome fell under barbarian dominion. Even in the later days of the empire, in the fourth and early fifth centuries, the proportion of Romans who were effectively literate dropped sharply. And after the fall of Rome, in the Dark Ages of the sixth and seventh centuries, the literate world in the West shrank to the cloisters of monasteries. As the governmental and economic structures of the Roman Empire collapsed, only the Church was able to maintain a coherent organization, and only the Church preserved the literate skills necessary for such an organization.

The struggle of oral societies merely to protect from oblivion the painfully stored skills and wisdom preserved only in memory was re-enacted in the ravaged literate society. When any text was embodied in only a few dozen, or at very most a few hundred, varying copies subject to loss, dispersal, and destruction, the bare survival of the literate heritage was threatened. And in the West most of the literate culture of the Roman Empire, including its Greek heritage, was for centuries lost as a living part of society. Much was lost forever. Copies have survived, for example, of only a few of the known plays of Sophocles, and probably the great majority of the lesser literary works of Greece and Rome have perished without our knowing that they ever existed. Much of what we now possess from those cultures was recovered only centuries after the fall of Rome from Byzantine and Arab sources and from diligent search in half-forgotten monastic libraries.

The idea of progress that had flourished in Greece and Rome expired. Once more, as in preliterate societies, the goal was less to advance knowledge than to clasp desperately what was held only in memory or now in scattered and perishable manuscripts. Rome became a legend, and Greece an even more distant one. Much of the high culture of Greece and Rome was lost in the waning of literacy and the dispersal of manuscripts, and more than once during the Middle Ages Western Europe slipped back from its own gains that could be recorded only in copies of manuscripts easily lost or destroyed.

Charlemagne's success in the eighth century in reestablishing a unified rule over a considerable portion of the original western Roman Empire brought with it a temporary revival of Latin literacy. He ordered that elementary schools be generally available (a remarkable ideal but one far from achieved), and higher education was offered in cathedral schools. But as Charlemagne's political empire crumbled after his death, so did the briefly achieved renaissance of Latin literacy.

A similar early renaissance occurred in the twelfth century with the founding of the University of Paris and a general revival of scholarship centered in the Church. But again, the fragile base of manuscripts was too small to sustain the progress, and the life of learning slid back into the darkness of earlier centuries. What made the similar revival of learning in the fifteenth century into the Renaissance we recognize and that changed history was that the invention of printing came in time to broaden and make permanent the base of recorded knowledge on which the revival rested.

Much the same thing happened in religion. Throughout the Middle Ages heresies had flickered and been extinguished or had continued to smolder underground without ever being so widely spread or so firmly established as to challenge the Roman Church. The Waldensian or Vaudois movement, based on Peter Waldo's teachings in eleventh-century France and Italy, and the Lollard movement, based on Wycliffe's writings and sermons in fourteenth-century England, are both examples. Each attempted to make use of writing; both made translations of the Bible, Waldo into Provençal and Wycliffe into English, in order to reach the people directly, independent of the established clergy. But with no abundant means to multiply copies of those translations and their sermons, and confronting a largely illiterate laity, they could rely only on oral pleadings of itinerant preachers. Although both heresies stubbornly maintained their existence and ultimately merged with sixteenth-century Protestantism, neither was able to become a mass movement to displace the Catholic church. The failure of Waldo and Wycliffe would contrast with the later success of the print-armed Luther and Calvin.

By the early fifteenth century Europe had recovered from the devastation of the Black Death. Numerous universities had been established, and the cultural life of Western Europe was buoyant. Writers like Dante, Chaucer, Villon, Boccaccio, and a host of lesser figures had already opened a literary revival. Scholastic philosophy had produced major monuments, especially in the works of Thomas Aquinas. Trade had revived across Europe, and prototypes of later banking institutions had come into being. Powerful monarchies ruled in England, France, and Spain, and the city states of Italy and many of the principalities of Germany were flourishing. Scholarship, trade, and government all required a greatly increased use of writing, and the universities and their students in particular demanded books in far larger quantities than had been available. The booksellers' trade flourished, especially around universities, and copyists in large numbers were hard-pressed to meet the demand. The coming into use of paper about 1000 C.E. had reduced the cost of books; by 1450 they were much more abundantly available than in any previous century, even than in the height of Greek and Roman literacy.

But hand-copied books were still prohibitively expensive and far too few to meet urgent demands. European literate society needed, and was ready for, a major breakthrough.

The printing press's time had come.

— 3 —

Printing

Booksellers and proto-publishers had striven mightily to meet the growing demand for books. Corps of scribes were often assigned to make simultaneous copies of a work from dictation, or a book might be divided into fascicles, each assigned to a separate copyist so that the work could be completed quickly. Individual documents or even very short works might sometimes be printed from wood blocks in which the text had been carved in reverse, and the same technique was used to produce block prints of illustrations.

However, none of these efforts to speed scribal copying sufficed. The solution came with a wholly new invention: the use of movable type set in a chase and employed in a printing press to impress ink on a paper or vellum page. This was actually a complex of related inventions. They included the technique of cutting a letter in hard steel, using this to press a matrix in a brass bar, developing an appropriate alloy of lead to use as a type metal that would be soft enough to mold in the matrix but hard enough to last for hundreds or a few thousands of impressions, and developing methods of casting letters with shanks of uniform height so that all the letters from which a page was printed would press evenly on the surface of the paper. Methods of casting from molds were developed from the skills of goldsmiths. The set of inventions also included modifications of the screw press, long in use in the production of wine and olive oil and for other purposes. Also of indispensable importance was the development of a sticky, oil-based ink that would cling to the type face and not run when pressed against the paper.

Many men apparently were experimenting in the development of these techniques in the mid-fifteenth century, but the first to bring them all together was Johannes Gutenberg, a goldsmith of Mainz. Gutenberg's career as a printer was brief, and the only major work of his that survives is a magnificent bible on which he was engaged from 1452 to 1456. But the importance of his invention was immediately perceived, and printing establishments were created, initially in Germany, quickly followed by Italy and France, with what was for the times amazing rapidity. Within fifteen years after the appearance of the Gutenberg Bible there were printing presses in Mainz, Strasbourg, Augsburg, Bamberg, Nurenberg, and Cologne in Germany, Basel and Beromunster in Switzerland, Venice, Subiaco, Rome, and Filigno in Italy, and in Paris and Seville. By 1480 there were presses in more that 110 towns in Western Europe, stretching from England to Poland.

By the end of the century presses were operating in more than 230 towns throughout Western Europe, indeed, in every city and town of consequence. They had produced more than thirty-five thousand editions in probably well over fifteen million copies. In the brief half-century following Gutenberg's invention, the increase in the quantity of material available to readers is difficult to conceive. There is no way in which an accurate count can be made, but it is clear that by 1500 there were hundreds—many hundreds—of times as many books in existence as in 1450. Individual printed books, although still very expensive, cost probably much less than 1 percent of the cost of comparable manuscript works. Books could now be the possession of the merely prosperous rather than, as in the past, of only the very rich and of members of scholarly communities.

It is of profound importance that the rapid spread of printing was confined to Western and Central Europe. Russia was not to have a printing press until nearly a century after Gutenberg; the Muslim Middle East, perhaps reluctant to see the sacred Koran committed to impersonal machine production, was reluctant to adopt printing in quantity even after the establishment of a press in Constantinople in 1527. The fact that Japan, China, and Korea did not use alphabets made it impractical for them to adopt Gutenberg's methods. Europe's priority in mastering the power of print laid the basis for its rise to political and economic dominance in the succeeding centuries.

The consequences of so vast an enlargement of society's public compendium of knowledge and such a broadening of access to it touched every aspect of European life. Here we can only point to some of its principal effects. When the railroad and steam locomotives were invented centuries later, their first use was to carry the same sorts of passengers and freight over the same routes to the same destinations as they had been carried by stage coaches and wagons, and to do so in very similar-appearing vehicles. In much the same way the printing press in its earliest years simply continued the work of the scribal copyists, producing the same sorts of books for the same community of Latin-reading scholars in volumes that closely resembled the manuscript work of scribes. Just as the railroad quickly achieved the ability to haul much broader classes of passengers and freight over far greater distances in newly developed types of cars, in the process transforming the whole economies and societies of the countries in which it operated, the printing press soon began to flood society with far more varied types of books reaching far broader audiences and remaking the world.

The press soon turned to the production of books in the vernacular tongues of Europe and to books that appealed to much broader audiences and dealt with everyday subjects, including practical manuals, popular histories, and light entertainments. Meanwhile, a growing literacy among the general public helped to produce a vast increase in the market for the newly cheaper books. And the relative abundance of books reciprocally helped to expand the literate audience. The result was a tremendous increase in the domain of the literate culture, which had so tentative an existence on the margins of the dominant oral culture of the Middle Ages.

In the area of scholarship, the first profoundly touched by printing, the most important immediate consequence was the ability of hundreds of scholars to have access to an identical document. So long as the culture and the knowledge of Rome was preserved in only dozens or at most a few hundred of varying manuscript copies of its great masterpieces, its memory could only be misty and legend-filled, and Greece could hardly be known at all in Western Europe. The failure of Western culture to sustain the brief renascences of Latin learning in the Middle Ages was due in large part to the paucity of texts. But the revival of learning that began in the age of Petrarch was still in flower when Gutenberg's invention suddenly made it possible to reproduce the classics not in dozens but in hundreds or thousands of comparatively inexpensive copies so that they could become the common possession of a community of thousands of scholars and readers across the whole of Western Europe. This time the revival became permanent as the Renaissance.

The very process of preparing texts for publication in printed form was itself a major stimulus to scholarship. It involved collecting and comparing as many manuscript examples of the text as possible and by careful analysis selecting the most accurate of the variant readings available. Textual criticism developed as a professional skill, and with it a devotion to precision and thoroughness. The development of the scholarly study of grammar and linguistics was an accompanying achievement. There resulted not only a much wider but also a much deeper knowledge of antiquity. The near mythical perception of Greek and Roman civilization was replaced by objective knowledge. Scriptural texts were subject to the same analysis, and the traditional Latin Vulgate of St. Jerome lost some of its authority. Order, thoroughness, and rationality were strengthened as the foundations of scholarship and learning.

The sciences were particularly affected. The newly abundant availability of classical texts may initially have drawn attention away from the tentative buddings of experimental science in the late Middle Ages, but the general effect was overwhelmingly positive. Although classical science was full of error and was too heavily based on theory rather than observation, a generally shared, accurate knowledge of classical mathematics, physics, and astronomy provided a useful basis for the work of fifteenth- and sixteenth-century scientists, even if only one to be tested and rejected in many of its elements. And the precision and skeptical determination to arrive at the truth that had been developed in the textual editing in the early days of print underlay the work of sixteenth- and seventeenth-century scientists.

But the great contribution of printing to the development of science came in the prompt, accurate, and broad dissemination of the work of contemporary scientists. Although publication of the work of researchers was painfully slow by modern standards, it was incomparably more rapid than in the scribal era. In reasonable time, the work of each scientist could be widely shared with the community of scholars throughout Europe so that bodies of knowledge could grow by collaborative action, even if the collaboration was unplanned, often unacknowledged, and at a distance. This wide dissemination of exact and identical texts was especially valuable in connection with astronomical tables and charts, maps, and anatomical and botanical drawings. Print made possible the shared compendium of exact, experimentally derived knowledge that became the bases of the extraordinary flowering of the seventeenth century, when the work of Galileo, Newton, Leibniz, Vesalius, Harvey, and others marked the beginning of modern science.

Of special importance in this connection was the role of print in publicizing the discoveries of early explorers. European voyagers had been reaching out for centuries. Phoenicians had probably circumnavigated Africa, and Vikings had certainly reached and temporarily settled North America. Probably on a number of occasions fishing or trading vessels blown off their courses had reached some part of the Americas. But because there was no effective means of publicizing their experience they passed into the mists of legend and were forgotten without having contributed to the knowledge or the settlement of the New World. How different it was when Columbus stumbled on the Bahamas in his search for the Orient and the report of his discovery was in print and widely read within a year of his return.

There was an eager market for the reports of the voyages of subsequent explorers, and promoters of colonization seized the opportunity to issue glowing accounts that would encourage investment and settlement in the New World. The outpouring of European expansion to Asia and the Americas in the sixteenth and seventeenth centuries could not have occurred without the flow of detailed printed information that provided both the incitement to explore and the technical navigational, economic, and anthropological data that could guide the explorers and settlers and enrich the scientific knowledge of the new worlds.

The religious life of Western Europe was also deeply affected by the new art of printing. Throughout the Middle Ages dissident religious leaders had faced almost insuperable difficulties in disseminating their views. Handwritten copies of their sermons could have only a tiny circulation. Such leaders and their immediate followers could go about preaching, when they could escape arrest and imprisonment or execution as heretics, but their efforts could be of little avail against the formidable apparatus for oral dissemination afforded by the hierarchy and priesthood of the Roman Church. Nor were oral sermons an effective means of setting forth the sort of systematic and organized theology that would be needed to persuade other priests or to lay a sound fundamental basis for a new creed.

Luther and Calvin and their followers found a new array of opportunities in the printing press. Their arguments were initially addressed to other priests and ministers and to highly literate rulers and political leaders. Printed texts were the ideal instrument for that purpose. They could present extensive and well-reasoned arguments that could be re-read and studied in detail. They could reach individual priests, scholars, rulers, and other leaders directly without being choked off in hierarchical channels. Although few among the mass of individual communicants could read the Latin treatises in which much of the early Protestant teachings were embodied, or even the vernacular texts that Luther preferred, these writings did reach, and in Northern Europe were remarkably persuasive with, political and clerical leaders who could bring their followers with them into the Protestant churches.

The strengthening of the role of the literate, as contrasted with the oral, culture that printing brought about affected the character as well as the success of the Protestant faith. With the decline of literacy in the early Middle Ages, orality reacquired much of its preliterate strength, in religion as in other areas. The austere monotheism of the early church and its Judaic matrix had been compromised by the panoply of near-divine saints that had arisen in the Middle Ages and by the ascription of divinity to the Virgin. An atmosphere of myth and legend and miracles typical of orality characterized much of medieval Christianity.

Not so the religion of Martin Luther and even more that of John Calvin, whose *Institutes of the Christian Religion* is a peerless example of the ordered, rational, fixed, step-by-step exposition that writing made possible and that characterized literate culture at its highest.

Print affected the nature of religion in other ways as well. The availability of the Scriptures in printed form, especially after they appeared in vernacular translations, enabled individual worshipers to approach the sources of their beliefs directly, without the necessary intermediation of a priesthood. In effect, salvation became an individual responsibility, dependent on the individual's faith and his or her conduct rather than on the sacraments of the Church. This process of individuation, of breaking the individual loose from the bonds of the corporate Church, spread into other areas as well. In Northern Europe, where print literacy and Protestantism were dominant, particularly among a growing middle class, the individual of the bourgeois classes was also broken loose from the cake of the feudal economy and polity. The basis was laid for the individual entrepreneurship and the budding democracy and rule of law that were to characterize the immediately following centuries.

The consequences of print affected government in other ways and underlay the rise of the nation-state. The power of print to establish large and continuing communities of scholars and religious dissidents across Europe was paralleled by its role in creating national political communities. The scant flow of books in the era before printing was too small to allow the crystallization of vernacular literatures or the extensive translation of Latin and Greek classics. There were, of course, vernacular literatures, even great ones, adorned by such writers as Dante, Petrarch, and Chaucer, who wrote in the particular dialects of their languages and primarily in poetry lending itself to memory and oral recitation. But their works, before they were multiplied in print, could have only a very small circulation, and a literary tradition could only with difficulty grow up around them. Because only by drawing on the resources of all Europe could a community of scholars be said to exist, Latin remained the medium of scholarship and most literature.

With the enormously increased number of readers reached by print, it quickly became possible for vernacular literatures to take form. German, Italian, French, Spanish, and English could be established as common languages through which tens and later hundreds of thousands of readers without Latin could command a common literature, a common body of knowledge, and a common history. The Latin universality was splintered.

But at the same time that print enabled the vernaculars to break free from Latin, it enabled them to suppress competing dialects. The German of Luther, the French of Paris, the Italian of Dante, the Spanish of Castile, and the Southern English of the Tudor court each became the standard for works printed in its vernacular. Each became the voice that unified the people of a country at the same time that it distinguished them from the people of other countries. For the first time, at least since Roman days, political identity could be determined not by tribal bonds or by the dynastic authority of rulers but by a shared sense of commonwealth among the people.

The possibility of the modern nation-state had its roots in the first two centuries of printing, both in the rise of a sense of shared national identity centered in a common national language and in the creation of a body of print-educated functionaries capable of staffing the bureaucracies and the armed services of nations. Not only did printing make possible a vast growth in the number of highly literate members of the upper and upper-middle classes, but the output of the press also increasingly included practical treatises on mathematics, bookkeeping, military strategy and tactics, technology, and other subjects useful in the administration of government. The England of Elizabeth and the France of Louis XIV could not have been governed by the limited cadres of informed and literate officials available to rulers before the age of print.

National governments were empowered not only by their command of a more effective bureaucracy but also by their newly acquired ability to make their laws, decrees, and judicial decisions widely and uniformly known throughout their realms. The rule of established and known law, uniform throughout a domain, became possible. The expressed will of the national government could reach directly to the individual subject. The dependence of the national ruler on a partially autonomous feudal hierarchy was lessened. This paralleled the developments by which papal encyclicals and commands and the theological conclusions of Protestant leaders could reach individual priests, ministers, and communicants, reducing the power of, or the need for, intermediate ecclesiastical hierarchies.

Government was affected also by the development of bodies of systematic political thought made possible by print. In the scribal era there was no way for any new body of political ideas to be shared with thousands or even hundreds of readers. This became readily possible with the advent of print. Political theory could be developed by thinkers like Machiavelli or Harrington or Hobbes or Locke, who in turn could draw on printed editions of Plato, Aristotle, Cicero, and other political theorists of antiquity. From the interplay of the ideas in these published works emerged the organized bodies of political thought that were to have increasing force in the seventeenth and eighteenth centuries. Because these political theories could be widely published, they could gain large bodies of adherents, communities of like-thinking individuals that could be the forerunners in later centuries of political parties.

The political thought of the era, like the religious thought, began to embody the rational and systematic characteristics of high literacy. The state came increasingly to be viewed pragmatically, as a social creation intended to serve certain ends and justified by its success in achieving those ends. The body of ideas began forming that were to achieve fruition in the Enlightenment of the eighteenth century. The English revolutions of the seventeenth century and the American and French revolutions of the eighteenth were grounded in the bodies of thought whose earlier dissemination and acceptance had been made possible by print, bodies of thought that bore the impress of the ordered rationality of the high-literate culture made dominant by print.

In all the ways in which it affected society, the coming of print achieved its impact primarily through its empowerment of literacy. In the Middle Ages the high-literate culture had retreated largely to centers of scholarship in the Church. Print enhanced its power in this environment and vastly extended it beyond. Large landowners, government bureaucrats, bourgeois entrepreneurs, and a swelling middle class generally were drawn into the net of literacy. The number of book-users was multiplied by hundreds if not thousands. And with the spread of the book itself came the spread of the rational and systematic patterns of thought characteristic of the high-literate culture.

The capacity to deal with extensive, organized bodies of ideas as expressed in treatises and literary works had existed since classic times, but only among a tiny elite. Almost all of humankind had continued to live in the timeless, traditional, poetic world of preliterate orality. The literate ways of perceiving the universe in more abstract and prosaic terms, with concepts in disciplined array, now became common among a much larger number who were both literate and able to gain access to books. Although still a very small minority of the total population, this newly enlarged literate community was the kernel from which the future society would grow.

The multiplicity of texts produced by print and the enhanced power of literacy made possible an unparalleled increase in the size and the accessibility of the public compendium of knowledge. Embodied now not in tens of thousands of manuscripts but in tens of millions of printed books, widely available not solely to a small community of Latin-reading scholars but to a broad segment of middle- and upper-class

Western Europeans, this public compendium became an enormous source of power.

Before the invention of printing, Europe was a small peninsula of the great Eurasian land mass, less populous than Muscovy, far poorer than the empire of China or the princedoms of India, threatened by the power of the Ottomans, ignorant of most of Africa, and totally unaware of the vast American continents. Yet it was this weakling domain alone that seized on the power of the press. Because scientific and technical skills could be cumulatively increased and widely shared, the productive efficiency and the navigational and military skills of Western European society were greatly increased. Education could go beyond the lecture hall and the painfully dictated notes to reach vast numbers through print, and cadres of trained men could be built up to administer powerful governments and large enterprises. Power could be centralized, in large part freed from dependence on feudal or hierarchical layers for its expression.

In these ways print vastly increased the power of human beings to control their environments and their future and, in the words of Genesis, to make possible whatever they proposed to do. This power was first achieved by Western Europe, where print first found full employment. Within two centuries after Gutenberg, European ships had traversed the globe, the Atlantic coast of the Americas had been settled, the beginnings of European commerce had reached across the earth, the military competence of Europe was unequalled, and the fountainhead of the overflowing new science was in that small peninsula.

Every new medium of communication affects the dissemination as well as the accretion of power. Print enormously enlarged the number of those who had access to the knowledge from which power is derived. A consequence was the participation in authority of a widening circle of highly literate upper- and upper-middle-class landowners, merchants, and entrepreneurs, although this circle as yet embraced only a tiny segment of the general population.

Although this participation increased the competence and power of the participants, it did less to increase their autonomy in a democratic sense. Rulers quickly realized what power flowed from the printing press. Most of them hastened to see that presses were established in their domains so that they could exploit that power. But they were equally concerned to see that the power that flowed from the press did not flow to their potential opponents. A panoply of controls was soon erected intended to prevent the use of the press to disseminate information or ideas likely to challenge the authority of those in power. These were varyingly effective. In centers of Catholic authority, such as France, Spain, and Italy, where Church and state could reinforce each other's control, they were likely to be enforced with substantial success. In Switzerland and the Netherlands and in Northern Germany, where Protestantism prevailed and where political authority was not centralized, greater freedom of the press existed. So did it in England, in spite of a strong central government. Independence from Rome, a tradition of personal liberty, and the existence of many unlicensed journeyman printers contributed to a greater freedom, both arising from and contributing to the growing tension between royal and Parliamentary authority. Although French printers were reasonably effectively controlled, the readily permeable borders with Switzerland and the Netherlands permitted a flow of dissident views from those more tolerant countries, a flow that was to grow to major proportions in the eighteenth century.

The net effect of the printing revolution in its first two centuries was to augment power within Europe, to nationalize it, and to centralize it within nations. But the steadily growing size of the literate audience and the diminishing effectiveness of censorship assured that in later decades print would make possible a wider and more nearly democratic dissemination of power as it did of the knowledge on which power would be based.

Perhaps most important of all, print freed Western Europe from the constant anxiety of preserving the achievements of the past that burdened oral and scribal societies. When the wisdom and skills by which a society lives are retained only in human memory and rare and fragile manuscripts, merely to hang on to them costs constant effort. They can slip easily away, as in the Dark Ages or the relapse after the Carolingian Renaissance. The whole mindset of such a society must be to treasure and cling to what is handed down lest it slip through the hold of memory and be lost.

But once the knowledge of the past had been captured and permanently fixed in print, this fear need no longer govern. Instead, now that each new discovery could be quickly shared across the continent and had become a foundation on which yet newer discoveries could be based, the hopes of humanity could be turned to creating the future rather than merely holding on to the past. There was a vast and slow redirection of a society now straining toward a world to be achieved.

The entryway to the modern world had been opened.

— 4 —

The Flowering of Print

In the three and a half centuries that followed Gutenberg's invention, the technology of print was little changed. In the eighteenth century as in the fifteenth, type was set by hand and placed in forms that were locked into wooden presses and manually inked by the use of leather balls. The presses were hand operated and required a considerable muscular strength. They imprinted, one side at a time, single sheets of paper handmade from rags. A journeyman printer magically transported from Mainz of 1475 to London of 1775 would have found himself in a very strange world but plying a very familiar trade.

What *had* changed, and changed dramatically, was the *quantity* of printing, especially during the course of the eighteenth century. By the latter years of that century, escaping limitations earlier imposed by governments, presses were everywhere. Hardly a large town in Western Europe or America was without its press. Publishing had emerged as a distinct and well-organized industry in which entrepreneurs made large investments; offered advances to authors; paid them royalties; marketed books through advertising, catalogs, sales representatives, and discounts to booksellers; and actively promoted their export. There can be no precise measure of the output of the press for either earlier or later dates, but it is estimated that in London alone more than 1,600 substantial books were printed and published annually by the 1790s in addition to large numbers of pamphlets, chapbooks, and newspapers and some magazines. There were at that time perhaps 350 publisher-booksellers in London. As Terry Berlanger has stated, "England in the 1790's was a well developed print society; in the 1690's, especially once we leave London, we find relatively little evidence of one" (6). Most of Northern and Western Europe experienced a parallel development.

The enormous increase in printing and the evolution of publishing into a large, well-organized, and highly commercial industry were associated with profound changes in eighteenth-century society and in its cultural and intellectual life. The opening of Asia and the Americas to European exploitation had produced an economic revolution that had a new capitalist organization of production and trade. A new class of entrepreneurs arose who bought and sold the spices of Java and the beaver pelts of Canada, sent their ships to Canton and the Coromandel Coast, traded rum for slaves in Africa, built speculative empires on land grants in the American wilderness, founded banks, and organized themselves in great trading companies. They saw the newly opening world of the eighteenth century as one vast arena for their unresting enterprise. National governments came to exercise enormous new powers, maintaining standing armies and large navies and administering whole empires on distant continents.

These dynamic thrusts pressed against the remaining structures of the Middle Ages: the local nobility, the traditional "estates" of the provinces, the monastic orders, and the city guilds. Power moved from those who held it by tradition to those who won it by success. New bodies of political and economic thought developed, drawing both on the rational, print-based worldview emerging from the scientific revolution of the seventeenth century and the pragmatic requirements of the new governments and capitalistic enterprises. Political writers rejected the idea that tradition sanctioned authority and held rather that governments and social institutions should be formed to meet society's needs and were sanctioned by their success in doing so. Companion bodies of economic thought emphasized the need to cast off traditional and governmentally imposed restraints to allow entrepreneurs to create wealth for society as they sought their own enrichment.

As these tensions grew between traditional institutions and the new pragmatic forces, the slow evolution of old institutions could not absorb the strain, and violent revolutions took place in England in 1649 and 1688, in America in 1776, and in France in 1789 to allow the creation of new institutions for a new era.

The classes and institutions coming into power in the eighteenth century were those that most extensively used and drew their power from print. The literate class, already enlarged in the early centuries of printing, had now grown from a small group of clerics, scholars, public officials, and important merchants and others who used books professionally to embrace a large urban middle-class and the more prosperous farmers of Northern Europe, England, and the American colonies. In some favored areas like New England adult white men generally, and perhaps a majority of white women, could read.

Throughout the first two or two-and-a-half centuries of printing, the popular culture of Western Europe remained primarily oral and preliterate. The world of print, although far more extensive than that of scribal literacy, was still but a thin crust over society, involving the higher levels of government and business, the church, the professions, and a few centers of learning. But most Europeans could not read, seldom saw a printed item, and inhabited a mental world shaped by long centuries of oral tradition.

By the mid-eighteenth century, print had penetrated far more deeply into society. Print was much more abundant, and far more people were capable of reading it; even those who could not themselves read were immersed in print-borne ideas through their contacts with the now broad class of readers. Folktales and ballads had been collected and printed, and it was now often from the printed text that the folk singers and tellers drew their stock of songs and tales. Political and religious views were shaped at secondhand from the ideas embodied in pamphlets and repeated in sermons and tavern talk. The late eighteenth century revealed a society increasingly shaped by print.

The great increase in the number of well-to-do, literate, middle-class book buyers provided a market and a source of income for both publishers and authors that made them independent of the patronage of church or state or wealthy nobility. Large publishing undertakings, like Diderot's *Encyclopédie* in France, Voltaire's major works in Switzerland, and Samuel Johnson's *Dictionary,* his *Lives of the Poets,* and his edition of Shakespeare in England could be planned, financed over a period of years, and successfully marketed as commercial enterprises.

During its first century or two, printing was a technology that had permitted the multiplication in vast numbers of copies of already existing works of the scribal era and of dramas, poetry, theological treatises, sacred texts, histories, and similar works that continued the traditions of the preprint era in form, patronage, and anticipated readership. By the mid to late eighteenth century the power of print had become so great that it served not only as a means of multiplying and disseminating the works of an already existing culture but also as a means of transforming that culture itself and the nature of its literary products. Authors were no longer dependent on royal or noble or ecclesiastical patronage, and the output of the press was no longer addressed primarily to the Latin-reading scholarly community who bought and read the books of the scribal era.

There were many consequences for literary form. Drama and poetry, the dominant types of the literature that had grown from the oral past and continued their importance in the early centuries of printing, were succeeded by the novel as the principal type of work read for entertainment. The novel would have been inconceivable as a major literary form until there was a large audience ready to buy books for their entertainment value and a publishing industry that could produce and market them inexpensively and in quantity. The light essay of Addison or Steele or Johnson or Montaigne was another product of the print-dominant era that (for all its precedents in Petronius and Lucian) could not have flourished in an earlier time. And certainly massive reference works like the *Encyclopédie* and Johnson's *Dictionary* could not have been conceived, much less accomplished, before print had firmly implanted the idea of fixed, orderly, alphabetically arranged works and a publishing industry existed capable of producing them.

The role of the author had changed as well. The very concept of "authorship" had been a vague one in the scribal age, when each copy of each book was a separate thing. Once a writer's work was reproduced in thousands of identical copies, with the author named on a title page, the distinction of being the creator of a book became an important one. The Act of Anne of 1709 granted authors a copyright for their work for fourteen years, renewable for another fourteen, and provided in England a legal validation of an author's creative rights.

By the mid-eighteenth century professional authors had emerged. In prior centuries men—and more rarely women—might write to advance their views, as did the Protestant Reformers. Those of means might write simply from pleasure or pride in their creative skill. Those without independent means of support wrote under the patronage of kings or the nobility or prelates. Only playwrights—writing to be performed rather than to be read—could hope to earn a living from the support of the general public. But by the latter 1700s, in both England and France, the book-buying public had become large enough, and the publishing industry well organized enough, to offer a chance for industrious authors to survive and even, with talent and good fortune, to prosper from the sale of their books. "Grub Street" and its French equivalent had arrived. Kernan (34) quotes J. W. Savage, who pointed out that in the period from 1520 to 1659 "nearly all the great important writers were either courtiers in their own right or satellites utterly dependent upon the courtly system." Genteel writers either withheld their true names from the title pages of their published works or affected to disdain income from their sale. Not so Samuel Johnson in the latter 1700s. He could say that "no man but a blockhead ever wrote, except for money."

Music as well as literature was deeply affected, and in parallel ways, by eighteenth-century developments in printing and publishing. The use of engraving rather than awkward letterpress printing to reproduce musical scores made practical the large-scale publication of music, including especially the extensive scores of symphonies and operas, and a highly organized music publishing industry came into being. This development was concomitant with the construction of symphony halls and opera houses and the broad public attendance that made it possible for musicians and composers to achieve an income increasingly independent of court patronage. The great composers of the eighteenth and nineteenth centuries were the creatures and creators of this flowering of music made possible in part by the outpouring of printed scores. Music, like literature, came to serve the enlightened middle classes.

With the rise of publishing as an organized industry and of authorship as a profit-seeking enterprise came the spread of printing throughout Northern Europe, England, and America by the end of the eighteenth century. A market-oriented rather than a court-oriented literature became possible. Not only did the new literary forms—the novel and the essay—largely displace the oral inheritances of drama and poetry as the literature of entertainment, but the content of writing as well as its form was also changed. Increasingly it was shaped by a rationality consistent with the abstract and orderly regularity of print and the interests of the wealthy bourgeoisie who now provided the principal market for printed works. Print served the ends of the powerful new classes emerging from the explosive economic growth of the late seventeenth and the eighteenth centuries.

The great thinkers of the eighteenth century—the Enlightenment authors of the Continent, the English and American political theorists, and economists like Adam Smith and the French Physiocrats—all were both creatures and creators of a print-centered body of thought: realistic, rational, international, orderly, and systematic. They built schools of thought that were made possible only by the wide international distribution of their works and the accumulation of a shared body of common ideas. All the thrust of these bodies of ideas responded to the interests of the wealthy bourgeois who had replaced the courts and prelacy as the market for books and the support of authors. They were directed at diminishing the authority of tradition and of the Church and enhancing that of reason, at supplanting absolutism with the rule of law, at asserting a role in government and a share of public power for substantial businessmen, and at freeing private enterprise from irrational constraints.

This drive toward the empowerment of well-to-do bourgeoisie corresponded closely with the sharing of communication provided by the flowering of print. It was only a substantial propertied class that produced a market and an important readership for books. Hand-operated presses using handmade paper could not have produced printing for the masses in any case, and the masses did not yet demand it. It was to that propertied class that the principal output of the press was addressed. And it was basically the ideas of that class that spread through simpler forms of print and oral retransmission.

The world of print of the late eighteenth and early nineteenth centuries was integrally linked to the restructured society that emerged from the revolutions of that era: rational, pragmatic, bursting bonds of tradition, and governed by men of property opposed both to the inherited and tradition-sanctioned powers of church and throne and to any uprising of the masses. Print was directed to those classes that made up a business-oriented oligarchy or, at its broadest, as in America, a tiered democracy in which power was concentrated in a core of active print-users and shared in diminishing degrees with those who made less frequent use of newspapers and pamphlets and, in turn, those who participated orally by hearing discussion of print-based ideas.

The printing press of the late eighteenth and early nineteenth centuries had helped to convey power to the newly strengthened propertied classes of Northern and Western Europe. It had also helped to fulfill the promise of power of Europe itself that had become evident in the earlier centuries of print. Europe now spread its power over most of the Americas, settling the Atlantic coasts and penetrating deeply into the interior. It had asserted its control over the subcontinent of India and much of coastal Asia save Japan and Siam. It dominated the Middle East and ravaged the coasts of Africa.

By the opening of the nineteenth century the enlarged domain of print was the residence of power, both among the nations of the world and within the social structure of each nation.

— 5 —

The Control of Print

In the scribal era the power generated by writing was necessarily closely held, as was the skill of writing itself. Printing generated vastly greater power and made possible its far wider dissemination. It empowered both those who used the printer and could thus spread their words among thousands and those who received the printer's products and hence could read what they chose for themselves. It early became an issue of importance to those in authority that they should control printing to assure that it should not become a channel of power to challenge or overthrow them. Equally important to those endeavoring to gain power was access to printing as a potential instrument of change. This drive to control the new medium as an instrument for the control of power would be repeated in future centuries with each new means of communication, and essentially the same techniques would be used.

At first, rulers encouraged the spread of printing, even offering encouragement to printers to come and settle in their realms, because of its promise to encourage learning and give them a more powerful instrument to convey their doctrines and decrees. Attitudes changed after the first revolutionary uses of print to spread the reformist preaching and writings of Luther, Calvin, Knox, and other Protestant leaders. The Catholic Church responded in the Council of Trent, which spent many years restating Catholic doctrine, considering reforms, and arming itself to combat spreading Protestantism. As part of this arming it adopted measures to control the press. The Church from its earliest days had denounced books it considered false or heretical, but now more systematic procedures were thought necessary. Bishops were given the authority to approve the publication of books through their imprimatur, and in 1559 there was established the *Index of Prohibited Books,* which defined whole classes of books and listed hundreds of others individually that Catholics (with certain exceptions for scholarly use) were forbidden to print, publish, buy, sell, or read. Works forbidden included those heretical in doctrine, hostile to the Church, immoral, or proposing scientific theories contrary to the teachings of the Church.

The Catholic control was very effective in Italy, France, Spain, and Portugal. Heretical works were not published in the Catholic bloc, and the center of scientific research and writing passed to Northern Europe after the banning of the writings of such authors as Galileo. Even where the authority of the Church was not sufficient to prevent the publishing of heretical works, inclusion in the *Index* limited their circulation and protected believers from exposure to them.

The freest publishing was in Switzerland and the Netherlands, where central governments were weak and authority rested primarily in small cantons and city governments having diverse religious commitments. With limited official control, the publishers of those countries were able to issue both Protestant and Catholic works, later the writings of the *philosophes* of the Enlightenment, and the work of scientists who were demolishing the medieval scientific system accepted by the Church. Exports from Switzerland and the Netherlands slipped across the border into France and across the Channel into England. Puritan works smuggled into seventeenth-century England helped to pave the way to the civil war and the Commonwealth. Smuggled Catholic works kept alive that proscribed faith in the same era. It was from Switzerland that the works of Voltaire and other Enlightenment writers entered France and played a role in laying the basis for the French Revolution. No censorship, however rigid and severe, was able to suppress completely the ideas it sought to ban.

England affords the most interesting examples of the various ways in which authorities attempted to control the press and in which those out of power sought to use it to attack dominant institutions. In that realm there was never either the absolute authority of French or Spanish or Italian rulers or of an unchallenged Church. During the sixteenth and seventeenth centuries parliament and Crown were often at odds, and for a time in the seventeenth at war. Two revolutions, in 1649 and 1688, and a counterrevolution in 1660 broke established patterns of government. The official religion shifted from Catholicism to an orthodox Church of England under Henry VIII, briefly back to Catholicism under Mary, to the Church of England again under Elizabeth, to Presbyterianism and Independent Puritanism under the Commonwealth, back to the Church of England under Charles II, to another flirtation with Catholicism under James II, and finally to a firmly established Church of England under William and Mary. Although this variety of political and religious control afforded a much greater interplay in control of the press than in the more consistent and more rigidly Catholic monarchies of the Continent, there was never the freedom of the Netherlands and Switzerland.

Both in the efforts to control the press and in the attempts to use the press to challenge authority, most techniques used in the twentieth century were developed in England between the sixteenth and eighteenth centuries. The Catholic *Index,* although never used by the British government, exemplified one method of control: the issuance of a list of proscribed works. An alternative method was to exercise prepublishing control at the level of the individual book, requiring each manuscript to be examined and licensed before being printed.

But to deal with individual works, whether by the preparation of a proscribed list or by prepublication licensing, placed an enormous burden on those in authority, one that grew insupportable as the quantity of works increased. Hence governments were impelled to devise means to shift the burden of censorship to associations of publishers or to individual publishers themselves. Four additional measures to attain such indirect control were developed.

One was to license printers, confining printing and publishing to a limited number of firms approved by authority. Another was to punish printers and publishers for having issued a publication that contravened more or less vaguely established rules, allowing the fear of punishment to instill self-censorship in the publisher or printer. A third was to reward printers, publishers, and authors who served the purposes of those in authority by the award of profitable monopolies or, in the case of authors, of sinecures or pensions. A fourth, and most important, means was to make use of the organization of printers and publishers, the Stationers Company, by limiting lawful publishing to its members and giving them authority to enforce the prohibitions against unlicensed publications.

Henry VIII had begun the practice of licensing printers, and in 1559 his daughter, Queen Mary, established the Stationers Company, a guild of printers and publishers whose members enjoyed the sole right to print or publish books. In addition to the general monopoly enjoyed by the company, specific monopolies were granted to particular publishers for individual types of books, like law books or almanacs, or even individual standard titles. But even if a printer were a member of the Stationers Company in good standing and enjoyed a patent for the type of book concerned, he was still required during most of the sixteenth and seventeenth centuries to submit every manuscript to an appropriate authority for review and for license to print and publish it. Works of religion, for example, had to be submitted to the Archbishop of Canterbury or the Bishop of London; law books, to the chancellor; and works of history or public affairs to a secretary of state. In practice, of course, the actual review of manuscripts was deputed to assistants to these officers.

A further restriction was achieved by limiting the number of printers. During most of the period there were allowed to be no more that twenty printers in London and none elsewhere save at Oxford and Cambridge, under the control of the universities, and at York. And each printer was severely limited in the number of assistants he might employ.

Parallel with the controls over the domestic production of books were restrictions on their import into England, intended both to prevent the circulation of books thought heretical or seditious and to protect English printers and binders from foreign competition.

The restriction of printing and publishing to the members of the Stationers Company and the limitation of the number of apprentices and journeymen, as well as the monopolies granted individual publishers, were intended to assure the prosperity of the favored publishers as well as to discipline the press so that it conformed to the religious and political views of the government. This strategy co-opted the press to carry out the censorship the government sought. The members of the Stationers Company had a strong economic motive to root out unlicensed competition, and they were given governmental authority to do so. And, anxious to preserve the good will of the government, the company was sedulous in reflecting the government's views. So, too, were major individual publishers who held profitable monopolies of individual types of books for which they were dependent on the favor of the Crown.

The controversies between Crown and parliament in the reign of Charles I that led to the English civil wars of 1642–49 and to the Commonwealth fractured this system of control. Both the king and parliament needed access to the press in order to present their opposing views to the public. Prior to 1642, when the conflict erupted into violence, discussion of controversial domestic political and religious issues was almost wholly suppressed. The corrantoes that were forerunners of the newspaper, for example, were confined to the reporting of foreign news, largely of the Thirty Years' War, and consisted principally of translations and adaptations of Dutch news sheets issued in Amsterdam. They dared not discuss the events and debates at home.

When warfare broke out between king and parliament and the king withdrew from London to Oxford in 1642, the gates were opened for the publication of domestic news and the contending positions of the parties. A number of newspapers openly critical of the king's policies and advisers, and increasingly of the king himself, were permitted in London; at first one and then other newspapers supporting the king and highly critical of parliament appeared in Oxford. Each side was supported by a vigorous output of pamphlets.

However, the freedom each of the contestants was now permitted was only a freedom to support its position in the controversies. Although parliament, ruling independently, abolished the Star Chamber Court, which had been frequently used for the prosecution and punishment of authors, printers, and publishers who had offended the Crown, it restored in 1643 the strict licensing of printers and of individual books, pamphlets, and newspapers that had lapsed in the early disorders of the conflict. It did this by issuing an "Order for the Regulating of Printing, and for suppressing the late great abuses and frequent disorders in Printing many false Scandalous, Seditious, Libellous, and unlicensed Pamphlets, to the great defamation of Religion and Government." This essentially restored the earlier machinery of control, relying primarily on the Stationers Company, and substituting parliamentary officers and Presbyterian ministers for royal and episcopal censors. Works critical of the king and the bishops of the Established Church could be freely published, but not criticisms of parliament or even reports of its proceedings. Equally forbidden were publications dealing with the growing differences between Presbyterians and Independents.

It was, surprisingly, not against royal decrees but against the parliamentary and Puritan restraints that the first great English defense of freedom of the press was written. This was the *Areopagitica* of John Milton, himself a leader in the parliamentary and Puritan cause. Milton recognized the paradox of the Puritan leaders, who had claimed a liberty of publishing to oppose the king and the Established Church, turning to censorship now that they were in power themselves in order to protect that newly won power from criticism:

> . . . while Bishops were to be baited down, then all Presses might be open; it was the peoples birthright and privilege in time of Parliament, it was the breaking forth of light. But now the Bishops abrogated and voided out of the Church, as if our Reformation sought no more, but to make room for others in their seats under another name, the Episcopall arts begin to bud again, the cruse of truth must run no more oyle, liberty of printing must be enthrall'd

again under a Prelaticall commission of twenty, the privilege of the people nullify'd, and which is wors, the freedom of learning must groan again, and to her old fetters. (24)

What Milton particularly attacked was the requirement that a license be obtained before any work could be printed. To subdue to the will and judgment of official hacks, as Milton thought the licensors likely to be, the creations of the wisest men and greatest scholars of the land seemed to him outrageous. But it was not only this procedural prior restraint that Milton opposed. He also saw freedom of publication and discussion as a positive and essential virtue. Only by exposing bad ideas and false doctrines to the test of public discussion could truth be found. Character was formed by exposure to all views and not by being sheltered from all but chosen doctrines. Proclaimed Milton, "and though all the windes of doctrin were let loose to play upon the earth, so Truth be in the field, we do injuriously by licensing and prohibiting to misdoubt her strength. Let her and Falshood grapple; whoever knew Truth to be put to the wors, in a free and open encounter" (31).

For all the eloquence with which Milton defended free discourse and asserted its necessity, even he conceded the propriety of the state's punishing improper speech or writing after the fact. While he would, for example, permit a complete range of expression of Protestant views, he said, "I mean not tolerated Popery, and open superstition, which as it exterpats all religious and civill supremacies, so it-self should also be extirpat . . . that also which is impious or evil absolutely either against faith or maners no law can possibly permit that intends not to unlaw it self" (32–33).

Of the writers of the time only Roger Williams, in a sense a disciple of Milton, went the whole way to freedom. In a debate with John Cotton, an orthodox Puritan minister, carried on in the distant New England coast but by means of pamphlets published in London, Williams demanded freedom for all religious views, even Catholic, Moslem, and infidel.

With the overthrow of the Commonwealth and Protectorate and the Restoration of Charles II in 1660, the system of control of the press was restored to its pre-1642 status. It sought different ends and was administered by officials of different views than under the rule of parliament and Cromwell, but it continued with essentially the same machinery. As the volume of publication increased, however, the controls began to break down. There were many out-of-work journeymen printers in England left unemployed by the limits on the number of master printers and the number of journeymen each could legally hire. Presses were inexpensive, and clandestine printing increasingly flourished. Even those who sought to obey the law were frustrated by the fact that the official licensors could no longer even begin to keep up with the flood of manuscripts submitted for approval. Increasing numbers of publications appeared without official sanction as the seventeenth century passed, and the authorities were little disposed to act unless their attention was called to a particularly offensive work. The Glorious Revolution of 1688 displaced James II, enthroned the Protestant William and Mary, and by the enactment of the Bill of Right in 1689 assured the preeminence of parliament and the rights of the subject. Censorship by prior restraint fell into disuse, and in 1696 the entire system of licensing, both of printers and of books, was ended.

The end of this system, however, did not mean the end of censorship itself. "Freedom of the press" became an accepted doctrine in England by the early eighteenth century, but it was not freedom as it is understood today. It meant that no one had to obtain a license before publishing what they pleased. It was clear, however, that the author—and publisher and printer as well—bore full responsibility for what was issued and could be punished severely for publications that offended the law.

Blackstone in his *Commentaries on the Laws of England* defined freedom of the press as it was understood in the eighteenth century: "The *liberty of the press* is indeed essential to the nature of a free state; but this consists in laying no *previous* restraints upon publications, and not in freedom from censure for criminal matter when published. Every freeman has an undoubted right to lay what sentiments he pleases before the public; to forbid this is to destroy the freedom of the press; but if he publishes what is improper, mischievous, or illegal, he must take the consequences of his own temerity" (quoted in *Freedom of the Press from Zenger to Jefferson,* ed. Levy, 104, emphasis in the original).

There were two principal kinds of offense with which the author, publisher, or printer might be charged. Under the common law, anything that brought government into disrepute or that might alienate the loyalty or affection of the people was a seditious libel, and its publication was a crime. The truth of the statements was not a defense; indeed, it was held that true charges against the government might do more damage than false ones and hence might be more to be condemned. It was for a judge to determine whether any published words were libelous; the jury's task was only to determine whether the defendant had issued the words or was responsible for them.

The other principal offense with which the press might be charged was a breach of the privileges of the parliament or either of its houses.

To report the votes or discussions or other proceedings in either the Commons or the Lords without specific prior authority was such a breach. So might be criticism of either house or its committees or even its individual members. Only the House of Commons or the House of Lords could determine what constituted a breach of privilege. Each could summon suspected offenders before the bar of the house, examine them, determine their guilt, and administer punishment without providing any of the protections afforded by the common law. Almost the only protection that authors, publishers, or printers had in such a case was that they could not be held in prison after parliament was no longer in session.

Throughout the eighteenth century, Crown officers brought frequent prosecutions for seditious libel, and parliament on numerous occasions summoned authors, publishers, and printers before its bar. As public opinion came increasingly to favor openness of public debate, juries became less willing to convict and grand juries even to indict in seditious libel cases, and parliament became more hesitant to assert its privileges against publishers. In the later decades of the century punishment of offending authors, publishers, and printers became much rarer.

Instead, the ministry attempted to control the press by less direct means. A rather high stamp tax made it difficult for small or poorly financed publishers—who were likely to be the more radical ones—to continue to issue newspapers. And, especially under Walpole's administration as prime minister, the government used subsidies and bribes to encourage its supporters among the press and to buy off opponents. Many leading writers, such as Daniel Defoe, were in the pay of the ministry. The enormous power of government, extending throughout society, and its ability to reward, assured that in general eighteenth-century publishing sustained the Crown, the Church of England, the role of wealth, and the ordered structure of society while allowing sufficient room for dissent to serve as a safety valve and to allow some flexibility of adjustment to changing circumstances.

The British had evolved a remarkably subtle and effective system, with little use of formal restraint, to assure that the press was a powerful support of the established order and at the same time facilitating changes and adjustments within that order. This successful system made a major contribution to the stability and the orderly evolution of the British political and social system over the three centuries following the Glorious Revolution, but it kept Britain a more class-ridden society with a narrower democracy than its former American colonies, where a freer press evolved.

Meanwhile, the techniques of control devised in the sixteenth and seventeenth centuries have survived to be used throughout the twentieth. The Catholic *Index* has lost much of its force, but in the 1950s and 1960s lists of books and films disapproved by the predominantly Catholic Legion of Decency were enforced by boycott and at times, before the courts intervened, by the police. In the 1930s several states required approval of individual films prior to exhibition, and the CIA requires prior approval of books by former employees. Broadcasting stations are licensed, as were early printers, and renewal of their licenses depends, at least in theory and in part, on the content of their broadcasts. The threat of prosecutions for obscenity, although now much reduced, remains an incentive to self-censorship. Pensions and monopolies no longer reward subservient authors and publishers, but conforming to conservative views can help to bring lucrative textbook contracts, and offending those views can bring loss of major markets. As the kings of England once relied on the Stationers Company to monitor its members, the U.S. government has leaned heavily on the Motion Picture Producers Association and the National Association of Broadcasters to lay down and enforce standards for their members, although the courts have now forbidden this devolution of censorship powers.

The media of communication may change dramatically from century to century, even from decade to decade, but the unrelenting urge to control the content of the media and the methods by which control is attempted seem unending.

— 6 —

Communications Policy in the Early American Republic

The United States was a new country, faced with the necessity of consciously establishing policies in many areas of national life, considering afresh what it would retain of English law and customs and what it would new-shape to its special needs. Communications policy ranked high in the concerns of the new nation, for its very coming into being was an achievement in communication. The scant resources of the American press had been used to form and to spread the ideological basis of the Revolution and of the constitution of governments in the new states and in the Union. The Founding Fathers were well aware that the creation of the new nation had been made possible only by the spread of information and the sharing of ideas and that its continued success would depend on an informed citizenry.

In a letter to William T. Barry on August 4, 1822, James Madison stated a view widely shared by his generation: "A popular Government, without popular information, or the means of acquiring it, is but a Prologue to a Farce or a Tragedy; or perhaps both. Knowledge will forever govern ignorance: And a people who mean to be their own Governors, must arm themselves with the power which knowledge gives" (Meyers, ed., *The Mind of the Founder*, 343).

There was, moreover, a recognition that the press must be a principal instrument in achieving the needed level of public information. As Thomas Jefferson wrote on January 16, 1787, in a personal letter to Edward Carrington, "The way to prevent these irregular interpositions of the people [he was referring to Shays's Rebellion] is to give them full information of their affairs thro' the channel of the public papers, and to contrive that those papers should penetrate the whole mass of the people. The basis of our governments being the opinion of the people, the very first object should be to keep that right; and if it were left to me to decide whether we should have a government without newspapers or newspapers without a government, I should not hesitate a moment to prefer the latter" (quoted in *Freedom of the Press from Zenger to Jefferson,* ed. Levy, 333).

The publishing establishment on which Jefferson so much relied had been slow to develop in the American colonies until the stimulus of the Revolutionary controversy forced its growth. Printing followed early upon the settlement of Massachusetts with the establishment of Stephen Daye's press at Cambridge in 1639. But nearly half a century was to pass before any other colony had a press. Maryland and Pennsylvania in 1685 and New York in 1693 were the next to follow, and the other colonies acquired their first presses at scattered intervals during the eighteenth century. Delaware in 1761 and Georgia in 1762 were the last two of the thirteen colonies to have their own presses. By 1755 there were twenty-four presses in fifteen communities in ten of the colonies, and Boston, New York, and Philadelphia had active and competitive if still small printing industries. Until 1696 printing in England had been confined by law to London, York, Oxford, and Cambridge and had expanded to other communities only in the eighteenth century. Hence the spread of printing in the colonies paralleled that in England.

A number of physical constraints limited the size of the American industry. The first American-made presses date only from 1769, and until the Revolution almost all presses had to be imported from England. So, too, was type, with only scattered instances of American manufacture in the colonial period. Some ink and an increasing amount of paper were produced locally, but American printers were largely dependent on imports even for these materials. There was simply not the capacity in the colonies to print in large quantities.

A more important constraint was the small size of the American market, or rather of the American markets, for it could hardly be said that any integrated American market existed. Overland routes among the colonies were extremely poor, and voyages among them infrequent. The trade connections of each colony were primarily with England and in some cases the West Indies rather than with each other. There was a small intercolonial book trade, with booksellers in New York accepting consignments from booksellers in Boston or Philadelphia and with some joint ventures. A few American titles found a small market in England. But the primary market for each colony's press was necessarily local.

The character of this local demand was reflected in the output of American printers. Acts of the local assembly, almanacs calculated for the local longitude and latitude, sermons and devotional works of local divines, especially of dissenting churches unlikely to be published in England, school books, and practical self-help books to meet the needs of local farmers and townspeople for medical, legal, and agricultural advice made up the bulk of the output. Occasionally a volume of verse or a history or other work of literature by a local author might be published, and in the middle and later eighteenth century a few popular English books began to be reprinted in America. But American readers were almost entirely dependent on imports from England for extensive works addressed to a general audience. Most of the great political thinkers of the seventeenth and eighteenth centuries—men like Milton, Harrington, and Hobbes—were known in the United States only through English editions.

In addition to their output of books, many American printers published newspapers. By the beginning of the controversy between England and the colonies in the mid-1760s, America had twenty-four newspapers, of which four were in Boston and three each in New York and Philadelphia. Portsmouth, New Hampshire, Newport and Providence, Rhode Island, New London, Hartford and New Haven, Connecticut, Annapolis, Maryland, Williamsburg, Virginia, New Bern and Wilmington, North Carolina, Charleston, South Carolina, and Savannah, Georgia each had one newspaper (Schlesinger, *Prelude to Independence,* 67). Of the thirteen colonies only Delaware and New Jersey lacked newspapers, and they were served by the presses of New York and Philadelphia.

The papers were small, usually printed on both sides of a single sheet and folded to form four pages. Almost all of them appeared weekly. Although by the later 1700s a few were issued two or three times a week, there was no daily newspaper until after the Revolution, when the *Pennsylvania Evening Post* began a daily edition in 1783 (Mott, *American Journalism,* 15).

There were no reporters and relatively little local news other than official proclamations and announcements of ship sailings and arrivals. About a third of most newspapers consisted of advertisements. The news was largely culled from English newspapers and those from other colonies and from correspondents. Vigorous statements of views, signed usually with pseudonyms, were submitted to the papers and published as contributions. Some of these were written by the editors or printers themselves, but these were usually disguised as contributions by others. Before 1764 there was relatively little political discussion in the newspapers.

The circulation of newspapers was very small throughout the eighteenth century but rose during the periods of intense controversy with Great Britain. A circulation of five to six hundred was probably about the average before the Stamp Act. By the early 1770s this figure rose to about 1,500 and was perhaps 2,500 at the height of the debate preceding the Declaration of Independence (Schlesinger, *Prelude to Independence*, 303–4).

The public interest in the political controversies from the Sugar Act of 1764 and the Stamp Act to the Declaration of Independence increased the number of newspapers as well as their frequency and circulation. The twenty-one newspapers at the beginning of the period had grown to thirty-one by the time of the Boston Tea Party in 1773. Five new papers were started during or immediately after the first Continental Congress, and by the outbreak of hostilities in April 1775, thirty-eight were being published. Because newspapers were passed hand-to-hand and many taverns and coffee houses kept copies for their customers to read, the number of actual readers of each issue of a newspaper was much larger than the circulation, perhaps even several times larger.

In 1764 there were probably fewer than fifteen thousand copies of newspapers printed in the colonies each week. By 1775 the thirty-eight newspapers, several with two and a few with three issues a week, and with an average circulation perhaps five times greater than in 1763, probably produced more than 125,000 copies a week—a ninefold increase in a brief twelve years. If each paper was seen, on average, by three or four readers, a very high proportion of all literate adult males saw newspapers with some frequency.

Newspapers were not the only form in which print entered the controversies with Great Britain. Many hundreds of political pamphlets were published in which legal, constitutional, and economic issues were argued at greater length than was possible in the newspapers. These closely complemented the newspapers. The same printers and publishers issued both; the same authors wrote for both. Many important newspaper series, like John Dickinson's *Letters of a Pennsylvania Farmer,* were subsequently published in collected form as pamphlets or books. And successful pamphlets, like Thomas Paine's *Common Sense,* were widely republished as series in newspapers throughout the colonies. Newspapers had an essential role in keeping citizens aware of developments and provided the continuing stimulus and support for the Whig cause. But it was in the flow of pamphlets that the Americans hammered out the basic constitutional theory and the perception of the issues on which the Revolution was ultimately based.

The improved postal service after 1758 inaugurated by Benjamin Franklin as deputy postmaster general gave special attention to the distribution of newspapers and other publications. This not only improved circulation within each colony but also made intercolonial distribution much easier. The principal Boston, New York, and Philadelphia newspapers achieved a considerable circulation among leaders in other, especially nearby, colonies. Their impact was further spread by the copying of material. The Boston papers' accounts of the violent controversies in that city were reprinted in other papers throughout the colonies, as were the major writings of Dickinson, the Adamses, Otis, and other Whig leaders. By the 1770s popular pamphlets could find a market throughout the colonies, and a work like Thomas Paine's *Common Sense* could become a best-seller in all of them.

John Adams pointed out that the American Revolution had been achieved before independence was declared, before the first shots at Lexington and Concord. Independence was achieved in the minds of Americans, and the Declaration of Independence simply announced what was already a fact: that the controlling majority of Americans had already thrown off their sense of allegiance to the British Crown and had committed themselves and their future to the new nation, although they could only dimly sense its form.

That this was true was due primarily to the newspapers and pamphlets of the 1760s and early 1770s. The allegiance of Americans had to be transferred from a real and long-revered Crown to a body of abstract ideas. A unity of commitment to those ideas had to be created among citizens of diverse colonies who had little direct contact with one another. The reality of the independent and united American nation that had to be achieved from the separate and dependent colonies was of necessity the embodiment of words.

Without the press no such embodiment could have been achieved. The basic ideas of the unconstitutionality of taxation without representation, of the right of the governed to choose their government, of the intolerability of subordination to a parliament in which the Americans had no voice, and of outrage at the punitive acts that followed the defiance of the Tea Act could come to be shared throughout the colonies only because the printing press carried them to every corner of the land.

The press played an equally important role in the creation of the new governments that replaced the Crown's authority. In each of the former colonies (except for Connecticut and Rhode Island, where colonial charters survived) a new constitution had to be drawn and adopted. In each, basic theories of government needed to be presented and debated as part of the effort to create a government whose legitimacy depended not on tradition or inherited authority but on a devolution of power from the people. In particular, the problem of an executive chosen by and responsible to the people had to be solved. Extensive pamphlet and newspaper discussion was essential to this process throughout the new states.

In the drafting and ratification of the Federal Constitution printing played an even more important role. Most of the fifty-five delegates to the Constitutional Convention were college graduates, and almost all of them shared a familiarity with works of Greek and Roman history and philosophy and with modern treatises on government. Locke, Hume, Harrington, Montesquieu, and Blackstone were quoted almost daily in the debates. Speeches on the floor of the convention were regularly buttressed by appeals to the authority of ancient or modern writers.

Once the Constitution drafted by the convention was published for debate and ratification, a flood of pamphlet and newspaper writing poured forth in every state. One series of newspaper articles, subsequently collected as *The Federalist Papers,* was not only probably the key instrument in winning ratification but also became famous as a presentation of the political theories on which the new republic was based and as an authoritative interpretation of the Constitution's meaning. Once again, only the forceful and effective use of print could achieve the shared understanding of new political beliefs that was necessary to the very being of the new nation.

How did the Founding Fathers' awareness of the importance of communication, and particularly of print, express itself in a communications policy for the United States? They were convinced that an informed citizenry was essential to free, democratic government, and they believed that a free press was the indispensable means of achieving such an informed citizenry. What they feared most was the power of those in authority to silence a critical press, for they knew that such a press had been the force that sustained their revolution. Hence almost every state constitution contained a provision guaranteeing freedom of the press. No such guarantee was included in the Federal Constitution as it was drafted and initially ratified. This was not, however, because the drafters wished to have the federal government's power over the press to be unconstrained. On the contrary, they wished to emphasize that the federal government had no powers not specifically granted it by the Constitution, and hence had no power to legislate in any way on the press. To include a bill of rights forbidding the Congress to legislate abridgements of the freedom of the press or of religion might be taken to imply that the Congress had other powers not specifically denied it even though not specifically granted.

Nevertheless, the forebodings of the ratifying conventions in Virginia and other states were great enough to force the adoption by the First Congress and the subsequent ratification of the first ten amendments to the Constitution. The first of these says, among other things, that "the Congress shall make no law abridging the freedom of the press." It imposed on Congress the same restraints imposed on most of the state legislatures by their respective state constitutions.

The force of the First Amendment at the time of its adoption, however, was very different from the meaning it has come to have in recent years. In the first place, before the post–Civil War adoption of the Fourteenth Amendment it was a constraint only upon the Congress. Each of the states was free to deal with the press in whatever ways were permitted by its constitution and laws and by the common law as recognized in the state. In the second place, and more important, most lawyers and judges of the time recognized freedom of the press only in its Blackstonian sense as freedom from prior restraint. Seditious libel and breaches of the privilege of the state assemblies, as successors to parliament, were offenses under the common law and were frequently prosecuted by individual states despite the provisions of state constitutions protecting freedom of the press. No one successfully asserted a position that the state constitutional guarantees forbade not only prior restraint but also subsequent prosecution for publications in violation of the common law or of state legislation. The most that was contended was that the truth of an alleged libel was an appropriate defense and that whether a statement was libelous was for a jury to determine.

These were the contentions that had been advanced in the Zenger case in colonial New York, in which Peter Zenger had been tried for seditious libel of the governor of the colony. Although the then novel plea had convinced the jury and had won Zenger's acquittal in that case, his attorney's views had not been accepted by other courts, either as to the availability of truth as a defense or as to the right of juries to determine it. The early state constitutions of Pennsylvania, Delaware, and Kentucky adopted the Zenger principles, but the silence of others left the issue at best in doubt (Levy, ed., *Freedom of the Press from Zenger to Jefferson*, iii).

The question remained as to whether the federal government might bring an action for seditious libel because it was not clear whether its courts could take cognizance of the common law. In theory, that government had no traditional or inherited authority but only that specifically conferred by the Constitution, so it could be argued that the power of the Crown and the courts of Britain did not descend to the federal executive and courts because they were considered to have descended to those of the individual colonies and thence to the states.

In 1798, during a period of intense controversy between the Federalist followers of John Adams and the Jeffersonian Republicans over

the policies of the United States with respect to the French revolutionary government, Congress sought to define the power of the federal
government by the passage of the Sedition Act. In an earlier generation
it would have been thought a liberal act; although it gave the federal
government the power for two years to prosecute seditious libels, it
granted everything that had been contended for in the Zenger case. In
order to obtain a conviction, the government must show that the defendant acted with criminal intent and that the alleged libel was false,
and the jury was given the power to decide both whether the defendant
published the statement with criminal intent and whether it was in fact
false and libelous.

Nevertheless, the reaction against the bill when it was first introduced in Congress was violent. Part of the objection was concerned
with the letter of the Constitution: that by reason of both the First
Amendment and its lack of powers not specifically delegated, the Congress was simply without power to legislate in any way on the subject
of freedom of the press. Federalists replied that prosecution for seditious libel was a right of government under the common law, available
to the federal authority as well as to the states, and that to define that
power and prescribe penalties was no abridgement of freedom of the
press, which consisted only in freedom from prior restraint.

The more meaningful argument involved a new definition of freedom
of the press itself as consisting not only of a freedom from prior restraint
but also a freedom from subsequent prosecution for whatever might be
published. Of special significance was a report of the Republican minority of a select committee of the House of Representatives to consider petitions for the repeal of the act. It stated a fundamental assumption with respect to the new American polity: "It must be agreed that
the nature of our Government makes a diffusion of knowledge of public affairs necessary and proper, and that the people have no mode of
obtaining it but through the press. The necessity of their having this
information results from its being their duty to elect all the parts of the
Government, and, in this way, to sit in judgment over the conduct of
those who had been heretofore employed" (as quoted in Levy, ed., *Freedom of the Press from Zenger to Jefferson,* 179).

The minority report took the provision of the First Amendment with
respect to the freedom of the press to be absolute. It denied the validity
of distinctions between the freedom of the press and the licentiousness
of the press, saying that if Congress had the power to draw the line
between the two it would be free to define as "licentious" any expressions to which it objected. This would give the Congress an unlimited
power to regulate the press in clear violation of the intent of the First

Amendment. The only limitation of the press countenanced by the minority report was the right of individuals to bring civil suits for damages in the case of personal libel.

Although the Republicans who opposed the Sedition Act were a minority in the Congress that enacted it, they controlled the governments of Virginia and Kentucky, which adopted resolutions denouncing both the Alien Act and the Sedition Act. These resolutions were in turn denounced by the legislatures of several states controlled by the Federalists. In 1800 the Virginia Assembly adopted a lengthy counter-reply drafted by James Madison. As Madison was a principal architect of the Constitution and the drafter of the First Amendment, his words had a special authority.

Madison's arguments had a dual thrust. The first went to the constitutionality of the act. The Constitution, he asserted, did not in itself authorize the Congress to impose any restraint on the press. He held that British common law, which recognized the crime of seditious libel, did not allow truth as a defense, and placed no limit on punishment, was not a part of federal law or cognizable by the federal courts. Hence the Sedition Act, even though it was more liberal than the common law, was an abridgement of the freedom of the press as it had existed before its passage. As such, it was beyond the authority of Congress under the First Amendment.

The second thrust went to the necessity of a free press to the functioning of the American form of government. All officials of the United States were elected, directly or indirectly, by the people. It was assumed that they would sometimes be incompetent or corrupt or otherwise abuse their offices. If so, the people must replace them at the next election, but they could do so only if they were able, through the press, to learn of the errant officials' misdeeds. If an official had behaved in a contemptible manner, he should be brought into contempt even though the common law of seditious libel made it a crime to do so. In general, where the people were the ultimate judges of men and issues, they must have complete freedom to inform themselves by a free press and complete freedom to express their views. Hence the position taken by Madison's report and adopted by the Virginia Assembly was absolute: "the liberty of conscience and the freedom of the press, were *equally* and *completely* exempted from all authority whatever of the United States" (as quoted in Levy, ed., *Freedom of the Press from Zenger to Jefferson,* 227, emphasis in the original).

The Alien and Sedition Acts expired by their own terms in March 1801. The Republican Party by that date controlled the presidency and the Congress and would continue to do so for decades to come. Hence the constitutionality of the Sedition Act was never tested in the courts. Madison's views were accepted by his followers and were for a long time generally unchallenged, but they never became incontrovertibly established in American law. In addition to many other later attempts to restrict freedom of the press in a variety of ways, Theodore Roosevelt as late as 1909 was to bring, although unsuccessfully, an old-fashioned criminal seditious libel action against Joseph Pulitzer and the New York *World* because it dared to accuse him of falsehoods and tolerance of corruption in connection with the building of the Panama Canal.

Throughout the debates over press policy in the new nation, a clear contrast was made between the aims of such a policy in the United States and that in Great Britain or the European powers. In Great Britain the king-in-parliament was sovereign, and it was important that the sovereign's power to govern not be embarrassed or weakened by attacks in the press. In America, however, the people themselves were sovereign, and it was important that their rights not be abused or diminished by the agents they elected. Hence the proper role of the press was not as a bulwark of the government but rather as a watchman to assure that the government was carried on in accord with the wishes of the people. Americans had seen that the exposure in the press of what they considered royal usurpations of power had been a major instrument of the American Revolution, which could not have been achieved without the long effort of newspaper publishers and pamphleteers. Jealous of the possibility of similar usurpations by those empowered in the new government, they valued above everything else in connection with the press its role as a vigilant watchman against the corruption and abuse of authority.

But they recognized, too, that if the ultimate powers of decision lay with the people, it was essential that the people not only be warned of abuses but also be well enough informed to decide wisely. In Jefferson's letter quoted earlier in which he emphasized the importance of newspapers even over the ordinary institutions of government he added, "But I should mean that every man should receive those papers and be capable of reading them." That is, the communications policy of the new nation should be concerned not only with the *freedom* of the press but also with its *accessibility* and with the popular education that would allow the people at large to benefit from it.

With respect to the latter two goals, achieving a broad distribution of the output of the press and an improved level of education, the Revolutionary generation, although it often proclaimed them, did little to achieve them. By and large, it was assumed that if no impediments were placed, the free working of private endeavor would produce the needed flow of information. There were, however, two measures, each foreshadowing later important policies, that were intended to encourage publishing in the new nation.

One was copyright. The British Act of Anne of 1709 had governed copyright in the American colonies. Following independence most of the new states had adopted individual copyright acts. The Constitution, however, recognized copyrights, along with patents, weights and measures, coinage and currency, and bankruptcy legislation as an inherently national concern and vested in Congress the power to enact copyright legislation. The First Congress did so, in an Act of 1790 that essentially continued the provisions of the Act of Anne but confined its protection to works of American authorship. Although it initially had relatively little importance for imaginative literature and the arts, it was very important from the beginning for mapmaking and for such publishers of educational materials as Noah Webster.

The other measure that aided publishing was the establishment of a national postal service that would be much more reliable than that available in the colonies or under the Continental Congress or the Confederation. Somewhat variable and inconsistent policies gave favored treatment to newspapers and to the few magazines that appeared in the early years of the Republic, with considerable freedom left to individual postmasters to arrange for carriage free or at reduced rates.

More important was the effort to achieve the popular education appropriate to a self-governing people. The Founding Fathers recognized that the educational level of the citizens of a democracy must be higher than that required for the subjects of a monarchical or autocratic government and were convinced that American education must be grounded in freedom, training youths not only in the basic academic subjects but also in the democratic principles of the Revolution.

Because the control of education was not vested by the Constitution in the federal government, the implementation of these ideals remained a matter of state, local, and private effort. The Congress of the Confederation, however, even before the adoption of the Constitution, had provided that one square mile of public land in each thirty-six-square-mile township in the Old Northwest should be dedicated to the support of common schools. This laid a far-sighted basis for education in what became the states of Ohio, Indiana, Illinois, Michigan, and Wisconsin. The New England states continued to require towns or school districts to maintain common schools, and there were nascent movements in other states to provide a scant and irregular state contribution to the support of local or even private schools, particularly for poor children.

The most comprehensive state plan for education was one proposed by Thomas Jefferson for Virginia in 1779 but never adopted. It would have provided three years of elementary education at public expense for all children. Further education would be at the expense of parents or guardians, except that the brightest children in each school would receive scholarships if needed for further education in grammar schools and, ultimately, the ablest of those would attend the College of William and Mary.

There was also concern for public support of higher education. The three southern states without well-established private colleges—North Carolina, Georgia, and South Carolina—established state universities, the first in the nation. Virginia followed, in 1819, with a larger, more advanced, and better supported state university. All of these were primarily dependent on tuition for support, together with income from land grants or gifts, with very little or nothing in the way of legislative appropriations or tax support. A number of other states gave some modest assistance in one form or another to private institutions in their borders; some, like Virginia, New York, Massachusetts, and New Hampshire, made efforts, all successfully resisted, to convert private colleges into state institutions. There was also a movement, strongly supported by Washington himself, to establish a national university, but Congress was never willing to approve or even consider seriously such a measure.

Although in the poverty of the post-Revolutionary years almost all efforts to win significant tax support for public education failed, the idea that education of the people was necessary in a free society and was a public and not merely a parental or philanthropic responsibility was implanted and would bear fruit in decades to come. In the meantime, the heightened concern for education expressed itself in greater exertion by churches and parents to support schools, which rapidly increased in number and improved in quality. A great many private academies were created, and their curriculum was broadened to include practical and vocational subjects suited to American society. Fifteen new colleges, including the state universities of North Carolina and Georgia, were established in the 1780s and 1790s. New textbooks, including Noah Webster's speller and Jedidiah Morse's works on geography, were published to reflect specifically American needs in education and enjoyed what for the day were enormous sales.

However unable or unwilling the American people as yet were to provide adequate tax-based support to education, by the end of the Revolutionary era the idea had been firmly implanted that a high level of literacy was essential, as was a free and accessible press, to the success of the democratic experiment.

But the communications system and policies of the new nation were consonant with the tiered rather than egalitarian democracy that existed in the early days of the Republic. It was an assumption so widely accepted as to be hardly debated that only a small minority of leaders could have the breadth of view and depth of information that would enable them to act wisely on complex national issues or choose national leaders. The Federal Constitution provided for the indirect election of the president by a College of Electors and of senators by state legislatures on the assumption that the people at large would not be well enough informed to judge among national or even statewide leaders. The people were to vote only for members of the House of Representatives, who would come from local congressional districts and would presumably be known to the voters personally or by local reputation. Qualifications for voters were whatever the individual states imposed for the right to vote for the lower house of its legislature. In general this limited the franchise to adult white male owners or lessees of real property. The whole concept of government assumed the existence of a small, well-educated, and broadly informed group of men who would provide national leaders; a much broader but still limited group who would be political leaders in their localities; and a still broader small-propertied citizenry, beyond which were the politically uninvolved: blacks, Indians, women, youths not yet householders, the poor, and landless laborers.

The communications system of Revolutionary and early national America was similarly tiered. Serious works of political theory—the products of such thinkers as Harrington, Hume, Montesquieu, and Grotius—were available only in British editions. So too were the histories of Greece and Rome and of England and most of the other writings that formed the intellectual underpinnings of the Revolution and of the drafting of the Constitution. In 1783 James Madison, at the request of a committee of the Congress of the Confederation, drew up a list of books recommended for purchase for the use of members of the Congress. This antecedent of the Library of Congress was never established, but of the more than three hundred titles in the list (more than four hundred if different editions and individual works under a collective heading are included) only collections of the laws of the various states and former colonies, histories of a few of them, and local Indian treaties had appeared in American editions—with the one exception of Locke's *Two Treatises on Government*. All the others so regularly re-

ferred to in debates in the Constitutional Convention and other delib-
erative bodies were known in America only in expensive imported editions, which were represented here only in a few dozens or at the most
a few hundreds of copies. The intellectual heritage of British and Continental thinkers that so powerfully affected the Revolution and the
Constitution did so by its direct influence on a relatively small elite of
highly educated Americans and indirectly through the pamphlets and
other writings of those leaders that circulated among the substantial
and literate members of the American populace. A few works like Thomas Paine's *Common Sense* probably reached the majority of the literate families in America, and probably most literate citizens saw a newspaper at least occasionally. But with rare exceptions individual
pamphlets and newspapers reached no more than a few thousand at
most, who in turn became the interpreters of politics to their less informed neighbors.

This was true of professional and well as political works. The writings of Blackstone, Coke, Grotius, Vattel, and others relied on by
learned lawyers were available only in scarce imported editions; rural
justices of the peace relied on simple, locally published handbooks.
Works on strategy for the professional officer were imported; the county militia captain used a locally printed drill manual. A few physicians
were educated abroad and used ponderous imported treatises; a plant-
er might treat his workers using an American printer's simple guide to
cures.

The readers of the scarce imported books were, for the most part,
the graduates of the few small colleges (nine at the beginning of the
Revolution, twenty-four by 1800) and the even smaller group who had
pursued their education in British universities or Inns of Court. Education, publishing, and power all had a similar central concentration.

A second tier both of power and of communication was represented
by the outpouring of pamphlets and newspapers during the Revolutionary and Constitutional eras and by their readers, people educated in
local schools, respected in their communities, owning property, and
interested in politics, who absorbed the ideas of the great political phi-
losophers as they were digested in the writing of men like Adams, Otis,
Jefferson, Dickinson, Paine, Mason, Madison, Hamilton, Jay, and other
American pamphleteers. These men in turn influenced their poorer and
less informed neighbors, who still were able to vote.

Tiered though it was, this was the most broadly structured political
democracy the world had known, as it was probably the most broadly
informed electorate. Freedom of the press, although not absolute, was

nevertheless firmly established. As technological progress would make possible cheaper and more abundant printing, and as the resources and public commitment to universal education would be strengthened, the way was open to provide a communications system consonant with the broadening democracy the nineteenth century would bring.

— **7** —

The Era of Print Dominance

By the mid-nineteenth century printing had become much more efficient than at the time of the American Revolution. Well-built iron presses had replaced those of wood, and cylindrical presses had come into use. Stereotype plates had made possible much longer press runs. Even more important, plates could be retained and used for successive printings over a period of years without the great expense that would have been required to maintain large numbers of forms of standing type. It became practical and relatively inexpensive to run off tens of thousands of copies of pamphlets and to reissue them repeatedly. Newspapers could increase their size and appear in much longer runs.

The demonstration of a workable telegraph in 1844 and its coming into widespread practical use in the 1850s enhanced the importance of newspapers, for now they could present news from distant points that was truly new. In the time of the American Revolution, and for decades thereafter, days or even weeks might pass between an event in Massachusetts and the awareness that would bring a response in Virginia. By the 1860s the nation had been brought to a state of simultaneity, when most citizens were aware of major events at the same time, so that they "happened," in terms of perception and response, all over the nation at once. The laying of a successful transatlantic cable in 1866 extended this simultaneity to Europe.

The midcentury was a time of democratic ferment. Jacksonianism had dissolved much of the elitist structure of the early republic. A wave of evangelical religious sentiment had swept over the cool deism of the Founding Fathers. Missionary efforts, especially to the frontier region and the recently settled West, became powerful. Impassioned movements, as for the abolition of slavery and the assertion of women's rights, stirred the country.

All of these efforts made extensive use of print. The evangelical denominations established offices with the sole function of producing inexpensive religious publications and created an extensive machinery, using itinerant ministers and colporteurs, to distribute them throughout the West and in other regions not well served by established churches. Print was also resorted to by the advocates of women's rights and even more by the abolitionists, whose principal weapons were newspapers like William Lloyd Garrison's *Liberator* and Frederick Douglass's *North Star* and a steady outpouring of pamphlets by the American Anti-Slavery Society. Election campaigns were also fought out in print as they had not been in the early Republic, with campaign biographies as a favorite weapon.

The market became large enough and printing became efficient enough to permit a wide publication of American novels and other literary works, almost unknown to the scant publishing of the Revolutionary and early republican years. Authors such as Washington Irving and James Fenimore Cooper became national figures whose works were read throughout the country. The publishing of books emerged as a business distinct from printing. The forebears of some of today's firms, like John Wiley and Sons and Harper and Brothers, were founded. Magazines gained a firmer footing, and ones like the *North American Review,* the *Atlantic Monthly,* the *Southern Literary Messenger,* and *DeBow's Review* attained national or regional importance for their literary content or their impact on public affairs or both.

This midcentury expansion of the role of print was, however, only a prelude to the predominance it attained in the last quarter of the nineteenth century. This was a time of explosive growth in the nation's technology and economy, which both sustained and were sustained by the growth in the world of print. The dynamic force of this economic growth was the railroad. The national network had been extended to the West Coast in 1869, and after a brief hesitation following the panic of 1873 railroad building continued at an intense pace. To the 95,000 miles of track in operation in 1876, thousands of miles were added annually to bring the total to 193,000 by 1900. In 1876 there were 16,000 locomotives hauling 15,000 passenger cars and 385,000 freight cars. By 1900 these figures had reached 37,000 locomotives, 35,000 passenger cars, and 1,365,000 freight cars. The expansion of the railroads itself created an almost endless demand for coal and steel. In 1876 steel mills produced 860,000 tons of rail alone; by 1900 the production had reached 2,671,000 tons.

Railroads affected every other industry as well by enabling raw materials to be assembled at factories and their products to be distributed nationally. Mining grew not only to supply the coal and iron ore demanded by the railroads but also the copper and nickel and precious metals needed in a growing economy. The total output of mines increased from $1,395,000,000 in 1869 to $5,475,000,000 in 1899. By 1880 cotton mills consumed 1,500,000 bales, most of which was brought by rail or coastal steamer from southern fields to northern mills to be reshipped as fabrics throughout the country. By 1900 the annual consumption was 3,687,000 bales. Factory production of furniture, stoves, housewares, shoes, and clothing superseded local handicrafts and again relied on rail shipment of both raw materials and finished products.

Between 1869 and 1899 the number of production workers in manufacturing increased from 2,100,000 to 5,100,000. The capital invested, measured in constant dollars, nearly quadrupled in the twenty years from 1879 to 1899. The horsepower of prime movers in manufacturing more than quadrupled between 1869 and 1899, and in the 1890s for the first time a considerable amount of the power came from electric motors. The production of raw steel, which was negligible as late as 1869, reached more than a million tons by 1879 and then multiplied elevenfold by the end of the century. A whole new industry came in the production and refinement of petroleum, initially primarily to produce kerosene for lighting.

The modern city was also the creation of the railroad. The early republic was rural or small-town in character; in 1790 no city in the United States had as many as fifty thousand residents and only three had as many as twenty-five thousand. Even as late as 1850, before the railroad afforded the means of concentrating population, the largest city was New York, with fewer than seven hundred thousand; only five others, all except Cincinnati seaport cities, had as many as one hundred thousand residents. By 1880 New York had more than a million, three others more than half a million, and sixteen more than one hundred thousand. By the end of the century, there were thirty cities with more than one hundred thousand: New York had reach nearly 3,500,000; Chicago, nearly 1,700,000; and Philadelphia, almost 1,300,000. Baltimore, Boston, and St. Louis had each well over half a million. Although 60 percent of the population was still rural, cities now dominated. Nearly 20 percent of Americans lived in cities of more than one hundred thousand.

Practical applications of electricity were second only to the railroad in the industrialization and urbanization of America. The telephone, the electric light, and the alternating current electric motor, although invented earlier, all came into practical use in the 1880s. The electrification of previously horse-drawn street railways and steam-powered elevated trains made it possible to extend the city, bringing workers and shoppers to central factories, offices, and stores from distances of several miles. Electrically powered elevators, replacing earlier hydraulic models, made practical much taller buildings and ultimately the early skyscraper, again permitting the compression of people and production within urban bounds. Electric motors powered from central generating plants made possible a much more efficient use of machinery than could be achieved when each machine had to receive power through gears and belts from a large nearby steam engine. Electric lights made city streets safer and more attractive and also made the illumination of large buildings more practical without the heat or fire hazards of gas or kerosene lighting. The telephone provided the network of communication for large offices and commercial establishments.

These developments involved enormous internal movements of population, not only from farm to city but also from the South to such manufacturing states as New York, Massachusetts, Illinois, and Michigan. Even more impressive was the constant flow of European immigration, which had been held in check for a time by the Civil War and the depression following the Panic of 1873 but averaged more than half a million a year in the 1880s. Again checked by the depression of the mid-1890s, it reached more than a million a year from 1900 to the outbreak of war in 1914.

These industrial and demographic developments imposed an enormous burden on the communications system of the United States. Similar developments imposed similar burdens on the communications system of other nations in comparable stages of economic development. Millions of workers were being employed not in agricultural or handicraft work where they would learn their skills orally by apprenticeship or from their parents, but in factories or mines or railroads requiring new skills, much of which were print-embodied and required the use of written instructions. Whole new professions of engineers and technicians were needed. The physical and chemical sciences that supported the new technologies required texts, treatises, and journals. A large administrative and clerical superstructure grew up in the offices of railroads and industrial companies, in the wholesale firms and stores that distributed their products, and in the banks and other institutions that served them. Two large masses of the population, the recently freed slaves and the millions of recent immigrants, in both cases largely illiterate, at least in English, had to be taught and acculturated.

These developments required an enormous expansion of the production and use of print, the only medium then available for impersonal communication, and a revolutionary increase in the publicly supported educational effort.

The technologizing of American industry that required so great an increase in print output also provided the means to achieve it, for the printing industry was mechanized in the same sweep of development that affected other industries. Powered rotary presses and the use of stereotype plates had been introduced earlier in the nineteenth century, at first in England and primarily for printing newspapers. But a greatly improved model, the Hoe press, was introduced in 1867, which printed on both sides of a "web" or roll of paper rather than from individual sheets.

One Hoe press had a potential output hundreds of times greater than that of the presses available at the beginning of the century. But its productive power could not be fully used without a new source for paper. The production of rag paper was limited by the supply of usable rags, the capacity of small mills, and its high cost. Three processes to produce pulp from wood were developed in the mid-nineteenth century—at first by mechanical grinding, then by the alkaline soda process introduced from England in 1854, and finally by the sulfite process, employing acids, which came into use in the late 1860s. All three used as their raw material softwood trees then available in limitless quantities. Large paper mills employing the new processes grew rapidly through the remainder of the century. Major improvements in machinery to transform pulp into paper further increased output.

Faster and more efficient printing and cheaper and more abundant paper made possible much larger editions at much lower prices. But the slowness of typesetting and the subsequent sorting and cleaning of type remained a burden. This was largely solved by the introduction of the Mergenthaler linotype and the Lanson monotype machines in the latter 1880s. These set matrices rather than type and cast fresh type from molten lead by the line or as individual characters. The used type was simply melted down, saving the cost of sorting and maintaining large fonts. The Benton boring machine, invented in 1885, made practical the production of the enormous number of matrices required by these processes.

These inventions permitted a vast increase in the sheer quantity of print pouring from America's presses. By 1880 there were nearly a thousand daily newspaper in the United States where there had been twenty-four in 1800, and their total circulation was about 3,500,000 as contrasted with little more than fifty thousand at the earlier time. Moreover, each issue was many times as large as its earlier counterpart, so that the daily physical output was hundreds of times greater. The number of daily newspapers would double again in the remaining years of the century, and circulation would grow another fourfold, to fifteen million, while each daily issue grew larger and larger. The total physical content of daily newspapers circulated in the United States in 1900 was more than a thousand times as great as in 1800.

Where there had been about forty magazines in 1800, most of them short-lived and with very limited circulation, there were 5,500 in 1900, many with large nationwide circulations and almost all founded in the last quarter of the century. They catered to every profession, learned discipline, trade, and personal interest. During the last quarter of the century, new magazines were founded at the rate of more than one a working day.

The handful of books published in the early years of the century had risen to more than two thousand a year by 1880, to four thousand by 1883, and to 6,400 by 1900, providing texts for schools, professional works for doctors, lawyers, and engineers, practical manuals for skilled technicians, religious treatises, political works, novels, children's books, and works of general information.

Probably well over 250,000,000 copies of printed pages were pouring from the press daily by 1900 in the form of newspapers, magazines, and books alone, in addition to pamphlets, broadsides, leaflets, and other job printing. A century earlier this output had been far less than half a million copies of pages a day, perhaps no more than 250,000. The population had increased greatly as well, but by 1900 the average American had available more than a hundred times as much printed matter daily as had his or her forebears of 1800. There had been a nineteenth-century revolution in the availability of print, not only in America but also in Northern and Western Europe, greater quantitatively than the Gutenberg revolution of the fifteenth century and perhaps as important in its impact on society.

To achieve this outpouring required not only the new technology of paper manufacture, typesetting, and printing, but also the creation of an industrial structure for the production and dissemination of print. The book publishing industry in the decades between the Civil War and World War I assumed, on a smaller scale, very much the form it would retain until late in the twentieth century. Older houses, such as Harper, Appleton, Putnam, Scribner, Dodd Mead, Van Nostrand, Dutton, Wiley, Lippincott, Houghton Mifflin, and Little Brown continued to grow, sometimes, as in the case of Harper, with a change of ownership but usually still under the control of the founding family. To them were added important new houses, such as Holt and Doubleday. Publishing became more sharply distinguished from printing, although some houses retained their presses. All the larger houses had distinct editorial, production, and marketing staffs and maintained sales forces to call on wholesalers, bookstores, schools, and other customers. Wholesale houses like Baker and Taylor, McClurg, and the American News Company became important factors. Most present marketing methods, including publicity, newspaper and magazine advertising, book reviews, and mail order, door-to-door, and subscription selling were well established. Earlier auctions and trade sales passed into disuse.

Throughout the period book publishing houses, even the largest, remained small compared to the great manufacturing and commercial enterprises of the era and were personally owned and directed, often remaining in the same family for generations. A relatively small total industry was divided among dozens of larger houses and hundreds of smaller, local, and specialized publishers. Only one effort was made to consolidate publishing houses with a view to controlling a sector of the market. That involved the creation of the American Book Company in 1890 by the merger of four of the largest publishers of elementary and secondary school textbooks. The new company later acquired others in the field. Although the American Book Company was for an extended period the largest textbook house, it was never able to establish a monopoly and saw its market share eroded over the years as other publishers entered this profitable field.

Small-scale and fragmented though it was, the book publishing industry had a fraternal and guildlike character that softened competition, economic as well as cultural. To entice away another publisher's authors or to offer higher than usual royalties or trade discounts was frowned on. Booksellers were pressed to maintain fixed prices. Publishers were much alike in being cultured and conservative gentlemen of means, and they discouraged the publication of works that offended their rather uniform political or moral sensibilities. Karl Marx on political grounds and Emile Zola on moral had difficulty in finding American publishers.

Somewhat outside the normal structure of book publishing was the enormous flow of very inexpensive books. These were essentially of two kinds. One consisted of reprints, primarily of British novels for which no copyright existed in the United States and on which no royalties were paid. These were issued by several leading publishing houses. First appearing in newspaperlike format, later in cheaply produced paperbacks at 25 cents or less, these enjoyed a wide market. In the 1890s their production declined because of the extension of limited copyright to the works of British authors and the depletion of the supply of reprintable British novels. The other kind were the even cheaper "dime novels," mass-produced tales of the West and of crime and detection, issued by houses specializing in such books and sold largely through the American News Company and newsstand outlets.

As in the case of books, the publication of magazines in the closing decades of the nineteenth century became a highly organized business. For a few companies it became a very large-scale one. The rise of national advertising, for which magazines were the only available medium, was a transforming force. Until after the Civil War, magazine advertising had been almost negligible in amount; by 1890 it had risen to more than $70,000,000 and by 1905 to $145,000,000. Advertising, rather than circulation, had become the principal source of income. Successful publishing came to involve assembling a large audience that could constitute a rewarding market for advertisers. The potential income was large enough to stimulate the most vigorous circulation promotion efforts and drive editors to devise the most reader-enticing content. It also provided the revenue that could support such major enterprises as the Curtis or McCall or Collier publishing companies.

Pre–Civil War magazines such as the *North American Review* or the *Southern Literary Messenger* reflected their editors' literary and intellectual tastes, catered generally to a highly educated elite, and had a correspondingly limited circulation. The advertising-driven magazines of the late nineteenth century were impelled to seek out very large or else very specialized readerships. The more successful had circulation figures in the hundreds of thousands; a few were to surpass a million. Except for specialized trade and professional magazines, readership had to be sought among Americans generally; editorial success consisted of divining the interests of ordinary Americans and appealing to them with a lively content. The great editors of the day, Edward Bok, George Horace Lorimer, Frank Leslie, Sam McClure, and James McCall, were great not necessarily because of their own intellectual leadership but because of their rapport with their readers.

Magazines also began to specialize in content in order to attract audiences appropriate to particular kinds of advertisers. Women's magazines, such at the *Delineator* (1873), the *Ladies Home Journal* (1883), and the *Women's Home Companion* (1897), achieved enormous circulations with a content that provided useful information on fashions, cookery, furnishings, housekeeping, and child-rearing in addition to entertaining fiction, often of high quality. Advertising was an essential part of their content, interesting and helpful to their women readers and a most effective medium for those wishing to reach the "women's market."

Others appealed to more specialized interests; bicycling and photography, for example, were each served by many dozens of magazines. Of particular importance were the trade or business magazines. They had a beginning much earlier in the century, with railroad magazines as early as 1832 and with *Debow's Review,* which covered business in general with special attention to the South. But there was an enormous increase in highly technical business journals in the latter decades of the century. Railroads, mines, the petroleum industry, textiles, steam power generally, and the new chemical and electrical industries engendered numerous publications that provided not only business news but also solid technological information essential to the industrial transformation taking place. The McGraw Publishing Company and the Hill Publishing Company, later to be merged, were already playing an important role in business and industrial publishing.

Also coming into importance in these years were scholarly journals, such as the *American Historical Review,* the *American Economic Review,* and numerous journals in medicine and the natural sciences. By 1900 every major discipline had at least one and often several journals, usually issued by newly formed learned societies, which sustained the new generation of professional scholars on university and college faculties and the scientific concerns of the new technologies.

The increase in the circulation and influence of newspapers was equally dramatic. Steady improvements were made in the already remarkable Hoe press, enabling it not only to print at very high speeds but also to cut, fold, and count papers as they emerged from the press. By 1882 it could produce twenty-four thousand copies an hour of a twelve-page paper. This speed had doubled by 1888, and continued to increase in response to the constant demands for longer runs of larger papers. The more successful publishers built imposing buildings with big pressrooms capable of housing a number of these giant presses. Because of the demand for speed, the invention of the linotype machine was even more important for newspapers than it had been for magazines and books.

Newsprint became abundant not only as a result of the use of ground wood pulp as the basic content but also as a result of remarkable increases in the efficiency of Fourdrinier paper-making machines, which tripled in the 1870s and 1880s. As a result, the cost of newsprint plummeted, dropping from about 12 cents a pound in 1872 to 3 cents a pound twenty years later.

The reductions in cost as a result of these technological advances made it possible to reduce the price of newspapers even farther in spite of their greater size. By the end of the century most major newspapers were selling for 1 or 2 cents a copy. This low price, which barely exceeded the cost of paper in the larger journals, was also made possible by a great increase in advertising revenue, which nearly doubled between 1870 and 1890 and more than tripled in the following twenty years. By 1914 the advertising revenue of newspapers had risen to $250,000,000 a year.

The growth in advertising reflected not only the growing prosperity of the country but also the increased effectiveness of newspapers as a mass advertising medium in consequence of their greatly increased circulation. In 1872 only two newspapers, both in New York, the *Sun* and the *Daily News,* had a circulation of more than 100,000. Twenty years later there were eight papers in this class, headed by the *New York World* with 375,000 and including papers in Chicago, Philadelphia, and Boston as well as New York. By 1914 thirty papers in twelve cities exceeded a hundred thousand and both Pulitzer's *World* and Hearst's *Journal* were at about a million.

Most of the thousands of newspapers in the country were small; many were still printed on old flat-bed presses, and some even hand-powered. Most appeared in weekly rather than daily editions. But the dynamic force of the press was concentrated in the great urban dailies. These had clearly become the instruments of men of great wealth. No longer could a newspaper, at least in a large city, be launched with a small printing press and a tiny staff. William Randolph Hearst invested at least $7,500,000 of his mother's fortune in the New York *Examiner* before he could make it profitable, and by the end of the century each of the largest papers represented an investment of tens of millions of dollars. The rewards of successful management were also great. The profits from Hearst's and Pultizer's empires enabled them to lead lives of great luxury, with yachts, castles, and art collections that put them in a class with such industrial and banking giants as Carnegie, Morgan, and Rockefeller. Other successful papers in smaller cities did not produce so enormous a flow of cash, but they did make their editor-owners men of substantial wealth and great importance in their communities.

Competition, however, was severe. Merchants and others sought to place their advertising in the journals that would reach the largest number of potential customers and hence of necessity to avoid those of more limited circulation. As a result there was an enormous premium on having the largest or one of the very largest circulations in any city. Success in that meant wealth; to slip out of this small circle was likely to mean a downward spiral into failure or bankruptcy.

Because of the intense competition and the high capital demands, especially successful publishers were able to buy up other papers and create powerful chains. The Hearst and Scripps chains had become particularly powerful, with papers in larger cities throughout the country.

By the turn of the century the output of print in the United States had become highly industrialized. It was now largely controlled by men and companies of great wealth and a predominantly profit-seeking motivation in their work. There continued to be thousands of small local newspapers, magazines of limited circulation, and small book publishers. There were no gatekeepers with monopolistic power to deny writers and viewpoints access to the public through the medium of print. But the great magazine, newspaper, and book publishers controlled the only *mass* channels to the public and were in a position to exercise enormous influence and to have power such as they had not had before and were not to have in the future after the coming of the new media of the twentieth century.

In the exercise of this power the tycoons of print had a dual motivation. Like the partisan newspaper publishers of the first half of the century, who produced what were essentially party organs, they had strongly held views. Pulitzer and the young Hearst campaigned stridently for their liberal and reformist convictions. The editors and publishers of the muckraking magazines were sincerely committed to the attack on the evils they exposed. There was not yet the impersonal corporate ownership of the great magazines, newspapers, and book publishers of the late twentieth century. But already the primary goals of publishers had become economic as they were drawn by the possibility of great profits and driven by competitive necessity. They sought readership as much as, increasingly even more than, they sought influence. They were impelled to seek out the interests of the mass readership they coveted and to shape their publishing around those interests. Readers gained a power over the media precisely and reciprocally as the media gained a power over the people. The flamboyant reform campaigns of many newspapers and magazines were intended more as a means of attracting readers than as expressions of publishers' zeal.

The American communications system of the late nineteenth and early twentieth centuries was shaped by public policy as well as by printing technology and the economic structure of the publishing industry. The belief in the indispensability of a free press so firmly implanted in the Revolutionary era continued to dominate public policy, at least so far as political discussion was concerned. The owners of newspapers, magazines, and book publishing houses offered little hospitality to anarchist or even to socialist ideas, and local police action might be taken, particularly against anarchist publications. But otherwise political discussion remained on the whole remarkably free. Election issues were robustly debated. Muckrakers mercilessly exposed corruption and monopolies. Political bosses like Tweed were savaged in the press. Utopian and idealistic writings challenging the whole socioeconomic system, such as Henry George's *Progress and Poverty* and Edward Bellamy's *Looking Backward,* were published in enormous editions.

But for the first time, censorship on moral grounds became widespread. Mass printing made the publication of salacious materials profitable. And the new abundant availability of print to children, the laboring class, and others of limited education aroused special concern. The intense and puritanical religiosity of the Victorian era gave further force to efforts to suppress not only the obscene but also anything that hinted of the risqué or that challenged rigid standards of sexual morality. These efforts were spearheaded by Anthony Comstock (1844–1915), a zealot of infinite energy, who in 1873 persuaded Congress to enact the so-called Comstock Laws making it illegal to send obscene publications through the mails and then got himself appointed a special postal inspector with authority to open and condemn shipments of printed matter. Comstock seized enormous quantities of books, pamphlets, and magazines, most of which would be considered quite harmless by late twentieth century standards and some of which contained material of substantial literary merit. Comstock's activities were not actively opposed by the publishing industry generally, whose conservative managements shared a disdain for works of taste or morals questionable under the standards of the time.

In the latter nineteenth century there was growing awareness of the need for a better educated and more proficient labor force, including white-collar and professional workers, to meet the needs of the merging urban and industrial society. There was also a growing concern that the health of democratic government was threatened by the presence of masses of uneducated voters. Hence federal, state, and local governments, especially in urban areas, moved aggressively to enlarge the flow of print, to make it more accessible, and to raise the level of education.

After long debate the Copyright Act was amended in 1891 to protect the work of foreign as well as American authors, provided the works of foreign authorship were promptly published in the United States in editions manufactured in this country. American authors were major beneficiaries of this act, for they no longer had to compete with pirated and royalty-free editions of the works of British and European authors.

More important in encouraging the widespread dissemination of print was the postal legislation of 1879, which provided for the free distribution of newspapers in the county of their publication (a boon to rural and small-town weeklies) and for a low, flat national rate for the carriage of magazines. This rate made it practical for magazines to use the newly extended rail network to achieve a truly national distribution at postal costs no greater from New York to the Pacific than to adjoining towns. In this way the postal service became a major factor in creating an integrated national culture bound together by the newly popular magazines that brought common points of view and bodies of knowledge to the entire country.

Of even more fundamental concern was public policy toward education as it developed in the latter decades of the century. The idea of tax-supported common schools, at least for white children, had won general approval by the time of the Civil War, but the support was minimal in much of the country, particularly in the South. One-room schoolhouses, presided over by untrained or half-trained teachers, were usual. Rural schools in particular tended to be poor, open only for short terms, and irregularly attended.

With the urbanization and industrialization of America came the realization that a soundly literate population was essential to the successful functioning of the more complex and rapidly changing society. Public schools won more generous tax support. Better school buildings with graded classes and with adequate physical facilities were built, especially in the cities. Professional standards for teachers were raised, and dozens of normal schools were created for their training. As a result of the demands of the new urban industries, manual and vocational training was introduced into the schools to prepare youths for the new kinds of jobs. The recognition that at least an elementary education was important not only to the children themselves but also to society as a whole resulted in the adoption in most states of compulsory education laws.

In the later years of the century there was also a growing recognition that primary and elementary education alone was not sufficient to society's needs. Secondary education prior to the 1870s had been almost entirely in private academies intended to give young men and, more rarely, young women the classical education needed to prepare them for college. As late as 1872 there were only twenty-five thousand students in public high schools. In the following decades there was a strong movement for tax-supported high schools, not only to prepare children of less affluent families for college but also to provide the vocational, mathematical, language, and clerical skills that would prepare graduates to go directly into the factories, shops, and offices of the expanding economy.

It was also recognized that higher education must be both expanded and made more responsive to the technological needs of society. A number of privately financed technical colleges were founded, such as the Worcester Polytechnic Institute in 1865, Lehigh University in 1866, and the Stevens Institute of Technology in 1871. The great thrust toward higher technical education came, however, as a result of the Morrill Act of 1862, which distributed to the states income from the sale of public lands in order to enable them to establish institutions that would provide higher education in agriculture and the mechanic arts. As a result of this legislation, during the remaining years of the century states created public universities that eschewed traditional classical studies in order to provide training in engineering, agronomy, and other subjects needed to sustain the new technological society that was emerging.

Scholarship and research became professionalized. American scholars who had studied in Germany brought back with them the ideal of the university as a center for research and postgraduate instruction. The ideal was embodied in the establishment of the Johns Hopkins University in 1876 and in the reorganization of postgraduate instruction in other major universities. The Ph.D. degree became a recognized certificate of professional scholarship and came to be awarded by the larger and more prestigious universities. Societies of scholars, like the Chemical Society of America (1876), the American Historical Association (1884), the Institute of Electrical Engineers (1884), the American Economic Association (1885), and the Geological Society of America (1888), defined and strengthened the professions.

Although libraries had existed in the American colonies from very early days and tax-supported public libraries had begun to appear, at least in New England, before the Civil War, the development of a library system as a major component of American education and communication occurred only after that war. As a result of the recognition of the need for resources that would enable adults to continue their educations and to equip themselves to deal with the more complex social issues and the more demanding technology of the postwar years, the library movement spread with great rapidity in the closing decades of the century.

The United States commissioner of education published the first comprehensive report on public libraries in 1876. "Public" libraries were considered to include all except personal collections and those of churches and Sunday schools. The report discovered 3,682 public libraries in 1875, of which 1,059 were school and academy libraries and 319 served colleges. Truly public libraries totaled 342. Of the libraries existing in 1875, 2,240 had been created in the previous 25 years, including 257 of the 342 truly public institutions, indicating that the surge of library growth was at its beginning. Almost all libraries were quite small, with the majority holding fewer than two thousand volumes. Only nine had more than a hundred thousand volumes; only two, the Boston Public Library and the Library of Congress, held more than two hundred thousand. But the foundation for growth and professionalization had been laid.

In the same year as the commissioner's report, 1876, the American Library Association was founded in Philadelphia as part of the celebration of the centennial of American independence, and the *Library Journal,* the first American professional periodical in the field, was initiated. In 1887 the first professional school for the training of librarians was established by Melville Dewey at Columbia University. The publication of Dewey's classification system and rules for cataloging provided a standard for the profession.

The public library movement received an enormous impetus from the philanthropy of Andrew Carnegie, who offered to give funds for the construction of a public library building in any community that would provide the site and obligate itself to fund the operation of the institution. By the time of World War I, almost every city and most large towns in the United States had a public library. Uniform cataloging rules, the availability of Library of Congress catalog cards, interlibrary loan practices, the existence of a number of library schools, and a strong national association knit these institutions into something loosely approaching a national library system.

Meanwhile, libraries were developing as resources for research as well as institutions for public enlightenment. Major universities, as they began to strengthen their programs of postgraduate instruction and to offer the Ph.D., developed their libraries to support advanced studies. Private philanthropy created the Newberry and the Crerar libraries in Chicago, devoted to the humanities and to science and technology, respectively. The Astor, the Tilden, and the Lenox families had created and endowed research libraries in New York, which were united in 1901 to form the New York Public Library. Public libraries in a number of other large cities, such as Boston, also developed strong research collections, employing both public and private funds.

The Copyright Act of 1870 provided for the first time that copies of all copyrighted works be deposited in the Library of Congress. This assured the rapid growth of that thitherto somnolent collection, almost forcing the creation of a great national institution. A magnificent new building was created for it and opened in 1897; a strong professional staff was assembled; and through its cataloging practices, the sale of its printed catalog cards, its bibliographical undertakings, and the comprehensive development of its collections, the Library of Congress quickly became a center of national library development.

———————

Through an enormous extension of its educational effort and other sound measures of public policy, through a large investment in paper mills and printing plants employing the new technologies of the era, and through the creation of an extensive and sophisticated publishing industry, the United States by the end of the nineteenth century had created a communications system appropriate to an urbanized and industrialized society employing new, scientifically based technologies. For the first time the mass of the population was drawn into direct participation in the print society.

These developments in the United States were paralleled in Northern Europe, where near universal literacy and a vast increase in inexpensive printed matter also coincided with the emergence of an urban and technology-based society. In all of the countries in which these developments were fully realized, the broadening of access to the flow of information was concomitant with the mass transfer of workers from traditional, orally learned occupations, primarily agricultural, into the new technology-based and print-learned economy and also with a major broadening of participation in political life. The reduction or elimination of property qualifications for the vote throughout North America and Northern and Western Europe enfranchised the newly literate working classes. The British Reform Act of 1867, the abolition of the monarchy and the creation of the broadly based Third Republic in France in 1871, the Bismarckian reforms in Germany, and the Reconstruction in the United States that attempted (although with limited success) to admit blacks to political life were all parts of the same broad movement.

In the United States the proportion of the adult male population voting in national elections rose to its highest, even though only the election of 1896 involved a well-defined clash on issues. Political parties assumed a more important, organized, and continuing role, in no small part because of the necessity of raising funds to meet the costs of the flood of printed materials that now became a major instrument in election campaigns. Fund-raisers like Mark Hanna became powerful political leaders, surpassing in importance the older generation of bosses who delivered votes by the use of patronage more than by publicity efforts. Print as a compelling force in political campaigns perhaps reached its height in the election of 1896. Both parties flooded the country with pamphlets and posters on the issues of labor and the free coinage of silver. The support of major newspapers, each reaching hundreds of thousands of potential voters, became of crucial importance. William Jennings Bryan's eloquence, displayed throughout the country as he went desperately by train from city to city, was no match for the print-voiced campaign of William McKinley, who remained at home meeting informally with delegations of supporters.

In Luther's day the availability of print to a small learned class made it possible for him to communicate directly with priests and monks who shared his concerns and to do so without going through the hierarchy. It was the opening of this channel that made the Reformation possible. Similarly, the mass availability of print in the late nineteenth century made new book-based religions possible, for now the prophet of a new order could communicate directly not only with a potentially dissident clergy but also with individual laymen. The Book of Mormon and *Science and Health, with Key to the Scriptures* were printed in hundreds of thousands—ultimately, millions—of copies. Supplemented by pamphlets, newspapers, and other printed materials, they made it possible for the formidable organizational skills of Brigham Young and of Mary Baker Eddy to create the Church of Jesus Christ of Latter Day Saints and the Church of Christ, Scientist as powerful national and later worldwide faiths.

The established denominations also made intensive use of print, with church periodicals and newspapers, Sunday school materials, sermons, and tracts helping to make the late nineteenth century a period of Victorian morality and public commitment to religious belief.

The mass availability of print also affected the forms of literature and of popular entertainment. Even by the late eighteenth and early nineteenth centuries, the rise in levels of literacy and the general availability of print to the middle class had enabled the novel and the light essay to displace drama as the predominant literary form. By the late nineteenth century reading had become an important source of entertainment for the population generally and not merely for the educated middle and upper classes. In consequence, the novel exploded in popularity, with the publication of well over a thousand titles a year, many in very inexpensive editions. Lurid tales of adventure, Westerns, stories of crime and detection, and other similar novels responded to a mass demand, but the period was one of the flowering of the literary novel as well, both in Europe and in the United States.

Poetry was also affected. During the course of the nineteenth century the classical and formalistic court-patronized poetry of the eighteenth century was succeeded by the emotional, popularly accessible poetry of the Romantic period responding to the tastes of the middle classes who had now become in effect the patrons of literature. The mass availability of print by the end of the century had evoked an out-pouring of pseudo-folk poetry corresponding to dime-novel fiction.

But the greatest of the effects of the print revolution of the nineteenth century was its empowerment of the societies in which it took place. Print carried to the furthest point the capacity of language to abstract selected components of reality and to manipulate them symbolically. It could "freeze" and preserve the formulations of language and dissem-inate them in fixed form throughout a society. It made possible the de-velopment of the sciences, the technologies, and the modes of thought that inform modern Western society.

Already by the end of the eighteenth century the surge of power that had accompanied the invention and early development of print had en-abled Western Europe to sweep out over the face of the earth, discover-ing, exploring, and settling the Americas, opening ways to Asia, and es-tablishing commercial outposts and a trading network centered in Europe and embracing the world. As yet, however, the print culture was a thickening crust on society; it did not penetrate deeply into the processes of production. The eighteenth century was still a time of handicrafts and peasant tillage, of wind and sail and trade, of muskets and light fieldpiec-es. It was not yet a time of steel and factories and railroads, of great cit-ies, of ironclad steam-powered ships and heavy artillery. These all came concomitantly with the diffusion of print culture throughout society and throughout the science-based technologies of its new industries and of its enormous new economic and military might.

In the half century before World War I the new print-related power of Western Europe and the United States exploded across the world, dividing Africa and dominating the societies of China, Southeast Asia, the Middle East, and Latin America where the powers of print reached only a small elite and had not availed to transform their societies. The predominance of print in that era was consonant with the outflowing power that came to bestride the world.

— 8 —

The Technology of the
Audiovisual Revolution

Until the late nineteenth century information could be preserved through time or transmitted over a distance only by embodying it in a written or printed document. To do this required selecting words to depict the scene or action or concept to be communicated, encoding the words into alphabetic or ideographic symbols, impressing those symbols on paper or other appropriate surfaces, and physically preserving or transporting the resulting document. Musical sounds similarly could be preserved or conveyed only by encoding them in a system of written notation. To recapture the recorded information or music required decoding the written or printed words or notes and mentally or actually reproducing their aural originals.

In the course of the nineteenth and early twentieth centuries a series of inventions made it possible to record information without the process of encoding or even of verbalization and to transmit it without physically transporting an artifact. The first of these was the telegraph. Although many scientists and tinkerers contributed to its invention, Samuel F. B. Morse and his associate, Alfred Vail, installed the first practical working telegraph between Baltimore and Washington in 1844. It rapidly spread into a national network accompanying the development of the railroad system, which provided the rights of way for the telegraph lines, while the telegraph in turn facilitated the control of train movements. The successful laying of a transatlantic cable in 1866, connecting American and European telegraphic networks, made it truly international.

The necessity of creating a large organization to establish and operate a national telegraphic network (the Western Union) and another national organization to collect and disseminate news through that network (the Associated Press) gave such structures an unprecedented power to affect, even in part to control, the flow of information and called for public policies to regulate the use of that power. Also, the cost of telegraphic communication demanded a terse, clear style that journalists adopted and that affected the writing of such journalistically trained authors as Ernest Hemingway.

The second major invention affecting communication was the telephone. In the 1870s several inventors were on the threshold of developing a workable means of audible communication through the use of modulated electric currents. Alexander Graham Bell achieved the most practical solution in 1876. The greatest contribution of Bell and his colleagues, especially Theodore Vail, was not so much the technological superiority of the instrument he developed as the creation of the Bell organization. This made possible the rapid establishment of a local telephone system in each city or town, connected by intercity lines.

The telephone made it possible to convey messages at a distance without encoding them into written form. It was much more rapid than the telegraph, as it avoided not only the delays in encoding and decoding but also those of delivery to and from the nearest telegraph terminal. Calls could be made directly to and from homes and offices, with instantaneous reply in dialog form. The oral qualities of pitch, tone, and emphasis of which writing is denuded could be preserved in telephonic communication.

Although the telephone system did not reach into most homes until well into the twentieth century, telephones were quickly placed in most business offices in the decades immediately following Bell's invention. It had a major effect on business communication, and the large corporations and national enterprises of the late nineteenth and twentieth centuries could hardly have functioned without it. However, because telephonic communication was inherently point-to-point or person-to-person, it tended to replace individually written letters or memorandums rather than newspapers, magazines, or other printed instruments of public communication.

As in the case of the telegraph, large organizations were necessary to create and operate telephone systems. In the United States these were private corporations, primarily the American Telephone and Telegraph Company, which grew out of the Bell organization. In almost all other countries it was a government agency, usually the national postal system. In either case, major problems were encountered in preventing or regulating monopoly control over communication through the system.

Artists had always been able to represent reality in their paintings or drawings without the necessity of describing it in words. Their work preserved images through time, preserving for us the likeness of those wealthy enough or important enough to have their portraits painted and images of important events or scenes. The slowness and expense of the artists' work, however, limited its use as a medium of recording and communication. What was needed were the means of producing images quickly, accurately, and inexpensively and also of reproducing them in quantity for public distribution. Both came in the nineteenth century.

Dozens of inventors contributed to the development of photographic techniques in the early decades of the nineteenth century, and by the 1860s photographers like Mathew Brady could capture reality, not as inexpensively and quickly or as conveniently as photographers today but with equal accuracy and representational skill. The leaders and men and women and the battlefields of the Civil War could now been seen by absent viewers as they could never have been envisioned through verbal descriptions or artists' sketches. However, there were no means of multiplying photographs directly in thousands of copies for use in newspapers and magazines. Until near the end of the nineteenth century such publications were still illustrated by woodcuts or engravings made from artists' drawings. The invention of the half-tone process in 1890 for the first time combined the convenience and accuracy of photography with print's capacity to reach a broad audience. By the coming of the twentieth century, print was free from an exclusive reliance on words and was able to convey visual images with equal facility. As the technology of photography, including color photography, and of printing improved over the decades of the twentieth century, this capacity was enhanced and the envisioning of the world was enriched.

As the telephone made it possible to transmit sound and speech without encoding, so the phonograph made it possible to record and preserve them. The first instrument to record and reproduce sound was invented by Thomas Edison in 1877. It employed a stylus to press grooves into the tin-foil covering of a cylinder. The quality of sound reproduction was very poor, however, and there was no practical way to make copies. The first usable phonograph was developed by Emile Berliner and Eldridge Johnson in the 1890s, using wax discs pressed from a master recording. Early in the twentieth century such instruments came into general use, and a wide range of both classical and popular music was made available on records. Music escaped the necessity of being encoded in notes that were then preserved or transmitted elsewhere to be decoded and the original sounds recreated by a performer. Now later or distant listeners could hear the music as it was originally performed without the translation into or the retranslation from written scores. Many kinds of music, such as folk music and music of other cultures that did not lend itself to recording in Western notation, could be recorded and preserved without having to be encoded in written form.

Over the course of the twentieth century the quality of musical recordings was transformed by new magnetic, electronic, and laser technologies, providing nearly perfect stereophonic reproduction. Public experience of music was enhanced beyond anything conceivable in earlier centuries. Although these recording techniques were used primarily for music, speech could be recorded as well. Recordings of poetry and drama were commercially available, and speech recording came to have widespread business use.

The technologies developed for musical and other sound recordings were to have their greatest use in radio and in the acoustical component of motion pictures and television.

As early as the 1820s it had been demonstrated that the presentation in quick succession of a series of images could create an illusion of fluid motion. This phenomenon became the basis of toys, especially after the development of photography reached a point at which it could provide rapidly succeeding images of a swiftly moving object. It was not until the invention in 1889 of cellulose film capable of being produced in strips that a true motion picture became practical. Thomas Edison produced a kinetiscope in 1891 that could exhibit a fifty-foot strip of film that lasted only a fraction of a minute and be seen by only one viewer at a time. It was first used commercially in 1894 but almost immediately replaced by machines developed independently in both France and the United States that could project the moving images on a screen, where they could be viewed by a sizable audience. The rapid development of better, lighter, and more mobile cameras and of projectors capable of handling long reels of film soon made possible the production of full-length dramas. The first theaters exclusively for motion pictures, usually converted store fronts, were not opened until early in the 1900s, but there were eight thousand or more by 1910 and the number continued to grow. Soon every small town in the United States had one or more "movies," with admission prices usually only 5 cents—hence the name "nickelodeon."

By the 1920s motion pictures had become the most universally enjoyed entertainment in the United States; most people attended dozens of times a year. The expense of film rentals and projection equipment, however, meant that it was practical for an individual to see films only as part of a relatively large audience assembled in a theater. This sharply narrowed the choice of films to be seen, because only in large cities would there be more than three or four theaters at most, and in many small towns only one. Moreover, only very large companies could meet the cost of producing major full-length films, and those companies soon came to own or control the principal distributors and large chains of theaters. Once more, a new technology gave large corporations a controlling voice in communications.

By the 1930s advancing technology made it possible to produce motion pictures in color and to accompany them with sound. For the first time it became possible to present a full image of life, in motion, in its natural colors, aurally as well as visually, and all directly, as one experienced life itself, without the necessity of abstraction expressed in words or in the encoding and decoding of writing. As yet, however, communication, other than by face-to-face speech or by telegraph or telephone, was still dependent on the embodiment of the communication in an artifact—which could now be a film or a photograph or a record as well as a book or magazine or newspaper—and the physical storage or transportation of the artifact.

Two inventions escaped this limitation. The first was radio. Initially, this was a form of wireless telegraphy. It was so called because it was able to transmit only the dots and dashes by which telegraphy encoded words. But it soon became able to transmit speech and music as well and became in effect a wireless telephone. Radio's initial uses, especially when its transmissions were still primarily by Morse code, were for point-to-point communication, to or among ships at sea, for example. Navies immediately saw its value, and the U.S. Navy sought at first to have exclusive control over its use in the United States. However, it soon became apparent that the true importance of radio lay in its capacity to *broadcast* a message, to make it available simultaneously to all within its range who had receiving sets and wished to listen.

This was a truly new function, in some ways more nearly analogous to the newspaper or other products of mass printing than to the technologically related telegraph and telephone in that it was able quickly to convey an identical message from a central source to a large and physically dispersed audience. At the same time, it differed profoundly from the newspaper in that it required the audience to own or have access to an apparatus that at first was relatively expensive, was able to carry the actual sounds of speech and music, avoided the necessity of coding into and decoding from written representations of words or notes, and escaped the necessity of embodying communication in artifacts.

Radio, like the telephone and telegraph, called for large-scale organization. Although hundreds of broadcasters undertook to send out radio programs, the economy of providing national programing from a central source was soon apparent. The Columbia Broadcasting System and the Red and Blue networks of the National Broadcasting Company were set up to provide such programing. By 1930 radio had not only reached most American homes, but it had also become embedded in a large, complex business structure whose characteristics had a major effect on what was broadcast. In the United States it had become the first medium in which the entire costs of communication were borne by neither speaker nor audience, but by third parties—advertisers. The fact had important implications for the social function of radio. Radio was also affected in important ways by the inescapable necessity of governmental control, which was required to prevent chaotic interference in the use of the limited radio spectrum.

The remaining new audiovisual technology was television. Its invention came in the late 1930s, but its development and deployment were delayed by World War II. In the decade following the war, however, the use of television exploded across the country. Soon almost every household had at least one television receiver, and the typical American spent dozens of hours a week viewing television programs. Television almost immediately became the most extensively shared and arguably the most influential communications medium.

In its economic organization and in the governmental controls under which it operated television followed in the patterns of radio. The same networks owned by the same corporations dominated national television as they had national radio. The same governmental agency—the Federal Communications Commission—regulated television in much the same way it regulated radio. But its content and impact were very different. Television took film's capacity to reproduce segments of reality directly rather than through the verbal description of an observer and added to it the capacity to disseminate that picture simultaneously to enormous audiences. By combining the technology and power of film and that of radio, television created a new communications instrument of incomparable power. By the late twentieth century, in the United States, throughout the industrialized world, and in many less developed countries, television had become the dominant, indeed, the overwhelming, means by which human beings entertained themselves and perceived the world outside the ambit of their daily lives.

Later ancillary inventions varied the patterns of television. The use of microwave transmissions via satellite freed television from dependence on wired connections between a source of programs and the station actually broadcasting them. News and depictions of important events could be viewed simultaneously worldwide. Conversely, by providing wired connections between sources of programming or powerful satellite receivers and individual television sets, cable systems freed viewers from sole dependence on the limited number of programs that could be broadcast over the air in one area within the available spectrum.

The invention of electronic cameras that recorded magnetically on tape rather than chemically on film and could transmit directly to a broadcasting station the images being viewed greatly increased the flexibility of television news services. Previously, live broadcasts could be provided only of planned events at which heavy cameras could be put in position in advance. Other scenes, as of fires, accidents, and battles, could be broadcast only hours later after film had been returned to the studio, developed, printed, edited, and put on the air. Televised scenes of the war in Vietnam, for example, like the movie newsreels of World War II, were usually days old when broadcast. The new technology could provide instant coverage with light, portable cameras.

The invention of videocassette recorders permitted individuals to record programs being received on their television sets, even to record one program while viewing another or to record programs when absent. The same technology made it possible to view purchased or rented videotapes on home television sets, in effect seeing movies at home. This further greatly increased the variety of programming that could be brought into homes through television receivers and also opened the way to a broad use of the technology for educational and training purposes.

By the late twentieth century the technologies developed for photography, motion pictures, radio, and television had combined to be able to unite practically the entire world into a single audience for an event like an international soccer match, the inauguration of a president, a royal wedding, or an atomic disaster. Almost every home in the industrialized nations could receive an enormously wide variety of programming by direct broadcast, cable, or cassette. The world itself, as viewed through the lens of cameras, could overflow us.

The effects of the audiovisual revolution made possible by these inventions were profound. It affected ways of viewing the world, ways of thinking, forms of literature, music, and art, the accumulation and the distribution of power in society, relations among differing cultures, the transmission of ideas and culture between generations, our capacity to govern ourselves, indeed, every aspect of our lives. And it did so with disconcerting speed. Humankind had had eons to learn to use speech and develop the structures and processes of an oral society. It had millennia to absorb and adjust to the powers of writing; centuries to develop those of print. But the radical transformations of the audiovisual revolution came within the span of a long lifetime. The problems of public policy and of social and individual adaptation this presented were unique and demanding, and we have by no means solved them. In subsequent chapters I shall endeavor to explore some of these changes, some of the ways we have adapted to them, and some of the problems of public policy that remain.

— 9 —

The Control of the Audiovisual Revolution

The shape of the audiovisual revolution and the impact it had on society were determined not only by its rapidly evolving technology but also by the controls exercised by government and by the economic organization of the media. American policy and practice in both these respects were quite different from those adopted in other technologically advanced countries. The production and distribution of phonograph records and motion pictures was recognized as appropriate for private business in Western Europe and Canada as well as in the United States. But those industries concerned with the electronic distribution of information, from the telegraph and telephone in the nineteenth century through radio and television in the twentieth, were viewed, except in the United States, as appropriate activities of national governments. The postal services of other countries took over the telegraph as a normal extension of their function and upon the invention of the telephone added that as one further step. On the basis of these precedents, radio was first seen as a wireless form of the telegraph and later of the telephone, and it too became a governmental activity except in the United States. Broadcasting was carried on by governmental ministries directly or, as in the case of the British Broadcasting Corporation, by semi-autonomous public agencies. Television followed naturally in the same pattern, carried on by the same agencies.

Although in the beginnings of the telegraph and later of radio there was discussion of public ownership in the United States, quite a different course was followed. Telegraph, telephone, radio, and television remained in private hands. Though this was a truly major policy decision, affecting in fundamental ways the whole future of audio-visual communication in the United States, it was taken as a matter of course, without significant debate or serious consideration of alternatives. This was in part because of a strong predilection for private rather than state management of all economic activity and in part because of a fear of placing excessive power in the hands of government through the control of important media of communication. Europeans and Canadians feared this power in private hands; Americans feared it in the hands of the state.

These fears were both moral and political. Throughout history, as each new communications medium came into being and widened the circle of those it reached, there was fear that the poorer and less educated given access to the new medium would be misled or corrupted by material that had been safely shared by the elite. The invention of printing brought the *Index;* the mass printing of the late nineteenth century brought the Comstock Act; and the inexpensive paperbacks of the mid-twentieth century were to bring an active revival of Comstockery. Even greater fears were generated by the movies, which could communicate directly and vividly with children and the uneducated, even the illiterate, as print could not and in which immoral or suggestive acts and scenes could be not merely read about but also witnessed. And those fears were further aggravated by radio, which could descend into every home without advance warning of content, and even more by television, which combined the ubiquity of radio with the vividness of film.

The availability of radio and television created political fears as well. It was recognized from an early date that radio could be a powerful instrument of political persuasion, and television quickly proved to be even more powerful. Except during the McCarthy era there was rarely major concern that broadcasting might become a tool of subversion, but there was a very genuine fear that control of broadcast outlets could invest one political party or movement or candidate with unchallengeable power over the opposition.

These concerns were heightened by the fact that all the audiovisual media quickly fell under the control of a very few large companies. The advantages of a centrally administered national network made both the telegraph and the intercity telephone service a natural monopoly, as was local telephone service within each community. The Western Union emerged as the dominant telegraph system, with limited competition from Postal Telegraph and smaller systems. The technology and economics of telephone service carried monopoly even farther in shaping both the national network and the local systems. Alexander Graham Bell's control of the basic telephone patents and the organizing ability of his associate and successor, Theodore Vail, built on these natural monopolistic tendencies. Bell's and Vail's creation, the American Telephone and Telegraph Company, emerged as the only significant intercity carrier and also controlled the local telephone service in the great majority of American cities. Its refusal to permit other than its own equipment to be connected to the network extended its monopoly to the manufacture of telephone equipment through its production arm, the Western Electric Company.

Although there was no similar technological reason for the concentration of ownership in the phonograph record and motion picture industries, economic and competitive forces had led to the domination of each industry by a very few firms. As each became a large industry, more and more capital was required for successful operation. It became especially important to have a broad and effective distribution network able to place films in theaters and records in stores throughout the country and later throughout the world. Small firms were absorbed into larger ones or they failed and disappeared.

In the motion picture industry it was a matter of survival to control the exhibition of films in the larger theaters. Production companies were driven to buy movie houses throughout the country, especially in cities, and to bring them together in chains. Thus they could guarantee the widespread showing of their own films and when necessary freeze out those of others. The more powerful studios could make independent theaters book their routine B films as a condition of acquiring rights to show the important movies with major stars. The possession of extensive studio facilities representing large investments, the control of big-name stars through long-term contracts, and the ownership of the principal theater chains gave big production companies a lock on the industry. By the 1930s six or eight companies almost totally dominated motion pictures, with independent and foreign producers occupying only those fringes of the industry in which they were tolerated by the few great firms that made up the Motion Picture Producers Association of America.

When radio and, later, television became major media there were compelling technological considerations that severely restricted competition. Only a limited number of frequencies could be used for transmission in any local region without interference that disrupted broadcasts. After an early period of chaos, it became necessary for the federal government to license all radio transmitters and to control their power and prescribe the frequencies to be used. Television broadcasts required the use of much wider bands of frequencies, and there were hence many fewer available channels. As a result, governmental licensing power became much more important in the case of television than in that of radio. Thus, for technological reasons, broadcasts that could be received in any particular locality were confined to those from a very few television stations, no more than three or four and frequently fewer except in the largest metropolitan areas, and from a larger but still restricted number of radio stations. The number of available channels was later to be considerably increased by the development of frequency modulation (FM) radio and ultra-high frequency (UHF) television, but it remained limited.

Economic pressures further confined the sources of programming. It was obviously impractical, or at the least uneconomic, for each station to create all its own programs. From the early days of radio, it became apparent that it was more efficient to have programs centrally produced and distributed by telephone lines to broadcasters throughout the country than to have hundreds of stations making separate efforts. Moreover, centralized programming could make nationally available performances by major symphonies, opera companies, popular musical stars, and acting and comedy groups that could not be afforded by individual stations, certainly not by stations outside the largest cities. Hence networks were formed to provide this service, first by the National Broadcasting Company, which in fact developed two networks, and then by the Columbia Broadcasting System. Individual stations continued to provide local news, weather, and similar programs as well as broadcasts of recorded music, which provided another means of permitting performers of national prominence to be heard locally. But networks increasingly provided major live presentations of music, drama, comedy, and national and foreign news.

The network structure was even more necessary to television, where the costs of creating programs was much larger and the consequent necessity of bringing them to large national audiences much greater. Locally produced television programming was to become increasingly confined to news and inexpensive discussion programs. Stations not affiliated with networks were to fill their hours by the showing of films and by reruns of network programs, analogous to the use of records by local radio stations.

The communications policies of the United States had been formulated in the period of the nation's founding and had been little changed by the end of the nineteenth century. They had been developed to deal with a world of print, and at first with a relatively tiered structure of society and communication. Although it was clearly recognized that a free press was an essential component in the American structure, required to make elected officials responsible in practice to the people, and that it was important that the product of such a free press be widely available to an electorate capable of reading and understanding it, Americans generally believed that an essentially negative policy would be sufficient to achieve these goals. The important thing, they thought, was that the press should be free of official constraints. If there were no governmental censorship, the private enterprise of writers, printers, and publishers could be counted on to see that diverse points of view were made widely available, at least to those adult white male property owners who could vote or to those local leaders to whom they looked for guidance. Hence the communications policies were addressed not to what the government *should* do but rather to what it should *not* do, for example, "The Congress shall make no law abridging the freedom of the press."

These policies had already been affected by the economic, social, and technological developments of the late nineteenth century. The democratization of politics, the transfer of tens of millions of workers from traditional agricultural and handicraft pursuits to factory and administrative work requiring the use of new technologies and written instructions and reports, and the development of mass printing all called for a more active communications policy. The response included, as pointed out in chapter 7, lowered flat national postal rates for newspapers and magazines and the beginning of the development of a public library system, both intended to make printed materials more widely available, and the commitment to nearly universal tax-supported public education, at least through the elementary grades. These measures were in recognition of the fact that public actions were necessary to assure that the products of a free press were in fact realistically available to a much broader public and that broader public would be able to read and use them. At the same time that the much wider availability of print was encouraged, it was also feared in terms of its possible moral effects, and substantial if often informal restrictions were imposed on the freedom of the press to deal with sexual or other moral issues beyond rather narrowly defined conventional boundaries.

Now the coming of the audiovisual revolution presented major new questions. The technology of printing and the economic organization of the publishing industry had imposed few barriers to entry. Save for local news in one-newspaper towns, no printer or publisher in nineteenth- or twentieth-century America had sufficient dominance to control what was available through print. But the technology and economic organization of the telegraph, telephone, record, motion picture, and broadcasting industries all required or encouraged monopoly or oligopoly, which American policy placed in private rather than public hands. Executives of private corporations now began to have the sort of power over channels of communication that at the time the First Amendment was adopted was feared only from government itself. Freedom, it now appeared, needed to be protected *by* the government as well as *from* the government.

At the same time, the new media spread more widely and penetrated more deeply than print, reaching less sophisticated audiences with a more vivid and compelling content. Sex, violence, and antisocial behavior could now be not only described but also depicted. The fears that mass print had provoked in the days of Anthony Comstock were aroused again, and more urgently. But now the concerns were broader and embraced political as well as moral issues. The vivid persuasiveness of the new media that reached so broadly into a not necessarily well-educated or sophisticated audience raised deep concern about the possibility of their demagogic use and about the power that those controlling or having preferred access to the new media might have to dominate the political process.

The first public concern relating to the new audiovisual materials was aroused by the perceived threat to public taste and morals by motion pictures and later by radio and television. This followed on the similar and still active concern, expressed by the Comstock Act and by innumerable state laws and prosecutions, for the effect that the outpouring of cheap books and magazines in the late nineteenth century might have on sexual morality. In their efforts to deal with this problem, the federal and state governments used all of the devices developed by the English government in the sixteenth and seventeenth centuries to control what were feared as the immoral and subversive dangers of the new invention of printing: licensing of individual publishers or producers, licensing of individual products on the basis of review prior to publication, control of imports, cooption of publishers or producers in order to exercise control through their organizations, and prosecution of those who exceeded the boundaries of tolerance.

The courts initially held that motion pictures were merely a form of entertainment, not embraced in the concept of the "press" protected by the First Amendment. This left films entirely vulnerable to censorship. Although the federal government refrained from action, save to bar the import of "obscene" films as well as books, all states felt free not only to prosecute producers and exhibitors of films thought obscene but also to exercise prior restraint. Some states required a film to be reviewed and licensed by a state agency before it could be exhibited within the state. As the film industry in the 1920s grew in size and in audiences and as competition became more intense, the Hollywood product began to press harder against conservative standards. The threat of strict comprehensive federal censorship evoked by this trend led the Motion

Picture Producers and Distributors of America, the industry trade association, to undertake systematic self-censorship. These efforts culminated in the adoption of an industry code in 1930 and the creation in 1934 of an office to enforce its provisions. The office could give or withhold its seal of approval, without which theaters controlled by members of the MPPDA were pledged not to exhibit the film. Most independent theaters also respected the decisions of this authority.

The provisions of the industry code were extremely conservative insofar as sexual matters were concerned. No nudity or near nudity was permitted. Kisses, limited in intensity and duration, were as far as sexual contact could go. It could not be shown or implied that couples not married to each other ever had sexual intercourse unless it was essential to the plot or meaning of the film, and then only if the matter were handled with great restraint and the guilty parties were shown to suffer for their misdeeds. Even between husband and wife sexual relations could never be dealt with in any direct way. Extramarital or premarital sex could never be regarded as acceptable behavior. Common terms for sexual organs or acts, along with those for excretion and even the mildest profanity, were forbidden.

But the restraints of the code went far beyond sexual morality. Drug use could not be depicted or implied. Social decorum in general was to be upheld, avoiding disrespect for family or public authority. Religion must be treated with great respect. Members of the clergy, police, and public officials were not to be shown as evil, brutal, or corrupt unless to do so were essential to the meaning of the film. And even then it must be shown that the offender was an exception, rejected by other clergy, police, or public officials and appropriately punished. Indeed, all wrongdoers must suffer punishment. Although the political standards were less explicit, no film thought to be unpatriotic or subversive could have won approval. Clearly the code not only protected conservative standards of sexual morality, but also effectively limited the opportunity of motion pictures to depict life realistically or to comment on it seriously.

The fact that by the 1930s the major motion picture producers controlled most large theater chains meant that foreign and independent domestic producers as well as members of the MPPDA were compelled to abide by its standards or be content with minimal income from small "art" theaters in large cities. On tacit behalf of the government the MPPDA exercised over film the same sort of control that the late sixteenth and early seventeenth century Stationers Company, as the implicit servants of the Crown, had exercised over books and pamphlets. And the MPPDA acted with the same motives: both to protect their members from prosecution and to suppress competition by foreign or independent producers who might win audiences (or in the earlier case, readers) by more daring productions.

Even greater fears were aroused by the power of radio and later of television to reach the minds of the masses, including children and youths. And in the case of broadcasting federal regulation was inescapable. The few experimental broadcasting stations serving the public in 1920 had exploded into the hundreds by the middle of the decade, and their interference with each other's signals was producing a chaos in which none could be heard clearly and dependably. The secretary of commerce had been authorized to license broadcasters, but with no authority to deny a license or to assign frequencies. The resulting confusion led to the passage of legislation in 1927 creating the Federal Radio Commission and giving it power to issue licenses to broadcasters prescribing the frequency on which they could broadcast, the wattage they could employ, and the hours during which they could operate. The same powers were continued in the Federal Communications Commission created in 1934.

These powers were granted primarily to permit clear reception through the elimination or reduction of interference. If there had been such an abundance of available frequencies that all applicants could be licensed, there would not necessarily have been any element of control. And, indeed, the 1927 act and subsequent statutes were emphatic that the commission should have no power to control the content of broadcasts. But in fact the radio spectrum was limited, and the available frequencies came to be in great demand—especially those assigned as "clear" channels for covering large regions and those in metropolitan areas. Choices had to be made among competing applicants.

The 1927 act had made it clear that the radio spectrum is a part of the public domain and that the use of any particular part of that spectrum was to be entrusted, on a temporary and renewable basis only, to licensees on the grounds of their service to the "public convenience, interest, or necessity." These terms were taken from public utility law and had their roots as far back as the medieval licensing of inns and ferries. It was easy to determine whether a ferryman served the public interest, convenience, or necessity, but it was more complicated to determine how a broadcaster should serve those ends, or whether one applicant for a license would serve them better than another. The commission was compelled to set standards for licensees that necessarily included judgments as to the content and quality of their actual or proposed broadcasts.

The necessity of setting standards on the basis of which broadcasting licenses would be issued or renewed was in constant potential conflict with the provisions of the 1927 and subsequent acts forbidding the Federal Radio Commission and its successor, the Federal Communications Commission, to exercise any control over the content of broadcasts. This conflict and the inherent problems in enforcing broadcast standards caused the FRC and the FCC to issue a number of statements of policy that were subject to frequent amendment and reinterpretation and seemed never to satisfy the broadcast industry, the public, or the commission members themselves. In 1928, shortly after its creation under the Radio Act of 1927, the Federal Radio Commission attempted a definition of "public interest" that could be used to govern its licensing decisions. Most of its provisions related to the public interest in the clear reception of broadcasts and were concerned with frequency allocation, transmitter locations, and similar problems rather than with program content. But there were some provisions regarding programming, including admonitions against extensive carriage of product advertising and playing of phonograph records, that seem strange in the light of later developments.

Within the year these provisions had been extended in connection with one of the first "comparative" hearings in which the commission had to decide between competing applicants for a license. In the "Great Lakes Statement" the commission made it clear that licensees were not to be common carriers, passively offering their facilities to those wishing to broadcast, but must accept responsibility for all programming over the station's facilities. It was further emphasized that the station must offer a diverse variety of programming appealing to all elements of the community it served and must provide "ample play for the free and fair competition of opposing views." Other statements made over the years in connection with proceedings on individual license applications built up a more extensive and complicated set of standards.

With the great increase in radio audiences during World War II, the greater role of the medium in the discussion of public issues, and the prospect of the early deployment of television, the Federal Communications Commission thought it necessary to codify and elaborate its standards. It did so in a lengthy statement of the public service responsibilities of broadcast licensees, issued on March 7, 1946, and generally known as the Blue Book. This was to be the basis for the more detailed review of performance in connection with license renewals that the commission had announced a year previously. The Blue Book restated the responsibility of licensees to serve the public interest and of the commission itself to evaluate the performance of that service in renewing licenses. The tests for determining the quality of public service were very broad, however, relating rather to general *kinds* of programming than to program content. For example, licensees were expected to provide a substantial amount of "sustaining" programming, not produced or paid for by advertisers, in order to assure balanced and varied programming that advertisers might not be willing to support. They were also expected to provide an adequate amount of locally produced live programming and of programs devoted to the discussion of public issues. This last requirement was described as "crucial." Advertising excesses were to be avoided. Discussion of issues was to be "fair" and balanced.

Although it bore ultimate responsibility for determining that only broadcasters properly serving the public interest were licensed, the commission saw only a relatively modest role for itself. It was rather the licensees who should bear the primary responsibility for devising effective means of performing their public service. Networks and industry associations like the National Association of Broadcasters were encouraged to erect more specific standards for such matters as avoiding advertising excesses. The commission believed that the public itself should define its interests and press local broadcasters to serve them, acting through listener (or later, viewer) associations.

The lofty ideals of the Blue Book and the promise of more detailed scrutiny of each licensee's performance, especially when licenses came up for removal, proved very difficult to apply in practice. It was simply impossible for the staff of the commission to examine in detail the day-by-day performance of the thousands of radio broadcasters and later the hundreds of television stations. In the absence of substantial listener or viewer complaint, reviews were generally perfunctory. Nevertheless the basic provisions of the Blue Book were elaborated over the years as decisions in individual proceedings created a kind of case law of broadcast regulation, emphasizing the importance of ascertaining and serving specific community needs, providing opportunities for robust debate and presentation of varied positions on controversial issues of public importance, meeting the needs of minorities and avoiding racial prejudice, and in general informing the public. In addition to the formal actions of the commission in dealing with license applications, renewals, and transfers, individual commissioners such as Newton Minow and Nicholas Johnson often made widely disseminated statements about the public responsibilities of broadcasters, and their statements had an important influence on the industry.

Commission actions were especially important in applying the so-called fairness doctrine, which required each licensee to provide for the discussion of controversial issues of public importance and to assure that all responsible points of view with respect to such issues were given opportunity for expression. In this particular area the commission went far beyond the evaluation at renewal time of general licensee performance. Rather, it received and acted on specific complaints of unfairness at the time they occurred and when it thought necessary issued specific orders to licensees to redress specific actions found to be unfair. This drew the commission into a kind of direct control over station programming that was otherwise avoided.

Control over, or influence on, the content of radio and television programming was exercised not only by the Federal Communications Commission and its predecessor Radio Commission, but also officially by federal statute and unofficially by industry codes of the National Association of Broadcasters. Federal law forbade the use of profane, obscene, or indecent language in broadcasting on pain of fine or imprisonment and, more important, required that if a station permitted any candidate in an election to use its facilities, it must allow all other candidates in the same election to use them for an equal time and on the same terms. This so-called equal-time provision exempts certain uses, such as regular news programs and broadcasts of public events. The Federal Communications Commission has primary responsibility for the interpretation and enforcement of these provisions. Under the "indecent language" clause it has forbidden the use of vulgar terms for sexual and excretory acts in broadcasts when children may be presumed to be among the audience, even though such words have been held by the courts not to be in themselves obscene and although they are freely used in other media such as books and motion pictures.

In their careful concern to avoid offending major elements in the audience, broadcasters in any case would almost certainly avoid the use of "indecent" words, so the effect of the statutory ban is slight. This is not, however, true of the equal-time provision. Most broadcasters for their own reasons seek a reputation for impartiality and fairness and would in any case treat candidates of the major parties equitably. The problem arises with minor party candidates. If Republican and Democratic candidates for the presidency appeared as contestants in a debate sponsored by a broadcast station, or were given a half-hour of free time each to present their views, the equal-time provision would require inclusion in the debate, or a free half-hour, for the candidates of each of a dozen or more tiny, little-known parties. Offered such a golden opportunity for free appearance on national television, political "parties" might be formed or candidacies announced for no other purpose but to claim the time. The consequence is that no candidate is given free time. Except in 1960, when special legislation valid only for that election permitted the Kennedy-Nixon debates, presidential debates have not been sponsored by broadcasters. Instead, such debates are broadcast under the legal fiction that they are merely news coverage of an event taking place in any case, usually under the sponsorship of the League of Women Voters.

This requirement has unfortunate consequences. Because candidates must buy all of their time, the better-financed candidates can make a much greater use of television. Moreover, parties and candidates have found it a much more efficient use of their funds to pay for thirty- and sixty-second commercials using advertising techniques and slogans rather than to buy expensive half-hour blocks that would allow a candidate to offer a reasoned expression of his or her views. Even in the staged debates that the networks cover as news events, the fact that the frequency and format of the debates must win the approval of both parties or candidates means that they have an artificial structure allowing only limited opportunities for an extended presentation of views.

Were networks free to set their own terms, without the equal-time provision, they could provide a very different format, perhaps nearer to that of the Lincoln-Douglas debates. The fact that otherwise his or her opponent could appear alone would substantially compel acceptance of the format by each candidate. But as it is, and largely because of the equal-time provision, wealthier candidates of better-financed parties have a very *unequal* opportunity to use this most persuasive medium and to use it in ways that minimize the provision to the electorate of information genuinely useful in deciding among candidates.

The Federal Communications Commission encouraged the National Association of Broadcasters to supplement and extend the official policies as to programming and advertising with its own industry-established standards. The association responded with various statements of standards running through many editions and revisions. The most extensive was the Television Code edition of 1976, further amended in 1977. Although the code no doubt reflected in part a sincere commitment to ethical standards on the part of responsible broadcasters, a primary motive for self-regulation in the broadcasting industry, as in the motion picture industry, was to avert governmental regulation.

The NAB code dealt both with program content and with advertising. The programming sections were, for the most part, very general admonitions to virtue and prudence and were largely addressed to the avoidance of sexual, violent, or other content that might be offensive to significant portions of the audience, although there were specific references to the treatment of gambling, alcohol and drug use, hypnosis, pseudo-scientific systems of prediction like astrology and palm-reading, quiz programs, and other problem areas. Sections relating to news and political programs paralleled and extended the commission's fairness doctrine. In 1975 provisions had been added reserving the first hour of prime time for "family entertainment" suitable for viewing by children. This section was apparently inserted under some pressure from members of the FCC who believed this sort of regulation to be desirable but beyond the powers of the commission to adopt.

The code provided much more detailed regulation of advertising. In addition to admonitions as to "good taste," particularly in the advertising of "personal" products, and the elimination of false or deceptive advertising, specific limitations were spelled out to cover the number of interruptions of programs for commercials and the number of minutes of advertising within programs of specified length in particular time segments. There were special provisions relating to advertising on children's programs, in particular requiring the clear separation of advertisements from program content and forbidding the use of characters from programs in commercials.

The effort to control content through official action or officially encouraged actions of industry associations reached its peak in connection with films in the 1940s and 1950s and in broadcasting in the 1970s. In both cases the efforts at control were benign in their intent. Public pressure was rarely sought to evoke any particular positive content other than during World War II, when the Office of Facts and Figures and the domestic division of the Office of War Information enlisted the enthusiastic and freely given cooperation of the film and broadcasting industries in emphasizing patriotic themes. There was requirement or pressure to devote substantial segments of broadcast time to discussion of public affairs, to news, to educational and cultural programming, to children's programming, and to similar public services, but no prescription of content within those broad rubrics. Official regulation, or quasi-official regulation through industry codes, was directed rather at preventing what was thought to be immoral or corrupting content and at assuring that the power of large and quasi-monopolistic media organizations would not be used unfairly on behalf of particular candidates or views. At the same time that regulatory effort sought to keep open an adequate opportunity for the expression of diverse views, including minority views, that lay within the mainstream, there was silent pressure not to go beyond that mainstream.

The mainstream itself was so relatively broad and commanded so nearly unanimous support that constraints to remain within it were taken for granted and hardly noticed. The freedom of Republicans and Democrats and of the larger third-party candidacies—like those of Henry Wallace, Strom Thurmond, and John Anderson—to use the airwaves was protected, as was that of Catholicism, Judaism, and a wide variety of Protestant faiths. Major religions outside the Judeo-Christian tradition, such a Buddhism, Islam, and Hinduism, were respectfully treated. But those outside the broadly defined mainstream, such as atheists, communists, or anarchists, found access blocked in practice if not in theory.

These various constraints on content were in uncomfortable tension with the traditional freedom of the press set forth in the First Amendment. Even when the government was acting to prevent what was feared as private abridgement of freedom of the press, there was an uneasy concern about the consequences of official controls or dominating influences over the content of the audiovisual media and particularly of radio and television broadcasts. The same statutes that gave the Federal Radio Commission authority to make determinations as to whether a broadcast licensee's performance served the public interest and to make or enforce a fairness doctrine denied the commission any right of censorship. Section 29 of the Radio Act of 1927 stated in part that "nothing in this Act shall be understood or construed to give the licensing authority [i.e., the commission] the power of censorship over the radio communications or signals transmitted by any radio station, and no regulation or condition shall be promulgated or fixed by the licensing authority which shall interfere with the right of free speech by means of radio communications."

This language was substantially repeated in section 326 of the Communications Act of 1934 and remains the law. It was such legal prohibition of censorship and the public concern it reflects that led the government to encourage industry groups like the Motion Picture Producers and Distributors of America and the National Association of Broadcasters to make and enforce standards that seemed desirable but were beyond the role of public authority. This again produced a tension of ambivalence because the control by private monopolies or oligopolies over communication was feared at the same time that it was encouraged as a means of establishing moral standards.

One result of these tensions was a continuing thrust to encourage a competitiveness in audiovisual communication sufficient, as in the case of print, to permit reliance on an open market to assure a free and diverse flow of communication. From an early date, statutes and common

law had established the common carrier status of telegraph and telephone systems, requiring them to be open to all at nondiscriminatory
rates, denying them any right of censorship or control over messages
communicated (except for the enforcement of bans on the transmission
of obscene matter, lottery information, and messages involved in fraud-
ulent schemes), and forbidding them to reveal or make use of information transmitted. Legal action had been taken to prevent the granting
by Western Union of favorable telegraphic rates to the Associated Press.
Such rates, coupled with regulations limiting the membership of local
newspapers in the Associated Press, threatened to give AP members a
potent barrier to competition in local markets. Monopoly in communication by telephone and telegraph, it then seemed, could not be avoided, but the fixing of rates by public authority could limit unjust profits
from such a monopoly. The enforcement of common carrier status
could also avoid the extension of the monopoly power to otherwise
competitive areas and prevent its use to control or suppress the flow of
information.

In the area of broadcasting as well there appeared no way to avoid a
monopoly over the use of a given channel in the broadcast spectrum and
hence at best local oligopolies. In addition to the insistence that the
monopoly powers conferred by license be used to serve the public interest, convenience, or necessity, federal policy from the beginning
sought to avoid the pyramiding of monopoly by placing restrictions on
station ownership and on networks. The Radio Act of 1927 limited licenses to three years, forbade licenses to those convicted of violations
of the antitrust statutes, and prohibited any cross-ownership of broadcasting stations and telephone or telegraph facilities. Subsequent legislation, or more frequently Federal Communications Commission action, limited the number of stations that could be licensed to a single
owner and prohibited the acquisition of a radio or television license by
the owner of a newspaper or another broadcast license in the same
community. Even already existing cross-ownership of a newspaper and
a broadcasting station in the same community could be broken by the
cancellation or nonrenewal of the broadcast license if such action was
necessary to preserve or restore competition in the media of communication in that locality.

Although the law gave it no authority over networks as such, the FCC
achieved a powerful role through its authority to deny or revoke licenses
to individual broadcasters on the basis of their relation to networks. It
has asserted that authority in order to limit the number of stations that
can be owned or operated by a network, to break up the control of two
or more networks by a common owner (as when the National Broadcast-

ing Company was forced to divest one of its two networks to form the basis of the American Broadcasting Company), to maintain the freedom of a network affiliate to accept or reject any network program (and, conversely, to maintain the freedom of a network to offer to another station in the same area a program rejected by an affiliate), to limit affiliation contracts to two years, to limit the amount of prime time that can be devoted to programming supplied by a network, and to prohibit the production and syndication by networks of programs other than its own broadcasts.

The purpose of these regulations was to provide as many different sources of broadcast material as practical and to limit the possible range of control of any one person or corporation. The technology of broadcasting itself, however, appeared to place a rather narrow limit (as contrasted with print) on the sources from which and the channels through which broadcast communication could reach the viewer or listener. In time, however, changing technology widened those limits. The carriage of radio signals by frequency modulation (FM) as distinguished from amplitude modulation (AM) greatly broadened the radio spectrum, making possible a multiplication of the number of radio stations. Although FM stations had a more limited range than AM stations, they gave a nearly static-free signal particularly suited for music. The FCC quickly seized the opportunity offered by the availability of a great many more channels. FM stations were freely licensed, and educational institutions and other nonprofit broadcasters were encouraged to apply. To assure an audience for the new stations, the FCC required that all newly manufactured radio sets be able to receive FM transmissions.

The great increase in the number of radio stations permitted the FCC to modify its earlier policy of requiring each radio station to offer comprehensive and diverse programming appealing to all significant audience interests. Now stations could be permitted to specialize in particular subjects or genres: all-news stations, talk-show stations, all classical music, all rock music or country music, or foreign language programs, or programs of special interest to black audiences. Special interests, especially in large metropolitan areas, could now be much more effectively served by diverse stations rather than by diverse programming on general stations.

Advancing technology also greatly broadened the available television spectrum by permitting broadcasting on ultra-high frequencies (UHF) in addition to the basic very high frequencies (VHF). Again a great increase in the number of licensed television stations was possible. This had special importance for public broadcasting enterprises which, coming late on the scene, often found all available VHF channels preempted. There were difficulties, however, in that UHF signals were weaker and less clearly received than those in the VHF spectrum. Although the FCC, as in the case of FM radio, required that all newly manufactured television sets have the capacity for UHF reception, special antennas were necessary and poor reception limited audiences, which in turn limited funding for attractive programming.

The coming of cable television presented new regulatory problems. Its original name, "community antenna television" (CATV), described the initial functions of cable television. Residents of areas blocked by mountains or other obstacles from clear reception of television signals with typical home antennas would join to pay for the use of a large professional antenna to which each of their homes could be connected by cable. It soon became clear that such antennas, especially after large "dishes" were designed, could not only improve the reception of local television stations but also bring in signals from distant stations serving other markets. Once their capacity was realized, services were also offered by satellite or by wired or microwave connection to the central receiver of a cable system, and thence distributed to individual homes connected with the system, without ever having been broadcast to the public over any licensed station.

Cable systems were at first subject to regulatory pressures from three directions. The Federal Communications Commission asserted jurisdiction over them, primarily to protect the rights and status of licensed broadcasters. Among the FCC rules was a requirement that a cable system must carry the signals of all broadcasters licensed to serve the market in which the cable system operated. Another requirement forbade a cable system to import from a distant station a work, such as a motion picture, when it had been notified that a local station had acquired the exclusive right to broadcast it in that market.

In the second place, cable systems had to come to the municipalities in which they sought to operate in order to get franchises permitting them to place cables under the streets or along poles on public rights of way. As a condition of such franchises, local governments imposed many conditions intended to protect consumers. Maximum rates were fixed, standards were set for the number of channels offered and the quality of service, and the owners of cable systems were frequently required to provide free channels for local governmental and educational services and to offer public access to one or more dedicated channels.

Finally, Congress moved to impose copyright requirements. Initially, the Supreme Court, apparently thinking of cable only as an enhancer of local signals, held that the distribution of signals through a cable system was not a "performance" within the meaning of the Copyright

Act. Motion picture companies and other copyright proprietors were deeply concerned at the failure to receive payment for the additional distribution of their products to markets beyond those of the station or stations licensed to broadcast them. Yet there was no way for a cable system to get prior permission to redistribute programs when it did not control or even know well in advance what works would be broadcast by the stations whose signals were retransmitted. An awkward compromise was finally enacted that required cable systems to contribute a percentage of their revenues to a fund that would be distributed among copyright proprietors by a Copyright Tribunal based on estimates of the frequency of use of works to which they held rights.

The cable industry mounted a major lobbying effort to rid itself of most of these restrictions, and with the passage of the cable regulatory act of 1984 it largely succeeded. The federal government preempted much of the authority of municipalities over franchised systems, in particular their authority to approve rates charged customers. "Must-carry" provisions were eliminated, leaving cable systems free to abandon carriage of stations with small or specialized (e.g., foreign-language) audiences. In practice, this latter change proved to be less important than expected because the increased capacity of most systems to carry a large number of channels reduced the pressure to confine coverage to the more popular stations or programs.

Cable, apparently because it was considered a service voluntarily sought and paid for, remained free of the "moral" censorship imposed on broadcasters by the FCC with respect to "indecent" language. And because the various services requiring extra payment, like HBO, were not advertiser-supported, they were not as sensitive to public concerns as to language or nudity. Films shown on the cable services were uncut and uncensored from the form in which they were shown in theaters, including occasional nude scenes and the frequent use of vulgar language, even though films shown by licensed broadcasters on adjacent channels had none of this freedom.

By the end of the 1980s, cable systems were in a very fortunate situation. Restrictions on ownership had been largely removed, except that Bell Operating Companies were under at least temporary court order forbidding their investing in cable and that television networks and, within their own markets, television licensees could not become cable owners. The otherwise general freedom to acquire cable systems led to most cable subscribers being served by one of a very few very large companies that came to dominate the whole industry. They enjoyed monopoly powers in their respective markets without the rate regulation or other controls that normally accompany the privileges of monopoly. They were protected from competition from television networks or telephone companies but were themselves free to compete with both. They could set up or take advantage of cable networks, like HBO or ESPN, that offered services competing directly with the offerings of the broadcast networks. And they could offer, as Manhattan Cable does among the banks and brokerage houses of the New York financial district, a broad-band, digital, point-to-point service competing with the local telephone company, especially in the high-speed transmission of computerized data.

Operating in this protected freedom, cable systems became powerful and profitable. They have been most successful, however, in serving relatively affluent suburban and small-city areas. Many urban areas, like the outer boroughs of New York City, and rural areas with widely scattered homes, in both of which installation is expensive, long remained and often still are entirely without cable service. Even in areas that have it, the relatively high cost of cable service, especially for so-called premium services like HBO, bar the less affluent from subscribing. Meanwhile, many programs that were formerly available on free television, especially in the field of sports, may now be seen only by cable subscribers.

The exploitation of their monopoly position by cable systems to raise their prices to subscribers provoked public resentment, which led to legislation and FCC action in the early 1990s to limit rates for basic cable services and reinstate some "must carry" provisions.

The more recent technological development, the use of video cassette recorders (VCRs) that enable tapes of motion pictures and similar products to be projected on the screens of ordinary television sets, escaped regulatory control almost entirely. The only governmental concern has been with their use to make unauthorized copies of copyrighted works, either by taping them from broadcast performances or by duplicating existing tapes. Motion pictures producers and other copyright proprietors sought to have all such copying held as infringements or to impose a tax on blank tapes that could go into a fund from which copyright owners might be paid in lieu of estimated royalties. Congress, however, refused to impose such a tax, and the courts held that the making of copies for personal use and not for sale or rental was a "fair use" not requiring permission or payment. The use of what promises to be one of the most important technologies of the audiovisual revolution remains almost entirely free of any official constraints, either as to content or commercial arrangements.

The tide of deregulation that swept through the 1980s affected traditional telecommunications services and broadcasting as well. The regulatory controls that had been most aggressively applied in the 1970s were largely dismantled by judicial decisions, FCC actions, or congressional statutes.

After the failure of many congressional efforts to achieve a major rewriting of the Federal Communications Act that would redefine the structure of telecommunications in the light of new technologies, such a redefinition was finally achieved by a federal district court in the course of an antitrust action brought by the Justice Department against the American Telephone and Telegraph Company. The operating companies that provided local telephone service in most American communities were severed from AT&T and grouped in seven large regional companies. The parent company was left as a provider of long-distance telephone service and, through its Western Electric subsidiary, as a producer and vendor or lessor of telephone equipment. In both areas it would be subject to competition; other carriers were given an equal opportunity to provide long-distance service, and the operating companies were now free to buy equipment from any source they chose. The local operating companies remained as licensed monopolies whose rates were controlled by state regulatory agencies. Because of its initial dominance of intercity service, AT&T's rates were made subject to FCC control for seven years, but other carriers were free to set such rates as they chose. AT&T was freed to enter other businesses, including the production of computers and provision of computer services, but it was initially barred from providing information services to be transmitted over its own lines, as were the operating companies.

This decision revolutionized telecommunications services and provided far more flexible and efficient services, especially in the field of data transmission and in intercity services, to large business users in particular. The fact that local services were no longer heavily subsidized, as they had been, from the profits of intercity and business services meant that the cost of local residential telephone service was substantially increased.

A sweeping relaxation of the regulation of broadcasting also took place. In part this was an expression of the determined laissez-faire policies of the Reagan administration, in part it was a rational response to the technological developments, such as FM and UHF broadcasting, cable, and VCRs, that made it more realistic to substitute competition for regulation in the control of broadcasting.

Former limitations on the ownership of broadcast licenses were sharply reduced. Group owners had been previously restricted to seven television stations, seven AM radio stations, and seven FM stations. This limitation was raised to twelve stations of each category, provided that no

group served more than 25 percent of the potential audience. Prior restrictions on "trafficking," which had prohibited the sale of a broadcasting station within three years of its purchase, were removed. Broadcasting licenses increasingly came to be bought and sold with frequency, like
any other property, without the evidence of long-continuing community
concern that had been sought by the earlier regulations.

Broadcast licenses came increasingly to be thought of in terms of
nearly fee-simple ownership rather than as temporary permissions to
use assigned frequencies on the condition that their use serve the public interest, necessity, and convenience. The term of the license was extended from three years to five, and a strong presumption of renewal
eliminated competition from other applicants unless there had been
major complaints against the licensee. Any serious review of performance at the time of renewal to determine whether the public interest,
necessity, and convenience had in fact been adequately served by the
licensee was abandoned. Requirements as to programming for children
were no longer effective. The fairness doctrine was rescinded by the
FCC, and President Reagan vetoed a bill to restore it. Meanwhile, the
courts had taken away the power of the National Association of Broadcasters to establish or enforce regulations affecting commercials and
program content.

By the end of the 1980s the whole structure of special regulation of
the audiovisual media had all but disappeared save for the equal-time
provision with respect to election campaigns, the requirement that
broadcast licenses be issued only to American owners, and the prohibition of "indecent" language in broadcasts. A penumbra of further
regulation still affected broadcasting because licenses remained necessary and the possibility always existed that the Congress or an FCC
with different membership might be provoked by a perception of abuses
within the broadcast industry to restore stricter controls. A fear of this
outcome no doubt served to reinforce broadcasters' sense of public responsibility. But with all regulation gone from films and records and
with broadcasting subject only to limited constraints, the audiovisual
media had become substantially as free as print.

In addition to such negative controls, public policy had affected the
role of the audiovisual media in American life by positive efforts to
encourage their use for educational and cultural purposes. From the
early days of films, of radio, and of television, enthusiasts had seen a
major, even revolutionary, role for each in education and in the popular diffusion of culture. Federal funding to encourage the educational
use of audiovisual materials was provided under the National Defense
Education Act of 1957. Radio and television channels were reserved for

the use of educational licensees. The creation of the Public Broadcasting System in 1969 provided a network type of support for local nonprofit radio and television stations, which have also been aided by federal funding through the Corporation for Public Broadcasting, which rose to more than $330,000,000 annually in the early 1990s and by state funding in many states.

Although educational and training films of all types and tapes for oral-aural language teaching enjoyed great popularity in the 1950s and 1960s, their use subsequently waned, in part because of the lack of material effectively integrated with the curriculum, in part no doubt because of the awkwardness of setting up screens, threading and operating projectors, and darkening classrooms for film projection. The availability of video tapes easily usable with already available television receivers may do much to facilitate the future classroom use of audiovisual materials.

By the end of the 1980s a decade of deregulation coupled with years of dizzyingly rapid technological progress and swift change in the economic organization and the structure of ownership of the media had radically altered the patterns of audiovisual communication. The sheer volume and diversity of sounds emanating from speakers and images projected on screens were overwhelming. Most Americans spent most of their leisure hours bathed in their flow. A relatively few large companies served as gatekeepers of that flow. Fortunately, those gatekeepers had few ideological objectives of their own. Their concern was rather to seek out and provide whatever their potential audiences wanted, especially potential audiences whose interests and demographic characteristics appealed to advertisers.

During the 1990s a wave of mergers brought together cable systems, motion picture companies, producers of cable and television programs, television networks, and some publishers in a few enormous combinations. This may well threaten the competition on which we have relied to replace regulation.

An enormous machinery, nearly free of external control, was intensely driven to use every possible resource of a rapidly evolving technology and every possible channel of communication to reach every possible audience with sounds and images that would catch and hold its attention. And our attention was caught and held. Increasingly, the audiovisual media provided the all-enveloping screen on which was formed our image of the reality about us.

— 10 —

The Audiovisual Media and Society

By the late twentieth century the audiovisual media had overflowed society. For all Americans, watching television, listening to radio, speaking on the telephone, listening to records, and seeing motion pictures in theaters or on VCRs had become a major occupation; most Americans were probably connected to these media for the majority of their waking hours away from work or school. It was thus that reality beyond the habit of their daily lives was perceived and that their conception of that reality was shaped.

A century ago an individual had to construct a perception of such external realities primarily through the use of his or her imagination on the basis of words decoded from a printed account by an observer who had had to abstract and organize what seemed significant, formulate his or her conception in words, and encode those words into print. To communicate at all, both the observer and the reader had to *think* about the reality in question and organize and formulate a conception of it. Not so with the newer media, which professed to allow the viewer effortlessly to hear or see the reality itself. (I say "professed to allow" because in fact the sounds the radio listener hears and the scenes the television or cinema viewer sees have been mediated in important ways by the selection of what is to be before the microphone or camera, the angle from which it is shot, the way in which recorded, and the juxtaposition of other scenes or sounds.)

As never before in history to the same degree, people responded not to reality itself, but to a mediated image of reality in which they were almost constantly bathed and to an image shaped by a kind of mediation never before known. The consequences of that fact have altered every aspect of American society. Our future as a society may largely depend on how full and how accurate that image may be and on how well, in the common and pervasive bath of shared images, individual autonomy can be preserved.

The different media have affected us differently. We need to separate those that record or transmit sound, including words, from those that record or transmit images. The former include the telegraph, the telephone, the phonograph and other acoustical records, and radio; the latter, photography, motion pictures, and television.

The telegraph enhanced rather than displaced the power of print. By making it possible to transmit words to a distant point almost instantly, and without the necessity of transmitting an actual object (letter or dispatch or newspaper) in which the words were written, the telegraph made newspapers far more important. They could now record, in extensive detail, news from very distant points within hours of the event. After the laying of the Atlantic cable, European news, which had arrived weeks old, could be as immediate as news from the next state. The telegraph also magnified the ability to manage large enterprises, whether of war or of business. Without the capacity of instant communication among headquarters, the conduct of the Civil War would have been very different. The techniques of rapid mobilization and movement of large forces in quick response to changing circumstances that characterizes modern warfare were born of the railroad and the telegraph in the Civil War. Without the telegraph, large railroad systems with numerous trains operating on varying schedules over complex networks could not have been managed. Nor, without the telegraph, could large mercantile, manufacturing, shipping, and financial enterprises respond as the times required to distant changes in markets and needs.

The telegraph was the first step in achieving the entirely new phenomenon of simultaneity that now binds the world together. Before the telegraph, an event in Europe did not become an "event" in America until weeks later. The Battle of New Orleans could take place weeks after the Treaty of Ghent ending the War of 1812 because the treaty did not become a "happening" in Washington until weeks after its signing and not in New Orleans until many days after that. The telegraph began the uniting of the world on the basis of a uniform real time, so that events could "happen" everywhere almost at once, an achievement of profound importance for modern society.

The telegraph, however, continued to rely on the transmission of words encoded in symbolic form. The dots and dashes of the Morse code foreshadowed the ones and zeros of the computer's digital code. The cognitive methods of written communication were unchanged. "Meaning" had to be abstracted from reality and formulated in words that were then embodied in texts.

The development of the telephone and of radio first enabled distant oral communication to take place. The confinement of speech to face-to-face communication had been one of its most severe limitations and had given writing much of its earlier importance as the only way of conveying messages to recipients distant in space or time. The new inventions permitted for many uses a return to orality after millennia in which only written communication was possible with those not immediately present. The telephone, especially as long-distance rates declined sharply in the latter twentieth century, largely displaced the letter as a means of personal communication. And radio came to compete with newspapers as a means of mass communication. Some, but by no means all, of the characteristics of preliterate orality reemerged. Telephone conversations between individuals were, like face-to-face talk, immediate transactions having existence only at the moment, without the presence of a text that could, like a letter, survive in time independently of both sender and recipient. (The later practice of taping some telephone conversations revived the possibility of text creation in another form.) The care and thought that were required by the composition of a letter might be absent, as well as the thoughtful rereading that might be devoted to extracting its full meaning. Even more important was the fact that the telephone made possible the recovery of the immediate back-and-forth of conversation that was impossible in written correspondence.

Radio, too, had the immediacy of talk without the delay in the dissemination of news that was inevitable in newspapers even after the advent of the telegraph and of high-speed presses. The most important aspect of the revival of orality by the radio was the fact that broadcasting made it possible for the emotional overtones of human speech, its warmth and persuasiveness, and its distinctive personality to be conveyed not only to those surrounding an orator but also to an audience of tens of millions. This raised the power of oratory, for good or ill, to unprecedented heights. A Hitler or a Mussolini as well as a Franklin Roosevelt or a Churchill achieved a power to sway multitudes that shaped the course of history. Print, by vastly expanding the audience for written communication, had shown its power to unite large numbers of people behind a common cause, whether of Protestantism or the American and French revolutions or such mid-nineteenth-century causes as abolition, temperance, or women's rights. But the power of radio was even greater and more immediate, achieving the intense mass commitments of the World War II era.

The telephone and radio escaped some of the strictures and forewent some of the strengths of writing and print, but they did not escape the web of words. With the important exception of music, conceptions of reality still had to be conveyed by abstracting particular qualities and

naming them with words. The world was still described, not seen. Nor
did it escape the impress of literacy. The words heard over radio were
in almost every case read from a text in the hands of the announcer or
reporter or actor. The thought-out, linear characteristics of written
communication largely survived in the sounds flowing from radio.

The consequences of the new aural media, especially the phonograph
and radio, were especially important for music. Here the bounds of
writing were truly escaped. The development of a written, later engraved and printed, musical notation had made it possible to preserve
musical compositions that otherwise would have had real existence
only at the moment of performance. Compositions so encoded could
not only be preserved through the centuries, but conveyed to persons
who could not otherwise hear them performed. As in the case of words,
the sounds had to be encoded into notes and then decoded by a performer to reproduce the original sounds.

Only musical sounds that used the traditional scales of Western
music and that had rhythmic patterns and other characteristics capable of being recorded in the traditional notation could be preserved and
conveyed in the written forms developed in Europe in the Middle Ages.
Only such music is left to us from prior centuries, and professional
musicians composed and performed the kinds of music that could be
accommodated by the notation system.

The phonograph record changed that situation profoundly. Music
could now be preserved, conveyed, and reproduced directly without the
encoding and decoding processes. And what was preserved was not the
bare framework of notes in the written score, but all the nuances of
individual performances. The creations of performers as well as composers, Caruso as well as Verdi, could survive not merely in tradition
but in living reality. Moreover, music whose characteristics were not
recordable or adequately recordable in Western notation, such as folk
music, African and Asian music, and much jazz, could now be recorded and preserved. Nontraditional music was enabled to flourish and be
introduced to Western and traditional audiences.

The opportunity to hear professionally performed music was enormously increased. Although the bulk and relatively poor quality of early
phonographs and scratchy 78-rpm records distorted what was heard,
they opened a whole world of music that people who lived in rural areas and small towns could otherwise never have known.

Radio further enormously increased the opportunity to hear both
popular and serious music. Live performances over the networks and
the playing of records by local stations were mainstays of radio programming from the beginning. Audiences of millions heard perfor-

mances of the NBC Symphony and Saturday afternoon broadcasts from the Metropolitan Opera House. Improved radio receivers and record players, the advent of FM stereo broadcasting, and the development of high fidelity long-playing discs, audio tape cassettes, and compact digital records transformed the quality of the music heard so that it substantially equalled that of live performance.

The consequences of the visual media for American society, for society generally, have been greater and more complex than those of the aural media. In this era of overflowing abundance of visual images, it is not easy to recall that before the invention of photography the look of a person or scene could be preserved or conveyed to another only by inadequate verbal description or by the individual drawings or paintings of an artist. Artists were few and competent ones rare, their work was expensive, and even for centuries after the invention of printing it was impossible to reproduce their work satisfactorily in quantity. Clumsy woodcuts could reproduce little more than heavy outlines. Copper engravings, which antedated printing, and etchings were steadily improved in the sixteenth to the nineteenth centuries and provided a much higher quality of reproduction than woodcuts. But the processes required high artistry and were expensive, and delicately engraved lines on soft copper plates could not survive the large number of impressions required for efficient use in book, much less in magazine and newspaper illustration.

Photography, developed in the mid-nineteenth century, provided part of the answer. More exact recordings of scenes and portraits could be achieved quickly, relatively inexpensively, and with less demand for great artistic skill. For the first time accurate portraits were abundantly available; probably few ordinary Americans of his day really knew what George Washington looked like, save from verbal description; Lincoln's visage, however, was familiar. The work of Mathew Brady and others made the Civil War the first visually recorded war. The country became familiar with images of dead and wounded, of weary soldiers, and of desolate battlefields as well as those of distinguished leaders.

Even after the coming of photography, however, it was not until the perfection of the halftone process in the 1880s that mass reproduction of photographic illustrations could take its place as part of the wave of mass printing. By the turn of the century, readers could see the world, at least in black and white, as well as peruse descriptions of it.

The development and improvement of color photography and color printing made faithful and inexpensive visual images almost universally available by the late twentieth century. The archaeological and art treasures of the entire world and of all history could be seen in vivid representation by hundreds of millions of persons who would rarely visit the sites where the originals existed. And the face of the earth itself, its jungles and mountains and rivers and deserts, the street scenes of its cities, and the dress and customs of its inhabitants have all been made real through illustrations presented by color photography and printing in such magazines as *The National Geographic*. The new media have enabled our eyes and our ears to reach out to the entire world. So far as the arena of direct perception extends, we live now not in the farmsteads and villages of our forebears but in the whole earth and the universe beyond.

By far the greatest impact of the new media on society has come, however, from the series of inventions by which images were made to move and then to speak and at last to be projected across the land to audiences of millions: motion pictures and television. In what, in historical terms, is only an eyeblink of time, our whole means of perceiving the world has been radically changed. A principal occupation of Americans, and most residents of industrialized countries, has come to be the nearly continuous observation of life, not as it is lived around us but as it is portrayed in an incessant image on a screen before us. There has never been anything comparable in history, and it is far too early to know all the consequences of this revolution in our perceptual relations with reality.

Most of what we see on the screen is fictional and offered as entertainment, but a large part, including news programs, documentaries, discussion programs, and sports presentations, profess to show us the world as it is. And even fictional programming is taken as showing what life may typically be; images of love, of family life, of violence, and of race and gender relations in movies, soap operas, and other television series implant a perception of what they are in reality.

And television, like print and like preliterate orality, impresses its own characteristics upon the images of reality it transmits. The fluid and unfixed character of oral accounts transmits a fluid and changeable conception of reality itself: history shimmers in the forms of myth; the boundaries of space undulate with each account; and men and gods are transformed from one telling to another. Writing, especially as frozen in the forms of print, could describe reality only by abstracting salient and meaningful elements, assigning terms for them, arranging those terms in structured sentences that expressed a determinate relation among the identified elements, and then fixing those sentences in an unvarying text. This very process assigns to reality an orderly and unchanging meaningfulness that exists only in the writing- and print-conditioned mind of the observer. Those who lived in a text-imaged world—an Aquinas, a Kant, a Jefferson, an Adam Smith, a Darwin, a Marx—could believe that the orderliness of their systems reflected an orderliness that really existed in the universe.

Something of the fluidity of oral perceptions returned with films and television. It is true that the movie director or the news program executive selects and arrays scenes to be shot and presented in ways that abstract meaningful patterns from the chaos of reality, but something of the unordered reality remains ambiguously before the viewer. Readers formed their pictures of World War II and other conflicts in the age of print from the reports of journalists and the statements of leaders who had striven to see and describe an intelligible order in the massive convulsions of reality; a necessary process of *thought* went into the forming of those perceptions. In contrast, the concepts of the Vietnam war came primarily from fragmented visual images. The reality was more vivid, but unpatterned. One *felt* about the war rather than *thought* about it or "understood" it.

Meaning must be actively wrested from a page of print; the images upon the screen flow by passive viewers and must be vivid to hold their attention. For this reason the controllers of the screen are led to select for presentation, whether real or fictional, elements with a dramatic visual content. Conflagrations, tornadoes, shootings, airplane crashes, and like disasters have extraordinary prominence in televised news as well as in televised drama simply because they can be *seen* and they reach out to grab attention. The evening news is likely to feature events, even trivial events, of these kinds to the near exclusion of less visible trends and problems and achievements that may have far larger importance for the community.

The characteristics of television have so insistently imposed a dramatic form on its perception and transmission of events that the events themselves have tended to lose reality as genuine happenings and become performances for the camera. Where the television reporter once came to a real event in order to record it, increasingly the event is created and brought to the camera to be viewed.

The quadrennial conventions of the political parties were once real and important events in which factions of the party fought vigorously over platforms and candidates, and the delegates met for serious purposes. The first widely televised conventions, in 1952, were fascinating revelations of politics in action. Once political leaders realized that an audience of tens of millions was gazing through television windows at their behavior, the whole character of conventions changed. Their primary purpose now is to be televised. Professional directors and experts are engaged to handle decoration and staging, and the timing of events is decided not in terms of the requirements of their agenda but in terms of attracting prime-time audiences. It is ironic that the effort to transform conventions from real events to carefully staged television dramas has robbed them of interest. They are rapidly losing the audiences they so actively seek to reach and in the future may no longer be broadcast except in excerpts.

Similarly, public demonstrations were once more or less spontaneous outpourings of genuine emotion addressed to those with power to redress the grievances felt. Once television cameras began to cover them, they quickly became staged dramas, put on simply to be televised and addressed to the television audience. Even in Arab countries the signs borne by protesters are likely to be in English and hence unreadable to the members and active witnesses of the demonstration and clearly intended for the foreign, mostly American, audience for the television show. Instead of the camera capturing reality, "reality" is created for the camera. There is a tendency for life itself to become a television show, enacted in conformity to the demands of the medium. People may speak the way they do, dress the way they do, and carry on relations with parents and children and spouses the way they do because that is what television has led them to accept as appropriate behavior. In a sense, the casual violence of city streets is another television show played off-screen.

Although we can only speculate on the overall effect of our spending hours of every day immersed in a flowing image of life shaped by the demands of the television medium, we can be more specific about the consequences for certain aspects of the American society—and, by extension, of other societies in which television is universally available. One such area is the organization and distribution of political power.

As each new medium has come into existence, permitting a more direct communication between a central source and the ultimate recipients of information, it has lessened the importance and power of the intermediate structures through which information was distributed. The printing press lessened the power of the Catholic hierarchy and the feudal estates by concentrating power in pope and king. The broadcasting media had a similar effect on the structure of American politics.

In the era of print dominance, organized political parties had great power. They were needed to fund the printing and carry out the distribution of enormous quantities of pamphlets and other materials. And their direct contact with voters enabled the "boss" of a city machine to deliver delegates to a convention and voters to the booth on election

day. The publishers of the principal newspapers, because of their control of major print media, were powerful political figures. The presidential and gubernatorial candidates of the Republicans and Democrats
were usually chosen by negotiation among the established leaders of
factions of the party, not by the voting public.

Radio began to change this. Franklin Roosevelt achieved such direct,
personal power through his "fireside chats" that no party machinery
could have availed against him. But the real change came with television. Dwight Eisenhower and Adlai Stevenson in 1952 were the last
candidates actually chosen by party leaders in convention. And 1952
was the first campaign in which television was a major factor. Thereafter, each candidate's success, both in seeking nomination and in the election, depended not on that candidate's relation to the party leaders but
on a direct appeal to individual voters, achieved almost entirely through
television.

The replacement of organized party strength by personal televised
appeal had several consequences, one of which was the importance of
telegenic attractiveness in the choice and success of candidates. The
notable example was Ronald Reagan, an indolent president almost
devoid of substance who nevertheless achieved extraordinary electoral
success and political power as the televised "great communicator." But
the same criteria also affected the choice and success of congressional
and gubernatorial candidates throughout the country.

The criteria of broadcast popularity changed as television replaced
radio as the dominant medium. The words of a radio speaker came
down as a detached voice from the heavens in a context that was appropriate to charismatic leaders. Good men and evil—Adolf Hitler and
Benito Mussolini as well as Franklin Roosevelt and Winston Churchill—were able to impress themselves on an adoring public as leaders
of almost superhuman force, able to command extraordinary loyalty
and willingness to sacrifice from their followers. Lesser demagogues,
like Father Coughlin, Joe McCarthy, and Huey Long, also made effective use of radio. The televised leader, in contrast is a diminutive figure
present as a guest in the audience's living rooms. A quiet and intimate,
unthreatening approach, such as that at which Reagan excelled, is
called for.

On the whole, television is the healthier medium. It can often penetrate insincerity and was the downfall of McCarthy and Richard Nixon. But it does diminish the power of dramatic leadership. Reagan used
it to great effect in part precisely because he indulged rather than led
his listeners, demanding from them no sacrifice or effort. It is open to

question whether television can be used to lead citizens to subordinate their personal interests to common purposes, as the great radio spokesmen were able to do. Certainly television does not encourage that type of leadership. When a rising deficit threatened to engulf the United States during the late 1980s, none were found ready to use television to demand the obviously needed cuts in expenditures and increases in taxes.

A second consequence of the lessened strength of organized political parties is a loss of party discipline, never strong at best in the United States. Candidates no longer dependent on party organizations to mobilize voters and get them to the polls can ignore party positions on issues. Many candidates suppress or minimize their party identification in the hope of winning votes of members of other parties. Members of Congress or of state legislatures feel only a very limited obligation to support the initiatives of a president or governor of their party. This loss of party discipline compounds the problem of leadership that television already produced. Political power tends to disintegrate and be scattered among innumerable legislators and executives, each seeking to protect his or her own individual position through direct television communication with constituents.

A third consequence is a broader and more egalitarian diffusion of political power. In the era of print dominance there was a highly tiered distribution of political information, made somewhat more egalitarian by the coming of mass print. But to the extent that television has become the principal instrument for the diffusion of news, tens of millions of viewers, of all degrees of income and education and in all parts of the country, see the same network news programs (for the news programs of all networks are substantially identical in coverage) and share a common body of information. Unquestionably this gives most Americans a far broader, if still shallow, knowledge of public affairs than that of their pre-television forebears. It also gives them corresponding power, for they can be instantly informed and mobilized about issues that arouse their interest. Hence broadly based public opinion can have an immediate and powerful impact, limiting the range of freedom of political leaders. In effect, the governors cannot be wiser than the governed. And since public opinion is more easily mobilized to oppose new measures by appeals to fear of the consequences than to support perhaps complicated initiatives, especially those demanding sacrifices, this more egalitarian distribution of political power imposes a further limitation on political leadership.

Other political consequences resulted not so much from the inherent characteristics of the medium as from the nature of television regulations, in particular from the equal-time provisions of section 315 of the Federal Communications Act, which, as has been pointed out, has the unintended result of denying free time to all political candidates.

In consequence, television time, essential to the success of any candidate at the state or national level, must either be sought with brief photo opportunities or ten-second sound bites that can catch the news programs or be bought. Because television time is expensive, there is tremendous pressure on candidates to raise very large campaign funds, far larger than were required in the days before television. Such funds are likely to come from affluent business sources; there is, in consequence, a heavy business-oriented influence on candidates and pressure approaching the purchase of general positions if not of specific votes.

Moreover, the economics of television make it much more efficient to buy time in thirty-second or one-minute units rather than in the fifteen-minute or half-hour segments that would permit a reasoned statement of a candidate's position or a presentation of an affirmative program. Because thirty seconds do not allow time for more than a slogan or an image in the manner of an ordinary commercial, and because negative statements can be made more briefly than positive ones, the use of television in campaigns has been increasingly not to inform or to set forth a candidate's own program but to attack, in simplistic terms, some aspects of any opponent's record or character. This dismal consequence of television's public role perhaps reached its nadir in the 1988 presidential campaign, when a thirty-second spot depicting a line of ominous-looking black men passing through a revolving gate while a voice-over invoked the name of Willie Horton obliterated the possibility of any discussion of the very real problem of crime in the United States, its causes, and possible programs that would offer a realistic opportunity to control and reduce it. It was so much cheaper and easier to say "Willie Horton" and show the black men shuffling through the gate.

Another political consequence of television arose from the ability of members of special groups to become aware of the existence of like-minded others through their depiction on news programs or even in entertainment programs. The intense motivation of blacks as a self-conscious group driving for the extension of civil rights in the United States owes much to televised scenes of early demonstrations and violent police actions and of the magnificent oratory of Martin Luther King, Jr., and other black leaders. Even so minor a figure as Al Sharpton, by persistent televised appearances, can become a focussing symbol. The feminist movement and the "right-to-life" movement each drew strength from its adherents' being able to see and hear speeches and demonstrations taking place elsewhere. Homosexuals were similarly emboldened to cease concealing their sexual preferences and to assert claims of rights. Members of dozens of other interest groups, ethnic and ideological, became more aware of the existence of their fellows throughout the country by means of television and developed a clearer and more self-conscious identity. They were enabled in consequence to make their demands on public officials more vociferously and effectively.

These developments left candidates and officials exposed to focussed and vehement pressures from conflicting interest groups, unprotected by national leadership and heavily dependent on interested campaign contributions. At the same time, the mediating role of party organizations in working out compromises and assembling coalitions has been greatly diminished. In such circumstances candidates are pressed toward defensive and evasive positions, more anxious to avoid offense than to assert leadership.

Television, which has certainly broadened the public awareness of conditions, both at home and abroad, and of issues, has the potential to offer the communications infrastructure for rational and effective national policy as well as a potential for demagogic monopoly. In practice it has done neither. It has not become an instrument of manipulation by government or by powerful ideological forces. But it has contributed to a politics of drift that may be equally ominous in a time of need for clear and decisive public action.

The social consequences of the audiovisual media, especially of television, are less easy to perceive. One obvious result has been a process of more nearly uniform acculturation. Motion pictures, even in their earliest nickelodeon form, began this process, familiarizing millions of immigrants in the early twentieth century with norms of middle-class American dress, furnishing, and manners. By the late twentieth century the standardizing influence of television is far more pervasive. New fashions and turns of phrase, especially among the young, spread almost instantly and uniformly across the nation and the world. Racial, ethnic, and gender characterizations, although often stereotyped, are generally intended as benign, and portrayals of blacks and women in positions of authority or in responsible professional positions and of interracial marriage and social interchange no doubt help toward the establishment of tolerance and equality as norms. The propensity of television, however, to rely heavily on sex and violence in its compelled search for larger audiences may also contribute to the acceptance of a looser sexual code, in particular of violence and the use of guns as norms of behavior.

It is impossible to untangle the web of causation in complex patterns of social behavior and to determine to what degree television reflects reality and "reality" reenacts television drama. How much of the constant play of gunfire on televised police, gangster, western, and other dramas reports an existing social reality? How much of the gunfire on the streets plays out the drama on the screen? Probably it is a phenomenon of reciprocal reinforcement, each helping to shape the other. But numerous studies carried on under the auspices of the surgeon general and others have almost uniformly found a correlation between the extent of exposure to violence on television and violent behavior on the part of children, a correlation certainly sufficient to give concern.

Television's thrust toward homogeneity extends abroad. Foreign television systems often have difficulty funding the production of entertainment programs with the professional slickness and popular appeal of those produced for American networks. Hence they have been heavily dependent on the importation of American programs, as they had long been on the importation of American movies. Even those countries well able to afford domestic production have imported a great deal of American programming, especially as independent television networks have been authorized to compete with government-owned systems, forcing both to move aggressively to win or hold market share. The development of cable systems and satellite transmission during the 1980s made it possible for televised programs to overleap national boundaries, especially in Europe, and further the exposure to American productions.

A consequence was a growing uniformity of life-styles, the same blue jeans and discos, the same clothing styles among middle and upper classes, the same popular music, the same modern architecture, and the same basic outlook of a secular, libertarian, free-market society. Aided by satellites, this same televised picture of life flowed through and above the Iron Curtain as well, giving Soviet and East European residents a picture of Western life-style in disturbing contrast to their own. Unquestionably, this daily emphasized contrast had a role in the upwelling dissatisfaction that shouldered aside the old regimes in the Soviet empire and Eastern Europe. The growing discontents in developing countries that have left many of them as simmering reservoirs of dissatisfaction proceed in part from the same televised contrast.

The impact of television on religion to some extent parallels its impact on politics in that individual preachers are enabled to reach large audiences directly without dependence on traditional denominational structures. The power of the denominations, like that of political parties, has been weakened and bypassed. And the substitution of audiovisual media for print has meant a more emotional and less reasoned approach to religion. The propensity of the audiovisual media to lead listeners or viewers to "feel" about rather than to "think" about issues is nowhere more clearly manifested than in the field of religion. The expression of their theological views in books (The Book of Mormon and *Science and Health, with Key to the Scriptures*) enabled Joseph Smith and Mary Baker Eddy to erect structured religions that have long survived them. But Jim Bakker and Jimmy Swaggart and even more established radio and television ministries such as those of Billy Graham and Jerry Falwell will have left little in established institutions after their transient images and voices have disappeared from the airwaves. The intimacy of an imagined personal contact through the audiovisual media, as contrasted with the impersonality and hierarchical distance of print, is evidenced in the near universality of nicknames among the "Billys" and "Jerrys" and "Jimmys" of the television priesthood. While texts perdure, it is precisely the illusion of person-to-person contact that proves evanescent.

By exhibiting the same models of dress and behavior to everyone, television helped to dissolve structures of formality appropriate to a more tiered society. Dress styles, especially among the young, seem increasingly classless. Speech patterns as well show diminishing regional and class variations and a greater openness to slang and vulgarities. Movie screens and pay-cable channels make public the dirty little words of what had been a private and unadmitted language. Life has became more informal as well as increasingly homogeneous. The casual use of first names on the basis of slight if any prior acquaintance is nearly universal. Patterns of etiquette have dissolved, and society, like religion and politics, is more of an unstructured mélange.

This loss of structure, common to so many aspects of American life, and of the life of Western industrialized democracies generally, may be grounded in a fundamental difference between the representation of the world in print and that in the audiovisual media. Print inevitably *structures* the conception and representation of reality, placing things and events in specific categories and asserting relationships among them. The kind of thought that underlies formal writing for publication in itself arranges life in coherent patterns. Whatever our attempts to democratize print through broadly supported education—indeed, universal education at elementary levels—and public libraries and programs to encourage reading, the use of printed materials remains highly differentiated. There is a wide gulf between those who are highly educated, widely read, and have access to good libraries and the habit of using print and the illiterate, who still include a major part of the world's population. And within that great gulf there are many loosely defined gradations. The tiered structure of eighteenth-century society is still reflected in softened form in the world of print.

The audiovisual media tend toward a relatively undifferentiated leveling of access, with many tens of millions watching the same programs and seeing the same films. They also tend toward a dissolution or splintering of patterns. Events are *shown*, not represented through abstraction and categorization. The necessity to "understand" in order to "state" is evaded. Television in particular presents short programs requiring only brief spans of attention. This tendency has been taken to extremes in recent years as a result of a number of factors: the relegation of much political discussion to brief sound bites in news programs and to thirty-second commercials, the division of most news programs into brief one- and two-minute segments, and the growing importance of the MTV style in which vivid kaleidoscopic splinters are shown in no discernible order. Fast-moving glimpses replace ordered contemplation.

Print embodies and realizes more clearly than any other medium the role of language itself in organizing and mastering reality. The reality represented in print is a series of abstract percepts in a fixed array upon which a meaning has been impressed or from which a meaning has been extracted. Print is an instrument to subdue that reality to the purposes of a user by organizing, conveying, and preserving functionally significant meanings. The audiovisual media, in contrast, are largely means for the passive and accepting *experiencing* of reality.

In the case of music, for example, print may record the abstract concept of a composition in engraved notes that may be studied and analyzed and used as instructions for recapturing the reality of the composition in performance. Or print may be the medium for description or comment or criticism or other intellection *about* music. A record or tape or radio performance allows the listener to sit back and effortlessly experience the actuality of the music itself. Similarly, print is an instrument for forming and conveying ideas *about* art; the audiovisual media are means to receive the art itself.

It is hence not surprising that print was the dominant medium in a period in our history in which the ethos of society demanded discipline, organization, and an emphasis on production and a suppression of consumption. The nineteenth century in America was, in fact, often unread, tumultuous, and undisciplined, with its life hardly arrayed in the fixed and orderly lines of print. But the commanding ideal of its print-based solid classes was one of mastering reality through purposive thought, disciplining consumption, and maximizing production and progress. Nor is it surprising that the audiovisual media have a predominant role in a time like our own, with its emphasis on enjoyment and the recreative consumption of life's goods.

The contrast may be embodied in two images: one of a young apprentice in a Franklin Institute library in the evening after a day's work, wrestling with a textbook on the new technologies of the late nineteenth century; the other of a contemporary youth, head nodding in pleasure, striding to the beat of music reaching him through his tape player or else more passively watching television from a living-room couch.

In the poem "McAndrew's Hymn," written in 1893, long before the dawn of the audiovisual era, Rudyard Kipling used the voice of a Scots engineer to record the spirit, the ethos, of his print-dominated time, when the massive and ordered powers of steam matched the ordered lines of print:

> From coupler-flange to spindle-guide I see Thy Hand, O
>   God—
> Predestination in the stride o' yon connectin'-rod.
> John Calvin might ha' forged the same—enorrmous, certain,
>   slow—
> Ay, wrought it in the furnace-flame—*my* "Institutio."
>
> . . . .
>
> Now, a' together, hear them lift their lesson—theirs an' mine
> "Law, Orrder, Duty an' Restraint, Obedience, Discipline!"

But in the same poem Kipling hinted at a different, passive, recipient ethos that was, in a way, to characterize an audiovisual time to come, when he wrote of a land breeze blowing across McAndrew's ship in the tropics "milk-warm, wi' breath o' spice and bloom" and calling him to come away and know the living God that "swells the ripenin' cocoanut an' and ripes the woman's breast."

— II —

The Coming of the Computer

Overlapping and following the audiovisual revolution came another—
the revolution of the computer and the satellite—with almost opposite
thrusts. The computer and related developments in telecommunications
made it possible to reduce not only words and numbers but also sounds
and images, to patterns of binary digits, to long series of ones and zeros
representing the "on" and "off" status of infinitesimally small switches.
These symbols, far more abstract and precise than words or letters, can
be input by striking keys on what resembles a typewriter keyboard or
manipulating a mouse or by optical or auditory scanning. The resulting
digital pattern is reflected in the state of circuits within the enormous
array of transistors embodied in the silicon chips that make up a computer's memory and can be transferred from that memory to magnetic
or laser-readable patterns on discs.

Such disc storage is so unbelievably compact that the equivalent of
a multivolume encyclopedia can be housed on a single disc. Data so
emplaced may be frozen as text in read-only memories (ROMs), or it
may be left in databases or random-access memories (RAMs) subject
to erasure, addition, rearrangement, or other manipulation. Elaborate
and complex calculations can be instantly performed with data so
stored, calculations that would otherwise consume years or be altogeth-
er impossible.

Both ROMs and RAMs can be "read" in ways that will reproduce
their contents or parts thereof by display on a screen or by instructions
to a printer, or they may directly instruct other equipment. And they
can be searched in ways that will select particular items according to
predetermined criteria, array them in desired ways, and otherwise manipulate them. The data can be sent from any point of storage to any
recipient with an appropriate terminal and connections to telephone
lines or an antenna for satellite reception. Enormous masses of data can
be transmitted almost instantly and relatively inexpensively in this way.

For many functions the computer thus provided a vastly more powerful and efficient alternative to print and is also often far less expensive. For any information to become part of the public compendium in
an age of print, it must be reduced to writing, edited, keyboarded or
otherwise embodied in type, and printed. For it to be widely available,
the printing must be in thousands, perhaps hundreds of thousands or
millions, of copies, and those copies must be physically distributed to
locations in which they may be used and stored in large, organized collections of similar materials for preservation or future use. Complex
systems of access must be provided. Physical units, such as books or
bound volumes of periodicals, may be cataloged by author, title, and a
few principal subjects and identified by numbers that indicate their location within a collection. Ponderous printed union catalogs and union
lists were needed to identify the libraries or other collections in which
copies of the book or journal could be found. At a more specific level
of control, periodical indexes might identify articles relevant to specified topics within selected journals. But the only indexes that led to
specific data within a work were those that might be contained within
individual books. In other words, the whole system of bibliographic
control was designed to lead to artifacts rather than to facts—to enable
users to lay their hands on a specific book or journal issue, not upon a
particular fact or idea.

Once committed to print, data could not be updated, rearranged,
corrected, or otherwise altered save by printing a new and revised edition, with the result that reference works almost immediately became
in some degree out of date. Entries could be arrayed by only a single
criterion (e.g., in alphabetical order) and could be used in calculations
only by a separate manual effort; they could be rearranged only in a new
or separate edition.

The cost of editing a manuscript, setting it in type, printing a large
number of copies that may or may not be used, and somehow distributing them so that they will be physically accessible to potential users
has always severely limited the amount of information that can be added to the public compendium. It has erected a threshold of cost that
requires evidence of relatively wide interest or special value before any
body of information can be printed. This means that only a small fraction of book manuscripts, scholarly dissertations and articles, and research reports ever see print. To overcome this barrier before the computer, various devices have been used. Reports not reaching the dignity
of print may be reproduced by mimeograph or similar methods, and
some of these are made available by the National Technical Information Service, which issues catalogs of the reports and will provide pho-

tocopied reproductions on order. Similarly, most unpublished doctoral theses are deposited with University Microfilms, which also issues catalogs and will provide microfilm or hard-copy reproductions.

The computer offers major advantages over such devices. The typing of the original manuscript, if done on a word processor, may in itself produce a machine-readable copy that can be fed into a national database with minimal additional expense. Once a document has been incorporated in such a national database it is automatically made available to anyone, wherever situated, who has access to a terminal connected with the database, without the necessity of reproducing physical copies unless and until they are actually needed. Moreover, the cataloging and indexing of a machine-readable document is relatively easy and may be made automatic. One may, for example, assign any number of subject headings to such a document without being limited to the few that can be used in standard cataloging practice, and these can be searched by a computer in any desired combination. Abstracts or even whole machine-readable texts themselves can also be searched by a computer to identify all appearances of a given term or combination of terms.

Computer developments have been complemented by equally striking developments in telecommunication, themselves made possible in large part by computerized switching. The use of optical fibers, of other high-capacity circuits, and of satellite-to-dish transmission has made possible the near instant and relatively very inexpensive transmission of enormous bodies of information in digital form.

These developments have enhanced, replaced, and complemented print. The enhancement has come in two ways. Computer-assisted photocomposition has made possible sharp reductions in the cost of preparing printing plates, bypassing the whole process of hot metal composition. If the author has used a word processor, it may be possible to compose directly from the author's discs without the necessity of a second keyboarding. The content of newspapers and magazines may now never appear as ink on paper until they are actually printed. In such cases, the reporter or other writer works on a word processor. His or her text is edited from a screen image; the finished article is composed and formatted on screen and transmitted electronically, usually by satellite, to a printing plant or plants where the paper or magazine is physically produced.

In the century following the invention of the linotype machine, technological advances in printing were devoted primarily to reducing the cost of printing and binding long runs of material. Such advances made possible, for example, the inexpensive mass-market paperback. But they did not lower the initial cost of preparing materials for the press and hence did not help with the problem of publishing short-run scholarly or specialized books and journals. Computer-assisted production lowers those initial costs dramatically and makes it much more practical to produce books and journals that may be important but have a limited potential market. The new techniques opened the door to the quadrupling in recent years of the number of books published annually and the explosion in the number of small-circulation scholarly and scientific journals.

A further enhancement of the role of print came from the use of the computer in cataloging and indexing. Earlier methods—Library of Congress printed catalog cards, reproduced in card catalogs of libraries throughout the country; printed union catalogs; printed union lists of serials; and printed periodical and journal indexes like *Index Medicus*—all collapsed under the flood of late twentieth-century printed materials. Now the kind of cataloging data provided on Library of Congress cards can be placed in a data bank such as those provided by the library's MARC tapes or by OCLC and other similar services. An individual library may draw from such a service the data needed to catalog its own holdings, embodying them in a card catalog or, as is now more frequently the case, in a local database searchable through terminals.

The limited and quickly outdated printed indexes or guides to journal articles have also been superseded by computerized services providing efficient, current, and more detailed and flexible access to articles within specific fields, such as *Chem Abstracts* and MEDLINE for chemical and biomedical articles. Other services, such as LEXIS for appellate court decisions and opinions and NEXUS for current news articles in a number of magazines and newspapers, go farther and provide whole-text indexing by all terms in the original text.

All of these devices combine to give a much more efficient and powerful access to the content of the public compendium of print than has ever before existed. Sitting at a computer terminal, a researcher can with relative ease quickly discover not only the books but also the journal articles and other materials relevant to his or her inquiry in many languages and located in depositories throughout much of the world.

The new technology enhances the role of print in these ways, and for certain functions it may even replace print. Such a replacement has already taken place for many bibliographical tools. Today one goes to the computer terminal where once one went to printed union catalogs or to Gregory's *Union List of Serials*. It is quite possible, for example, to envision the replacement of scholarly or scientific journals of limited circulation by incorporating edited and refereed articles in a database that is indexed by key words in abstracts. This would greatly speed the publication of new scientific or other scholarly contributions because there would be no arbitrary space limitation or need for waiting for monthly or quarterly issues. Abstracts could be readily scanned on a terminal and articles of interest called up on a screen or printed out. The advantages of such a system as a replacement for highly specialized journals are so obvious that the failure to make broader use of it may appear to be due more to academic conservatism and the pressure for printed publication as a prerequisite to tenure and promotion than to practical considerations, although problems in devising arrangements for meeting the costs of such a system are also an important factor.

In general, however, the new technology is unlikely to replace print for extensive documents such as novels, histories, biographies, and longer treatises; for works read for pleasure; and for works likely to be demanded in their full form, as distinguished from works, like telephone directories or dictionaries, consulted only for individual data. Print enjoys formidable advantages in convenience, portability, ease of reading, and economy in the case of widely used works. Works, particularly reference works, may exist in both forms: telephone directories are in print in homes and offices, on-line in directory assistance offices and central switchboards; airline guides are available on-line to travel agents and through some information services as well as in print; and some general encyclopedias are available on-line and in ROM discs as well as in traditional form.

The most important role of the new technology as a medium for the embodiment of information, however, is not in doing what print does, replacing or paralleling printed documents, but in its capacity to bring into the public compendium vast quantities of information too detailed or specialized or evanescent ever to be embodied in print. A vast ocean of recorded data now lies beneath the scattered islands of print. Of course, there were always enormous quantities of information that lay below the level of print, recorded in written files. Individual census data, income tax returns, the ledgers of banks and stores and offices, the records of individual transactions, the notes of laboratory experiments, and doctors' files on patients have all embodied information that may be the raw material for printed documents. But access to them has been blocked by their unique physical form; they could be consulted only at the one, usually securely restricted, place in which they were housed. And consultation of any large number of records by manual inspection and tabulation was impossibly expensive. Once such data are embodied in machine-readable databases, as they now commonly are, it is at least technically possible for the raw data to be accessible to any person with a terminal and modem and be easily manipulable for analysis.

The cost threshold limiting the inclusion of data in the public compendium has thus been dramatically lowered. This broader accessibility has many benign consequences. The management of large enterprises has been dramatically improved by the enhanced ability of central offices to have direct access to details of distant operations, thus reducing the need for intermediate levels of management and permitting early detection of problems. Similarly, the ability of hundreds of thousands of stores, restaurants, hotels, airlines, and other vendors to have instant access to information on the credit of individuals has made possible the nearly universal use of credit cards. Contemporary banking and financial services would be inconceivable without such instant data access.

For research as well, the ability to arrange and manipulate raw data, especially data from varied sources, makes possible analyses and correlations that could never previously be undertaken. Economic studies have been particularly aided, but other disciplines have also. Contemporary cosmology and astronomy, molecular biology, and environmental medicine are examples of the many fields revolutionized or even made possible by the computer.

But there are potentially menacing as well as benign consequences of the enlargement of the public compendium to include records of individual persons and transactions. Although various means exist to confine database access to restricted groups of authorized users, these means are not impenetrable. A possibility exists for private information about individuals' financial or medical or personal affairs to come into improper hands and be misused. And even authorized uses of personal data brought together from various sources, as by governmental agencies, may give an undesirable power over individuals.

Every significant new medium of communication has had important effects on the power of societies employing it and on the distribution of power within those societies. The impact of the computer has been equal to that of print and far greater than that of the audiovisual media. Where cinema, recordings, and broadcasting conduced to a fuller *experiencing* of reality, the computer, like print, has been addressed to its *mastery*. Of all the empowerments of the word that have come since humankind first devised speech, the computer is the most compelling.

Economic and military power in the late twentieth century was directly dependent on mastery of the new computer and communications technology. The mastery of print in Europe and its neglect in the Middle East, Africa, and the Orient had thrust the formerly weak European states of the seventeenth and eighteenth centuries past such previously more powerful states as China, Japan, the Ottoman Empire, and the principalities of India. So in the twentieth century the United States, Western Europe, and Japan used the technology of the computer to open an even wider gulf between their power and that of not only developing countries but also of the Soviet bloc. The quick overwhelming of an Iraqi force, equally equipped with conventional weapons, by the high technology of the American and allied forces was a dramatic demonstration of its irresistible power. So was the practical abandonment of the Soviet Union's effort to maintain military equality with or superiority over the West and its pretensions to comparable economic power.

It was not a question only of the capacity to manufacture computer hardware, which was dominated by the United States, followed by Japan, with the major Western European powers struggling to maintain viable industries. Nor was it the ability to use the computer for a few select undertakings: the Soviet Union had made brilliant use of the new technology in its space program. What made the difference was the permeation of a society by the *use* of the computer so that it could transform the economy as a whole. And here the United States, Japan, and Western Europe have achieved unparalleled success. Similarly, Western Europe was not able to extend its commercial dominance over the Middle East and Asia until print had become more than an instrument of a small scholarly elite and had permeated the urban bourgeoisie. And the achievement of the nineteenth-century Industrial Revolution in Western Europe and the United States came only when the technology of cheap paper, steam, and electrically powered presses and new typesetting machinery extended the use of print throughout the entire society.

The Western economies were transformed not only by the use of the computer in science and in such advanced technology as that of the exotic weapons they now possess but also by its use in day-to-day life: in the management of large enterprises, in enabling a swift response to changing markets, in ordinary factory operation, and in reducing costs in the daily conduct of business.

The consequences of the computer revolution in the empowerment of societies are clear. Less clear are its consequences in the distribution of power within those societies. Again there is a parallel to print. So long as the distribution of print was limited to select groups or classes, and so long as its content could be controlled by rulers, print served to concentrate power, enhancing the authority of the papacy within the hierarchy and of royal courts within the feudal order, of national over provincial authorities. As the middle classes used print more actively, and as it escaped rigid censorship, it played a role in the empowerment of the bourgeoisie and rural proprietors in the late eighteenth and early nineteenth centuries. And the wide availability of mass print in the latter nineteenth century was concurrent with the movement toward universal suffrage.

So it was in the case of computers. The first generation of these powerful instruments was enormous and extremely costly. Their use was practical only for large governmental agencies and very large corporations. They seemed likely to concentrate power further where it was already greatest. But technological change came quickly; compact, efficient, and less expensive computers came within reach of much smaller operations. There was a reduced threat of further concentration of power in a few potent centers but still concern that society would be divided into a broad group that had access to computers and were competent in their use and a much broader group who lacked that access and competence. But even further technological progress has made inexpensive personal computers available to even the smallest businesses and to millions of individuals. The increasingly widespread use of computers in schools promises to make ability to use the new technology commonplace in the rising generation. The use of modems, moreover, has made possible the easy connection of individual personal computers with enormous and powerful databases.

At the same time, further developments in computer use have reduced the advantage of the very large and expensive mainframe computers that had centralized and controlled the access to databases. They are increasingly replaced by networks of small personal computers linked to distributed databases. Even within large corporations and governmental agencies, access to information and the power to organize and use it has been decentralized and spread throughout the organization.

The computer, like print by the end of the nineteenth century, now promises to be an instrument for widely disseminating a particularly powerful means of access to large bodies of previously completely or nearly inaccessible information and hence to become an instrument for the further democratizing of information and of concomitant power.

Using print to diffuse through most of society the enormous power of the written word once closely held by rulers had one unhappy consequence. It left at the end a small class of illiterates more hopelessly than ever excluded from opportunity by the very fact that a society now built around literacy had no place for them. Just so, the fact that computers are becoming nearly universal in advanced societies will mean that those elements in such societies that do not share in the new technology may be increasingly condemned to powerlessness and exclusion. And the gulf between technologically advanced societies and those without that advantage will become even wider.

The computer, coupled with the more discriminating sensors and measuring instruments that it makes possible, may have effects on our basic conception of reality more fundamental than its effects on the possession and diffusion of power. Words have been our system of symbols to represent reality. They are often blunt and imprecise, always metaphorical and subjective. To describe a particular group of colors, we have only a limited range of words: "red," "pink," "rose," "vermilion," "scarlet," or "crimson." None are exact; all are evocative of remembered colors and associations but incapable of precisely defining a color in a way that permits its exact duplication. But an electronic scanner can perceive the color in terms of the exact composition of wave lengths refracted from it, and the computer can record this in lines of binary symbols, far beyond the capacity of words to perceive or record. Again, we have only a handful of vague words to record a voice, which may be husky, light, hoarse, high-pitched, deep, squeaky, or mellifluous. Blindfolded, we can readily recognize friends by the sound of their voices, but there is no way we can record that perception in words sufficiently precise to enable another to recognize them. But the computer can make possible a digital recording that can let another computer confirm the identity of a speaker.

The veil of ambiguity that words raise between ourselves and reality has been rent by computer-assisted instruments of mensuration and by the computer itself. The recording of objective perceptions in a precise and potentially infinitely detailed digital code instead of the subjective perceptions recorded in the broad and metaphorical symbols of words has brought to a wholly new level our grasp of, and our mastery over, reality. Now indeed has humankind's symbolizing of reality been so empowered that, as God foresaw at Babel, "Nothing they propose to do will now be impossible for them."

The principal developers of computers and of the information sciences they served were engineers and mathematicians who conceived of reality in precise and discrete terms. And the information systems served by the new technologies were funded and developed by agencies whose concern was to provide as complete information as possible about individual subjects and events: travel agents and airlines that needed to know the availability of every seat on every flight; credit card banks and others that needed instant information of every one of hundreds of millions of daily transactions; intelligence agencies that wanted every scrap of information on an enormous number of persons and events of concern; and scientists and engineers who need to calculate precisely the orbit of satellites into months and years of flight.

In consequence, the uses of the computer have tended to reinforce conceptions of the universe as fractured arrays of discrete data stripped bare of emotional connotation and absent holistic unity. It is a sense of the universe cognate with that expressed in much contemporary art, music, and literature, in which scantly patterned items of sound or description or color seem bare of overreaching meaning and unlinked by patterns of melody or narrative or depiction.

Recent developments in computer programming have strengthened the capacity of computers to integrate as well as to analyze and to learn from experience. Computers can now be programmed to play chess better than any but a very few grand masters and to sense patterns of relationships among bewildering masses of data. Some exponents of so-called artificial intelligence believe that in time the computer can be empowered to do anything that the human mind can do, for they conceive the human brain as itself a computer whose transmission of electrochemical signals across neural synapses parallels the computer's electronic signaling across transistors.

The conception of the brain as essentially a machine and its intelligence as programming analogous to the programming of a computer avoids questions of conscious self-awareness, of "meaning" as a conscious awareness of pattern, and of the emotional components of cognition. All of these are functions that we have embodied in or expressed through words and are related to the human investment in their metaphorical and connotative rather than to their denotative use. A distinctly "human" perception of reality is still in the domain of words, uncaptured by the computer's digital patterns.

We have seen that the power of a society is related to the amplitude of the public compendium of knowledge at its command and its ability to make effective use of its content. Similarly, the distribution of power within a society depends on patterns of access to that public compendium. The computer, in a quite revolutionary way, has enormously expanded the public compendium, making it possible to create an accessible record of oceans of data that could never be embodied in print. And the extraordinary heuristic power of the computer has had an equally revolutionary effect through the dramatic increase in our technological power to find information within that compendium and arrange and manipulate it in ways that make possible its far more effective use. Thus, through a much ampler public compendium that can be far more effectively used, comes the revolutionary increase in the power of the technologically advanced Western societies. At issue are two basic questions. One is how to realize more fully the heuristic and manipulative potentials of the new technology so that we can more effectively use the enriched public compendium. The other is how to extend access to that compendium as broadly as possible without invading the privacy of individual data so that the new, vastly greater power may be as fully diffused as possible throughout society rather than further concentrated in the hands of those who can control access.

Our arrangements for preserving, organizing, establishing bibliographical control over, and providing access to the public compendium of printed knowledge evolved over many decades, in part even from the early days of printing. The complex system involved a variety of publishers as gatekeepers of the compendium, with constitutional protection of their freedom; government publishing programs and subsidy of nonprofit publishers to assure that entry into the public compendium will not be confined to commercially profitable materials; copyright laws to assure an orderly market in which private publishing and individual authors can create without the need for governmental support and hence control; systems of wholesalers and bookstores for the distribution of books and of postal services for periodicals; libraries to act as reservoirs for the collection and preservation of the flow of print; uniform cataloging and classification rules and systems of subject headings to permit a standardized organization of materials in the public compendium as stored in libraries; public support of libraries to enable free access; and interlibrary loan systems and photocopying arrangements permitting a user to have access to materials in distant libraries.

This elaborate and largely voluntary system of interlocking institutions and practices had two objectives. One was to permit the entry into the public compendium of any communication that in some relevant judgment was sufficiently worthwhile to justify the threshold costs of publication, whether the judgment was based on estimates of popular sale, or of scholarly worth as by a university press, or an advocate's conviction that it was worth the cost to send such a message. The other was to approach the ideal goal of making it possible for any user anywhere to have access to any item in the public compendium, an ideal far from complete achievement but realized with fair success for skillful and persistent inquirers.

We should have the same objectives for the communications resources of the new technology. The economic threshold for addition to the public compendium has been radically lowered now that it is no longer necessary to print thousands of copies for this purpose. Tremendous quantities of data are now accumulated in forms appropriate for inclusion in the public compendium. The limitations are now questions primarily of policy rather than of cost. Many large and potentially useful databases have been created to which the public is not allowed access and which are hence not effectively in the public compendium. Some are in the hands of large corporations and relate to their internal operations or to their markets (e.g., specialized mailing lists of potential customers). These will no doubt continue to remain under private control. But many governmental agencies have even larger databases that, although accumulated to serve the operations of the agency creating them, have great potential secondary value to other users. Some need to be restricted, of course, for security reasons, for example, the files of intelligence agencies, and others, such as income tax returns, to protect the privacy of individuals. But others could, in most cases, quite properly be opened to public access: the records of the Bureau of the Census with personally identifying data deleted; the data banks of the Bureau of Labor Statistics, the Federal Reserve Board, and other economic agencies; the research files of the Bureau of Standards and the National Institutes of Health; and the enormous files created by congressional committees.

But merely adding databases to the public compendium so that there is no legal barrier to their use obviously does not assure realistic access. Once books are in bookstores and libraries and newspapers and magazines are available on newsstands and by subscription, complex bibliographical systems and catalogs enable a user to locate and buy or borrow them or read them in a library or obtain photocopies. Although the user who can afford to buy the book or subscribe to the magazine or newspaper will have an advantage, public policy expressed in the support of free public libraries helps to provide a more egalitarian access.

Much of this elaborate infrastructure that facilitates the use of printed materials is lacking in the case of machine-readable databases. No comprehensive bibliography of databases exists. Systematic cataloging is in its early stages. Most databases are proprietary and may be entered only by customers who have paid a substantial fee. Access requires an appropriate terminal and a modem to connect with a central database or else a disc drive that will permit the use of data recorded on ROMs. The required equipment is expensive, as are access charges and telephone line costs. These are charges that can be justified easily only for those who use given databases frequently for business or professional purposes. Moreover, a considerable specialized skill is required to use a complex database. A law firm, for example, must not only meet the considerable costs of access to LEXIS but also must have staff experienced in computer use and who have also mastered the rather complex skills specific to the use of that enormous and powerful database.

These various limitations of cost, equipment, and skills mean that the use of large databases is in practice largely confined to a limited number of individuals and organizations that rely on them for business and professional purposes. The proprietors of databases in turn design them to respond to the needs of that limited market. Giant databases like COMPUSTAT are designed primarily to meet the needs of large investors, brokers, banks, and corporate merger and acquisitions departments and similar large users, not to meet the quite different needs of small businesses. Bibliographic databases like MEDLINE or *Chem Abstracts* are designed to serve the needs of the specialist who seeks to learn of *all* the reports on a particular limited topic, not for the occasional user who wants to know the best or at least a good book or article on a broader subject.

What are badly needed are intermediary institutions that can provide the facilities and skills needed for full database access, that have subscriptions to the appropriate proprietary databases, and that can make all these available even to unsophisticated individual and small organization users. Many such exist. Travel agents, for example, have sophisticated on-line access to complex airline and hotel reservation systems that are used for the benefit of individual travelers. Social service offices may have access to databases with information about various institutions and sources of assistance that they can draw on for the benefit of their clients. A high school counselor may have a terminal to search through curriculum offerings, tuition fees, admission standards, and financial assistance offerings of hundreds of colleges and better advise a graduating senior where to apply.

But the only general institution that can provide this assistance to an inquirer seeking not help in solving a particular problem but rather information itself is the library. This has always been a function of libraries with respect to print. Probably most middle-sized and larger libraries are now able to provide assistance with bibliographical databases. They will either help readers search DIALOG or the OCLC catalog or similar bibliographical tools or perform the searches for them. These are databases that the library must be able to use for its own internal purposes. But few are connected with textual databases such as LEXIS or NEXUS or with factual ones such as COMPUSTAT. They do not have the funds, nor do they often consider it their function.

Although computer "literacy" has become widespread, personal computers are widely owned, and the use of computers in routine business transactions has become commonplace, these various limitations have tended to restrict the effective use of informational databases to large organizations and specially trained professionals. The situation is analogous to that of print. Almost everyone can read and has reasonable access to newspapers and popular books and magazines but only a very few have the opportunity, the interest, or the capacity to use the full resources of major research libraries, with a consequent further clustering of power around centers of sophisticated competence in the use of information.

A whole new infrastructure, comparable to that existing for print, is needed in order to make the enormous compendium of machine-readable information more fully available. This will require both public support and a broadly based cooperative effort of creators and marketers of information in that medium and of libraries and other institutions. And, above all, it will require a different mind-set. We have for centuries identified information with the artifacts in which it is embodied. Publication has meant incorporation in an artifact—a book or journal or newspaper. Dissemination has meant the physical distribution of the artifacts. Preservation of the information has meant storage and preservation of the physical documents containing the information. Organization of information has meant arranging the documents according to a predetermined pattern. Cataloging has meant preparing means for locating a given physical document within a collection. Access has meant the ability to get the desired document in one's hands.

All of this changes when we conceive of information as disembodied from any artifact, attached to no place, and existing as a potential capable of being made manifest in any terminal. Connections replace collections in our thinking. In some sense the qualities of orality are restored, with information stored in the memory of computers as in human memory, capable of being evoked on demand, of being kept constantly current with additions and corrections, and of being manipulated and combined with other elements of information.

We are but at the threshold of reconceiving the storage and communication of information, of realizing the enormous power the new technology offers us, and of learning to harness it to the public good.

—12—

Printed Media in the Audiovisual and Electronic Era

The era of print dominance ended in the United States and in much of the rest of the industrialized world during the 1920s, when radio and the movies became almost universally available. There were now other sources of news, more instant and less demanding. Important speeches and ceremonies could be heard live, the voice of a president or other leader could enter every home, sports events could be followed play-by-play as they took place on the field, and dramatic events of every kind could be reported from the scene in the moment of their occurrence. Radio could in part displace the newspaper; together with the movies it threatened to take over the entertainment function of books. Who would read a novel when the theater beckoned her to a vivid portrayal of the scenes and characters on the screen, or when he could use the time to listen to Amos and Andy or a major league baseball game or a radio drama in his living room?

Many publishers, especially the ever-lugubrious publishers of books, foresaw the doom of their industry in the new media. Newspaper publishers fought vigorously to forestall or limit the news-bearing functions of radio. Many refused at first to publish the schedules of radio broadcasts. They sought to bar or severely limit the availability to broadcasters of the news services of the press associations they controlled.

It did not, of course, turn out as the pessimists feared. The 1920s instead were an abounding decade for print. The circulation of newspapers increased, and their voices remained powerful. The role of print in the dissemination of news was in fact enhanced by the initiation of *Time* and other news magazines. Within a couple of years in the mid-1920s the launching of several remarkable book publishing houses, including Random House, Viking, and Simon and Schuster, and of the Book-of-the-Month and Literary Guild book clubs, along with the coming into full flower of the Knopf house, brought a new vitality to the industry and a new sensitivity to European writing and to new schools of American authorship.

The depression of the 1930s was a much more powerful factor than competition from the new media in curtailing the income of print publishers and the flow of their products, and the print media, like all industries, suffered during those years. But the hunger for news in World War II was so great that all the news-bearing media achieved a new importance. Radio became indispensable, newsreels were in every theater, news magazines flourished, and newspapers achieved added vigor. Book publishing, although held in restraint by paper shortages, sold out a high proportion of printings and was very profitable.

A far greater impact of the new media began with the 1950s, when television first achieved a nearly universal reach and when the potentialities of the computer began to be perceived. The future of print seemed now to be a diminished if not a doomed one. When the movie screen could be moved to the living room and made free of charge and enhanced with news and live coverage of events, who would beguile themselves with reading or rely on stale print to provide news, hours-old at best, of events that could be seen on the screen as they happened? And the computer promised to make the storage and retrieval of information and the processes of education and training more efficient than print could ever make them. Books and magazines, it was thought, might shrivel in importance; the reading of books, like the riding of horses, might become the elegant and archaic pastime of a small elite.

The exhibition of films in theaters turned out to be the principal victim of television. The number of motion picture theaters in the United States declined from 12,291 in 1958, when the number had already begun to shrink, to 9,150 in 1963. Over the same period their receipts fell from $935 million to $808 million. Although it suffered initially, the motion picture industry in time learned to deal with television as a new market rather than as a competitor and was able in consequence to remain powerful and profitable.

The print media suffered less from a loss of audience then from a loss of advertising. Until the coming of radio and, far more significantly, of television, magazines offered advertisers the only means of reaching a general national audience, and with a visual message radio could not offer. But television soon dominated this field. One by one, great national magazines aimed at a general audience went under: *Saturday Evening Post, Life, Look, Liberty, Colliers, American*—journals some of which are now almost forgotten, but powerful instruments in their day. Television was not efficient in reaching specialized markets, and

magazines aimed at more limited audiences managed to retain advertisers of products appealing to their kinds of readers. Women's magazines survived and prospered, even those, like *Ladies Home Journal,
Women's Home Companion,* and *Good Housekeeping,* aimed at a
broad female audience. So did hundreds of magazines addressed to the
followers of particular occupations, businesses, or hobbies, so long as
the audience of each constituted a coherent market for a particular
group of products or services. It was easy for magazines to survive by
catering to tennis players, golfers, stamp collectors, computer enthusiasts, or the like because their readers were ready markets for tennis
racquets, golf equipment, stamp catalogs and albums, and computer
software and peripherals. But it was nearly impossible to publish a successful magazine for lovers of poetry or short stories; their readers did
not provide a coherent market for any particular class of product.

One special class of periodicals throve in the new era: scientific and
scholarly journals. The tremendous increase in enrollments in advanced
education and in employment requiring advanced scientific, technical,
and professional knowledge provided a dramatically expanding market, and computer technology made practical the publication of highly
specialized journals with very small circulation. The result was an explosion in the number of periodicals using the new technology to meet
the newly expanding need.

Newspapers suffered a loss of circulation, especially of urban afternoon editions, as the hunger for news at day's end was satisfied by early
evening network television programs. Local television also captured a
significant part of the advertising budgets of urban department stores and
other major newspaper advertisers. Direct mail marketing proved to be
an even more serious competitor as the computer made more efficient the
pin-pointing of mailing lists for catalogs. The number of urban newspapers declined steadily, and ultimately only the very largest cities were able
to maintain more than one daily newspaper. And even in those few cities
with competing papers, one of them, like the *New York Times,* the *Washington Post,* and the Los Angeles *Times-Mirror,* was dominant, and its
competitors were left marginally profitable at best. Usually, however, its
monopoly or near-monopoly position left the only or principal paper in
each city quite profitable. Suburban papers also gained ground in the
television era. They served markets too small for television to be an effective competitor and were able to reduce costs and expand and prosper by joining networks so that they could share the cost of production
and of providing features and national and international news.

Newspaper content also changed substantially. Even the most successful papers realized their inability to compete with radio and television in

the immediate reporting of headline news. The public would inevitably turn to the screen to find out quickly what happened. The newspaper's role would hence tend to be to explain why it happened, its background and its consequences, and to fill out details. Interpretive analyses came to occupy a more prominent place, along with syndicated columns and extensive editorial features other than spot news, so that newspapers came to play something of the role of news magazines. The copious weekly "Science," "Home," "Travel," and "Arts and Leisure" sections like those of the *New York Times* could be afforded by few other papers, but similar content on a smaller scale came to characterize most newspapers.

The most surprising response of the print media to the audiovisual and computer revolutions came in book publishing. Far from the doomed future foreseen in the early 1950s, books in the subsequent decades flourished as never before. By 1990 more than six times as many titles were published annually as in 1950. By 1993 publishers' sales, most at wholesale prices, had risen to $18 billion, more than thirty times the sales volume of 1950, an increase several times greater than the level of inflation. The number of bookstores increased equally dramatically, not only of the chain stores now seeming to appear in every suburban shopping mall but also of well-stocked individual shops. Book sales, even when measured in copies rather than dollars, tripled.

This extraordinary increase in the flow of books, which was so contrary to conventional expectations, was due to a number of factors. Some were technological, just as advances in presses, typesetting machines, and methods of paper manufacture had made possible the flood of printed materials in the late nineteenth century. The adaptation for book production of high-speed magazine presses and the development of better glues and means of laminating paper bindings made practical the very inexpensive mass-market paperback sold through magazine channels. This new product flourished from the late 1940s onward and created an enormous new market for popular novels and for some nonfiction. Computer-assisted accounting, mailing, and administrative procedures facilitated a rapid expansion of book clubs. More important, the computer and related technology lowered typesetting and platemaking costs, permitting the annual publication of many thousands of additional titles for specialized markets.

But a more important factor was demographic. In the years immediately following the end of World War II, the annual birthrate in the United States increased approximately 60 percent, and this unusually high fertility continued until the mid-1960s, with four million or more births annually compared to fewer than 2,500,000 in the war and prewar years. The first fruit of this baby boom entered the first grade in

1953, and grade-by-grade produced a sudden increase of 40 percent or more as it plowed its way through the school system. The size of the adult population was not materially affected until the late 1960s, but the 1970s and 1980s saw a rapid increase in the number of adults as the postwar children matured and entered the work force.

Public policy may have played an even larger role. The principal benefit voted the veterans of World War II was a generous program of educational scholarships, resulting in an immediate major increase in college enrollments. By 1950 the percentage of youths eighteen to twenty-four who were enrolled in college as degree candidates nearly doubled the prewar figure, and doubled again by 1970, as other forms of public assistance succeeded the G.I. Bill of Rights scholarships. In the early 1970s the confluence of the higher proportion attending college and the baby boom's reaching college age produced another surge of enrollments. Soon more than twelve million were in postsecondary institutions, including community and junior colleges, compared with a prewar enrollment of little more than one million.

Similar expansions of public policy were taking place at the elementary and high school level and in relation to public libraries. The National Defense Education Act of 1957 established a precedent for federal support of public education, with substantial appropriations for audiovisual materials and equipment and for the teaching of science, mathematics, and modern foreign languages. More important was the Elementary and Secondary Education Act of 1965, with very large funding for poverty-impacted school districts and special funding for school libraries. Public libraries also benefited significantly from the Library Services Act of 1958, initially addressed primarily to the extension of public library services to rural areas but later extended to general library support.

These factors all combined to produce an enormous demand for books, at first for children's books and elementary school textbooks to accommodate the new wave of children and for college textbooks for the beneficiaries of the G.I. scholarships. As college enrollments leapt upward in the late 1960s and the 1970s with the entry of the baby boom generation, hundreds of new colleges were created; small teachers' colleges were enlarged to universities, as in New York; and schools with small enrollments grew to enormous institutions with twenty thousand students or more. This growth created a demand not only for college textbooks but also for materials for the stocking of hundreds of new or vastly enlarged college libraries. Federal support under the Elementary and Secondary Education Act and the Library Services and Construction Act and greatly increased state and local support multiplied the demand for books for school and public libraries.

The organization and ownership of the American book publishing industry were radically transformed by the problem of meeting this surging demand for books. For every thousand dollars a publisher receives from the sale of books, at least an equal amount must be invested in advances to authors, salaries and overhead, design and composition, inventory, and accounts receivable. The swift rise of book sales from about $500 million a year in the early 1950s to about $1.5 billion a decade later required an investment of something in the order of a billion dollars. It was impossible that this be achieved by the reinvesting of the industry's own profits, which were probably hardly more than $25 million at the beginning of the period. Outside capital, and in large quantities, had to be drawn into the industry.

Until the post–World War II years most American book publishers were small, independent, personally or family owned companies. The owners themselves lacked the capital for rapid expansion. Instead, new capital came from outside the industry in a variety of ways. One was to transform the privately owned companies into publicly held corporations that could issue stock to draw outside investment. The rapid expansion that made this necessary also made it possible, and for the first time the industry began to seem attractive to investors. Many major publishers did "go public" during the latter 1950s and 1960s.

A second source of capital came from magazine publishers. While book publishing must devour cash in order to expand, magazine publishing is a great cash generator because subscriptions are paid for in advance and cash is collected promptly from newsstand sales and advertisers. McGraw-Hill, at the time primarily a magazine publisher, used the cash flow generated by *Business Week* and its other journals to finance a rapid expansion of its book business until it became for a time probably the largest book publisher in the country. Time, Inc. became the proprietor of Little-Brown and Book-of-the-Month Club, in addition to starting its own line of books. Dell, a publisher of comic books and pulp magazines, became an important factor in mass-market book publishing.

As the market for textbooks and other educational materials grew with almost explosive rapidity, electronics companies, convinced that their technology could transform education, entered book publishing in order to acquire the pedagogical experience and contacts of textbook publishers. Xerox, Raytheon, General Electric, IBM, RCA, CBS, and ABC all acquired major stakes in educational publishing. A period of disillusion ultimately followed. The marriage of electronic technology and traditional textbook publishing did not at the time generate the hoped for flood of triumphant new educational materials, and most of the electronic companies in time withdrew from or minimized their book publishing endeavors, but not before having invested large sums in the industry's growth.

In the 1980s two convictions drove the further growth and restructuring of book publishers. One was that very large size was essential and that small publishers were not viable. Firms like Atheneum and Scribners found it necessary or expedient to merge, ending in their cases as part of the Macmillan empire. The other conviction was that publishing had become a global enterprise, both in geographic terms and in relations among the various media. The ideal company was thought to be large, international, and multimedia. The print media continued to grow together: Companies rooted in magazine publishing, like Time, Inc. and McGraw-Hill, sustained and expanded their roles in book publishing, and newspaper publishers like the Newhouse chain and the Times-Mirror Company became important in the book world. Newhouse in particular not only acquired the *New Yorker* but also succeeded RCA and General Electric in the ownership of the enormous Random House-Knopf-Pantheon conglomerate.

Perhaps even more significant was the entry of film and cable interests into book publishing. Paramount became primarily a book publisher, and a major one, with the acquisition of Simon and Schuster and Prentice-Hall. Time, Inc. had become a major participant in the cable industry, and Warner, originally a film company, had become an important paperback book publisher. Their merger created a giant company in films, cable, hardback and paperback book publishing, and book clubs. The entertainment conglomerate MCA acquired Putnam's. The primary motivation for this type of merger or acquisition was the conviction that it was important to be able to exploit an author's work in all forms: original hardcover book, paperback reprint, book-club selection, and film for theater, cable, television, and VCR use. Hardcover houses without a paperback affiliate feared that they might be handicapped in selling reprint rights, and independent paperback houses feared that they might be handicapped in acquiring them. Similar attitudes existed with respect to book clubs.

Some publishers also became convinced of the importance of being able to control the international rights for books they produced. Some American publishers, notably McGraw-Hill, and also Harper, Wiley, Prentice-Hall, and others, had long had foreign subsidiaries to market their titles abroad. But as the international strength of the American economy declined, American publishing investments abroad tended to contract. Foreign publishers in turn saw in the opulent American market a very attractive area. Rupert Murdoch, the Australian turned American to qualify for the ownership of television licenses, acquired Harper and Row and, as Harper-Collins, merged it with a large British publisher he already controlled. Murdoch was also owner of the New York *Post,* of television stations in New York and Boston, and of a fledging television network. He had similar multimedia interests internationally. Robert Maxwell, a Czech émigré to Britain and a major British printer, newspaper publisher, and broadcaster, had already been active internationally as the owner of Pergamon, a worldwide publisher of scientific journals and monographs. Having failed in an effort to acquire Harcourt Brace Jovanovich, he bought control of Macmillan and further strengthened his position by merging its school textbook operations in a joint venture with those of McGraw-Hill and becoming thereby a leading figure in that sector of the industry. He capped his American role by acquiring the New York *Daily News,* whose daily circulation was enormous, only to have his entire empire collapse shortly thereafter in bankruptcy and come to a mysterious death himself. Paramount thereupon acquired Macmillan (other than its elementary and high school textbook business, taken over by McGraw-Hill). Viacom, primarily a cable television company, subsequently gained control of Paramount and all its publishing subsidiaries. Time-Warner, with all its publishing enterprises, merged with Ted Turner's broadcasting and movie concerns, leaving Turner the largest shareholder in Time-Warner. Other mergers, as of the Disney company with the American Broadcasting Company and of Westinghouse with the Columbia Broadcasting System, although less directly affecting print, contributed to a growing coalescence of the producers and distributors of entertainment and information into a few dominant companies. It was a development that justified increasing concern.

Meanwhile Bertelsmann, the major German publisher and book-club owner, acquired Doubleday and along with it Dell, the Literary Guild, and a host of smaller book clubs in addition to the previously Italian-owned Bantam Books. These acquisitions made Bertelsmann one of the largest if not the largest book publisher, both in the United States and in the world. Smaller investments by Canadian and Dutch publishers, the steady growth of Cambridge and Oxford University presses, and the indirect entry of the Japanese through the acquisition of MCA had resulted by the early 1990s in an extraordinarily large role for foreign book publishing interests in the United States.

It is impossible to say with any precision or assurance how these remarkable changes in the structure and ownership of publishing houses affected the character and quality of books published. Save in the few remaining small independent houses directly managed by their owners, like Farrar Straus and Norton, there would appear to be less opportunity for personal taste and judgment to determine publishing decisions than in earlier days. Of course, even the most fiercely independent publisher in the nostalgically remembered past was bound by the demands of profitability. It was as necessary for Henry Holt or Alfred Knopf or Cass Canfield to make money to stay in business as it is for managers of book departments of international conglomerates to make a profit to keep their jobs, and the old-timers were very good at it. Indeed, the demands on them may have been more unbending, for rarely did they have corporate reserves to call on to redeem a bad decision or make up for a disappointing year, as all the major publishers have today.

But the size and diversity of today's multimedia global companies make profitability the only practical criterion for decision. How, on the basis of intrinsic quality, can today's corporate executive at a company like Time-Warner decide whether to invest several million dollars in an advance to sign up a renowned public figure as an author, or to meet part of the cost of acquiring a local cable system, or to begin the launching of a new magazine, or to meet part of the budget of a new film? On what basis *can* that executive decide except on the basis of which investment is likely to prove most profitable? Such decisions at the corporate level are, of course, rarely made on the basis of individual titles. It is normally a question of deciding how much of the investment flow should go into each of the corporation's major areas of enterprise: how much to book publishing (and perhaps within that area, how much to textbooks, to trade books, or to children's books); how much to magazine publishing; how much to overseas programs; how much to film production; and how much to other areas and to general management. Although the head of each of these sectors may have wide freedom to decide what books, what magazines, and what films he or she will support, it is necessary to make every decision with a view to maximizing the profits of the division for which these executives are held accountable, for only thus can they protect the division and, indeed, their own jobs. The bottom line is likely to be an iron criterion of employment and promotion in a large corporate setting.

The mass media make possible the assembling of massive audiences. Tens of millions may watch the television broadcast of a film or a sporting event; millions may buy the hardcover edition of a popular novel; tens of millions may buy a paperback reprint; and another audience of many tens of millions may see a filmed version. Few attain this command of the masses, but for the athletes, performers, and authors who do, wealth awaits unheard of when print stood on its own. The lure of the many millions of dollars in royalties for authors and in profits to publishers that may flow from a major bestseller unquestionably focuses the attention of publishers, especially of the larger houses, on the possibility of such coups to an even greater extent than in the past. And a different kind of book achieves superstardom: the novel of terror or suspense, the erotic romance, the celebrity's account of his or her life, or the psychological fix-it book. Literary merit or thoughtful content are rarely the characteristics that reach out to seize the available and highly profitable mass audiences. Being a successful editor in the acquisition of such books is a different occupation from the long nurturing of serious authors that earlier editors may have seen as their role.

The preoccupation with highly commercial bestsellers does not mean, however, that worthier books go unpublished or may not, in fact, sell quite well. An outpouring of tens of thousands of titles are now published annually that would not have reached print without the improved technological capacity of the industry. New literary contributions that cannot yet win the backing of major mainstream publishers find a home on the lists of the hundreds of small independent houses that venture along the frontiers of the industry. University presses flourish in increasing numbers and have taken over the publication of much poetry and of those scholarly writings addressed to a general public as well as the monographs they have long published. It is unlikely that any contribution seriously deserving the attention of the general public or of one of its specialized sectors will fail to find an actively sought publication.

Even though it is the audiovisual media that bring most of their news to Americans and perhaps do most to form the pictures in their minds of the world beyond their daily experience, the role of print remains powerful. Particularly is this true because the background of information and perceptions of those who speak to Americans through the audiovisual media is itself largely print-shapen. The tiering of information dissemination that was characteristic of the late eighteenth and early nineteenth centuries has not disappeared in the late twentieth. The content of news programs broadcast to the American people is shaped by persons whose own knowledge and perceptions are derived in large part from their reading. And the writers of serious newspaper dispatches work from knowledge derived in part from journals like *Foreign Affairs* and from thoughtful books.

Print thus survived the new media, one might say triumphantly, at least in its outpouring abundance. Never had so much printer's ink been pressed upon so much paper. Even to dispose of the daily flood of newspapers, magazines, and catalogs required recycling lines across the country to forestall the overflow of landfills with the product of the press. There remain problems, however. How fully and how broadly is this rich resource available to all the American people? How can we control its very abundance so that needed information can be found within its mass? How effectively can, and do, people generally make use of print? How do the print media affect the possession and location of power in our society?

Although the availability of books, scholarly and technical journals, and magazines was certainly far from perfect by the end of the 1980s, it had improved enormously in the postwar decades. In 1950 there were few more than 1,500 bookstores in the United States, most of them quite small and almost all of them in cities or reasonably large towns. By 1990 there were estimated to be more than eleven thousand bookstores, much larger on the average and serving smaller towns and suburban areas as well as cities. The fact that a great many of them were parts of large chains may have made them less personal, but it also made them more efficient and more able to handle special orders promptly. Computer controls had also improved the efficiency of the order services of both publishers and book wholesalers and the management of book clubs. The number of book clubs had multiplied, now appealing to almost every interest and each offering a much broader range of titles. Toll-free telephone numbers and the use of credit cards made it practical for publishers and specialized wholesale services to accept retail orders from the public. It was never so easy for anyone to buy any book he or she wanted and could afford.

Although newspaper circulation had declined, as had the number of major mass-market magazines, it was easy to subscribe to whatever one wished and could afford among the many thousands of magazines and to get at least local newspapers. The new technology made it possible to print identical magazines at a number of places across the country, speeding the delivery of news magazines in particular. The same technology enabled the *New York Times,* the *Wall Street Journal,* and *USA Today* to become national publications, printed at a variety of locations and available daily almost everywhere it the country.

Thus it was easier than it had ever been for those who could afford it to dip as they wished into the current flow of tens of thousands of magazine and newspaper issues and books issuing monthly from the press. A more severe test was how well we succeeded in capturing this flow into reservoirs where it could be preserved, organized, and made available as part of the public compendium of knowledge—in other words, how well the library system functioned.

In the immediate post–World War II years few institutions could truly be described as research libraries, and their holdings were relatively small by later standards. There was limited cooperation among them in terms of acquisition programs, cooperative cataloging efforts, interlibrary loans, or the availability of photocopies of material that could not be lent. The beginning of more active cooperation was induced by the evident need to work together in the postwar years to acquire materials unavailable throughout the war; to build resources of American libraries relating to areas of Eastern Europe, Asia, Africa, and Latin America that had been on the margins of American scholarly concern; and to preserve through microphotography endangered manuscripts and rare books. But in the late 1940s and 1950s such cooperation was only beginning.

Public libraries typically had only local support. Large cities generally had strong central libraries and branch libraries; smaller towns and cities had libraries but were less well served. With few exceptions, rural areas had no library service at all, and any that existed was minimal. There was a great geographic disparity in library services, with the South in particular having far less adequate library service, as it had less adequate schools and bookstores, than the rest of the country.

The following decades saw vigorous measures to increase the magnitude of library resources and make them more widely available. Most states undertook or greatly enlarged contributions to the support of local public libraries. College and university libraries were increased in number and size to accommodate the enormous influx of students already described and the outpouring of research materials. Federal support under the Library Services Act of 1958 and the Elementary and Secondary Education Act of 1965 encouraged a rapid growth of rural, small-town, and school libraries.

The 1960s saw a peaking of library support as part of Lyndon Johnson's educational programs. In 1966 he appointed a National Advisory Commission on Libraries, which after extensive hearings and the review of a number of specially commissioned studies submitted its final report in the closing months of the Johnson administration. It made a strong case for considering the varied library systems of the country—federal, state, and local, and school, university, research, and public—as an integral national resource essential to economic growth, informed democracy, and the individual self-realization of citizens. It recommended increased support at federal, state, and local levels, especially for measures that would encourage interlibrary cooperation in acquisitions, cataloging, bibliographical controls, and service to help libraries operate more effectively as a coordinated national system. A specific recommendation was for the creation of a National Commission for Libraries and Information Science that would be charged with planning and recommending such measures and reporting to the president, Congress, and the public on the status and needs of libraries and related information services.

Although legislation to create such a commission was enacted and signed by Richard Nixon, the dreams of the original Advisory Commission were largely dissipated by the indifference or hostility of the Nixon administration and most of its successors. Far from increasing federal support, the Nixon budget sought to eliminate entirely appropriations to implement the Library Services Act, a recommendation later followed in the Reagan and Bush budgets. Although Congress regularly restored funds, it was not at a level to keep pace with growing needs. State and local funding, which had increased dramatically in the 1960s and 1970s, leveled off or grew but slowly in the 1980s and was severely constricted in the recession of the early 1990s.

However, libraries helped themselves in the 1970s and 1980s by an increasing use of computer-based technology. Not only did major libraries change to on-line cataloging, with the controls over their collections embodied in databases searched on terminals rather than in card catalogs, but they also used the computer extensively to enlarge their cooperative endeavors. Several groups, of which the largest was OCLC, undertook to pool the cataloging of member libraries in central databases, from which bibliographic data and catalog entries could be provided to member libraries. Information on holdings could also be provided to facilitate interlibrary loans. OCLC files in a sense came to provide a constantly updated national union catalog. Computerized systems for acquisitions and circulation were also developed and made widely available.

In the early 1990s there remained many weaknesses and unevennesses in national library resources and constraints on their availability, particularly in outreach services to the large part of the population that rarely thought of the library as a means of meeting their often serious information needs. But a skilled and persistent inquirer could, more effectively than ever before, reach into collections throughout the country and much of the world and find and gain access to whatever information or documents he or she might need.

Print no longer had the unique role of earlier times, but its power within its own realm had never been so great.

—13—

Now and into the Future

The human capacity to communicate has grown with explosive force in the last half-century. We are flooded with print. The television screen in the United States now offers a choice not only among four networks and a few independent stations but also among a hundred or more cable channels and the choice of many thousands of videocassettes. Even in the poorer homes in developing lands, television aerials draw in programs from across the world. Databases ensconced on hard discs record the details of trillions of transactions and the lives of hundreds of millions of individuals. Thanks to satellites, all these untold quintillions of bytes of data can surge back and forth across the world with the speed of light, as can the instant news photography of CNN and the private telephone calls of individuals. Reality is pressed upon our eyes and ears through a panoply of varying media, bombarding us with pictures and speech and music and printed words and symbols. Never has such a flood of information poured out so abundantly to so many. So much of our time is spent in receiving the pictured world that we have limited time for embracing reality itself.

The daily flow of communication is enormous, far above the capacity of any individual, indeed, of society itself to absorb as it passes. It is captured for preservation in networks of libraries, gargantuan linked reservoirs with elaborate computerized systems of control, and in computer-readable databanks capable of maintaining uncountable trillions of bytes of data in organized and accessible form.

This revolutionary capacity to communicate, to store, and to recall information in quantities and with speeds never before conceived has come with unparalleled suddenness. Speech evolved over hundreds of thousands of years, and, even after a capacity to speak with a fully formed grammar and syntax was achieved, tens of thousands more years passed before our ancestors began to write down their words. Thousands more years went by before we could print what was written. Printing remained our sole means of public communication for more than four centuries until the telegraph, the telephone, and late nineteenth and early twentieth century audiovisual inventions began to find their place. And then decade by decade, almost year by year, the new technologies came tumbling one after the other—radio, motion pictures, television, the computer, and satellite communication, interconnecting among themselves and with one technology reinforcing another. The changing communications technology in turn has hurried along accompanying social change, one pressing the other, so that there is no time to pause, take account, and integrate the kinds of communications systems that are evolving with the kind of society we seek.

One concomitant of the power of communication is the power of society itself. God forebodingly saw that the power of words would make nothing impossible that humanity might propose to do, and that prophecy has been abundantly fulfilled as the empowerment of words by our computerized instruments and stored banks of knowledge enable us to look back to the beginning of time, outward toward the billions-of-light-years distant margins of the universe, and inward toward the infinitesimal particles within the atoms and to send human beings to the moon and satellites into the infinity beyond the solar system. The two go hand in hand. Without advancing science, the new communications technology could not be created; without computerized and satellite-borne communication, contemporary science would be impossible.

The capacity to convey and to accumulate knowledge, to record and share experience would seem to have approached a consummation in which every event in the surrounding reality can be captured—not only every heard sound and seen image but also events imperceptible to the unaided eye and ear, from the tiny fluctuations in light traveling over billions of years from the outer reaches of the universe to the even tinier changes in subatomic structure. Just as words first enabled us to seize aspects of surrounding reality and use them as elements of a constructed and usable image of that reality, our technologically enhanced capacity enables us to seize previously imperceptible aspects and do so in a previously inconceivable depth and precision and hence to construct a vaster and more precisely usable image of reality.

If when we add to this power the power of almost instant and universal communication and of almost limitless accumulation, where lie our problems?

A major problem is simply one of magnitude. The sheer quantity of the public compendium now assembled overflows our capacity to house and organize it. In part this is the consequence of the rapid growth in print, with the outpouring of tens of thousands of books and hundreds of thousands of serials and the far greater outpouring of materials produced by new near-print processes far outrunning our capacity to organize and catalog or even to store them. It is in part the flood of recorded audiovisual materials: motion pictures, still photographs, records, compact discs, audiocassettes, and tapes of television programs, which we have never learned to preserve and organize even as well as we do printed materials. But in even greater part it is due to the whole new order of magnitude of stored data embodied in digital form in computer discs. The sheer recorded volume of knowledge possessed by society has multiplied many times over in the present generation alone. We are in danger of being so choked with knowledge that we cannot effectively use it.

This abundance is increasingly unevenly shared, and so is the power that grows from it. This is our second and even greater problem. It is true that broadcasting has been a great equalizing force, allowing almost everyone, at least in the industrialized states, to hear and see events and persons thought newsworthy. And it is true that access to the world of computers and the data they control is being greatly broadened. But the gulf is deep and widening between the Western powers with integrated information and communications systems and those developing countries—and even the former communist countries of Eastern Europe—that lack the mastery over the stores of knowledge and the capacity to communicate on which the strength of advanced powers is based. The same evening news program may show an American astronaut capturing an off-course satellite and bringing it to a space shuttle for repair and a village of starving Somali peasants, dull-eyed above their swollen bellies and shrunken limbs. The reality behind those images represents the shattering of the hopes of an earlier day to bring the developing countries into the circle of shared abundance the new technology provides. And it defines a problem far more formidable than we dreamed in the early days of foreign aid programs.

Even within the advanced Western powers, the contrast in power and wealth between the corporations and individuals trained and equipped to use the information resources of those societies and the marginally literate poor tears at the social fabric and is perhaps the greatest threat to the public welfare. This is particularly true of the United States, where the information resources are the most powerful and those lacking access to them probably among the most numerous.

Not only the distribution of power and wealth within societies but also the very structure of societies has been deeply affected by the new technology of the media, particularly by satellite transmission of television programs and computerized data flows. Print had contributed greatly to the power and the separateness of nation states. It provided an effective medium for the internal dissemination of information essential to government in the form of laws, regulations, judicial decisions, and orders of the central government. It provided the information base for the administration of bureaucracies and of large industrial corporations. It permitted the standardization of national languages, surmounting the divisive force of medieval regional dialects. At the same time, because the dissemination of print required the controllable physical transportation of artifacts, dissident and "subversive" publications could be stopped at the border. The cross-border flow of even entirely welcome publications was very small compared to the distribution of publications within each nation itself, thus emphasizing national distinctiveness.

In contrast, the satellite transmission of television programs leaps over national boundaries and, when received by dishes, circumvents control over national networks. The elaborate programs proposed by some European powers for controls over transborder flows of digital data among banks, airlines, travel agencies, multinational corporations, and other businesses, which might have been feasible so long as they were transmitted by terrestrial telephone lines under national control, were simply overwhelmed by satellite transmission. Automatic digital switching of telephone calls further diminished the possibility of effective control, even over those transmissions that continued to use the national telephone network. The result has been the near obliteration of national information boundaries and the dilution of national sovereignty insofar as control of information or of multinational economic activity are concerned.

At the same time, the availability of inexpensive means of reproducing audiovisual materials in cassettes and of texts produced on word processors and printers in small editions has made it possible for cultural and ethnic minorities to create informational and cultural enclaves.

These dual trends have helped lead to the dissolution of the Soviet and Yugoslav states and to ethnic tensions within the former Soviet republics and in many other states as well. Other states whose territorial integrity has remained uncompromised, like England or France, have been weakened in the maintenance of national cultural inheritances as a largely American pop culture has swept across the world and a common theme of liberal individualistic capitalism become prevalent everywhere. The collapse of the Soviet Union may have been due in considerable part to the availability throughout its territory of televised images of the free-and-easy affluence of the West.

And business has become internationalized just as have culture and economics. Investments in the billions of dollars flow from country to country at the touch of a computer keyboard, free of any effective national control. Multinational corporations whose owners, managers, factories, offices, employees, and markets are scattered across the globe are bound together by computer consoles and are beyond the control of any one state. No national state can any longer pursue an autarchic policy with respect to interest rates or monetary or fiscal policy, or types of regulation that may affect the competitive strength of its industries in a fluid market that knows few national boundaries.

We have no governmental entities whose structure and scope correspond to the structure and scope of today's information flows or of the cultural and economic realms those flows support, and this is another of the great problems presented by the radical information developments of our time.

Those developments have also created problems by their effects on the internal structure of our societies. Every new information medium that enhances the power of a central source of information to communicate directly with individual recipients weakens the role of intermediate authorities. Print strengthened central royal and papal authority against feudal and ecclesiastical hierarchies. Mass print in the nineteenth and early twentieth centuries made possible the mobilization of such causes as abolition, temperance, Populism, and women's rights by pamphlets and articles communicating directly with individuals throughout the country. New religious denominations could grow from publications like the Book of Mormon and *Science and Health, with Key to the Scriptures* and the overflowing abundance of evangelical pamphlets. Political parties could seek a mass base through a flood of printed material.

But much communication continued to take place through smaller traditional structures and face to face. Religious messages continued to be conveyed primarily through sermons within individual congregations, and the hierarchy of the principal denominations had great influence on the content of doctrine. The face-to-face contact of district leaders and local politicians with individual voters was the principal means of campaigning. Basic values and perceptions were implanted within families and communities by personal contact.

The newer media, particularly television, have made it possible, far more than print did, to bypass these traditional intermediate structures. Television evangelists can reach millions of followers directly, drawing worshipers and funds from the established churches. Political candidates can address the voters and seek campaign contributions directly, releasing them from reliance on the party organization. Television diminishes family and community in providing the matrix for the development of beliefs and values. Although attendance at plays, concerts, and sports events has been sustained and has even increased, we now typically experience them not in association with others and in the actual presence of performers, but alone at home before a television screen or sound system.

The consequences for politics have been particularly striking and go far beyond the weakening of traditional party organizations. For national and statewide elections, television has become the dominant and essential campaign tool, as it has in many congressional districts outside major metropolitan areas. However, the purchase of substantial blocks of time up to half an hour, which would enable candidates to state and explain their positions on important issues, is expensive, and candidates now avoid it. Instead, they fall into the format not of substantive programming but of commercial announcements of ten to thirty seconds, bought to advertise a candidate just as they are bought to advertise toothpaste or beer. Because thirty seconds allows no time for any significant presentation of the substance of a candidate's program, there has been a growing tendency to use these brief spots for negative attacks on opponents. One result has been that in the relative absence of meaningful discussion of real issues and in the presence of a flood of brief, skillful attacks discrediting each candidate public trust in political leaders and the political process has been eroded and often replaced by a "curse on both your houses" negativism and apathy.

Such television campaigns are extremely expensive, and much of the time of elected politicians must be devoted to continuous fund-raising, not only during but also between campaigns. Only the well-to-do are likely sources of contributions, and the need to appeal to them draws the votes and programs of political leaders toward the service of their interests. The existence of political action committees, which can aggregate the funds of those having special interests and place them strategically in the hands of powerfully placed members of Congress, gives those interests a further and disproportionate voice. Hence television, which might have been an informing and democratizing political force, has instead become a corrupting and disillusioning one, contributing to a cynical political apathy.

These problems of overwhelming flows, of inequalities of access to information and to the power it gives, and of structural change are compounded by problems of control over input into the mass media. The problems of access are not only problems of recipients who may confront such barriers as inadequate literacy, poor schools and libraries, and the inability to purchase materials. They are also problems of those who have positions to advocate or information to give and yet lack opportunity to present them. In a society dominated by mass media, even though people may be completely free to speak their minds, if they cannot speak it in the columns of the widely read press or on a broadcasting network they are in large degree silenced. The fact that enormous audiences, measured in the millions or tens of millions, are gathered by a limited number of national publications, press services, and networks gives great power to the gatekeepers of those points of access to the people. Not everyone can have access to the columns and microphones of the media without creating a meaningless babel. The traditional Miltonian view that all voices should be allowed to speak so that the truth can be winnowed from debate is impossible when the structure of the media permits only selected voices to be effectively heard.

Society has a great stake in who exercises that gatekeeper function and by what standards of fairness. In most countries the fear that private interests might control the process has led that concern to be expressed by keeping the gatekeeper function in governmental hands. Except in the United States, both radio and television broadcasting was initially made the responsibility of government ministries or, as in Great Britain, of autonomous public bodies like the British Broadcasting Corporation, although private networks have now been admitted into competition almost everywhere. In the United States governmental control was more feared than private, and broadcasting facilities, like the press and film, were kept in private hands and jealously guarded from government censorship. Broadcasters were, however, constrained by legislation and federal regulation to deal "fairly" with controversial issues and equally with candidates for office, creating an ambiguous area of governmental influence. Otherwise policy in the United States has generally been directed toward attempting to assure a diversity of competing gatekeepers through encouraging new technologies such as cable television and VCRs, through antitrust actions, and through regulations affecting ownership of broadcast facilities and the power of networks.

The American system has probably worked better than might have been feared. The controllers of the media have been less prone than were the newspaper magnates of the preceding century to use their power to press their own political aims. Professional commitments to objectivity have tended to govern reporters and newscasters, and the owners of the media have been more concerned to maximize their profits than to propagandize their views. And to maximize their profits they need sedulously to give their audiences what they want and to win their confidence by avoiding obvious biases in their presentations.

One need not, however, imagine a conspiracy of media owners to slant and control their programming in any sinister way to have concerns about the gatekeeping function. Because those who control the media have established wealth and position and because they are moved by their business concerns to keep their programming within the broad mainstream of their audiences' prejudices, even the widening variety of sources tends to produce a stultifying and uniform blandness of output. A significant problem concerns how the gatekeepers of the information flow can be led to admit a wider representation of novel and not yet widely held views and cultural products and minority positions.

This problem is related to the fundamental one of who pays for the flow of information. One possibility, of course, is that producers or disseminators of information will pay because it serves their purposes to have the information or views made known. Examples are the publication by the federal government of pamphlets on agricultural practices or child care, broadcasts and publications of doctrinal material by religious bodies, campaign materials put out by candidates for public office, and press releases by publicity-seeking corporations. They may, like the child-care pamphlets, serve an important public interest, but it is the interest of the originator of the material that controls.

The opposite alternative is for the recipient to pay, as when one buys a book or a ticket to a play or concert or movie theater or rents a VCR cassette. Similarly, one meets at least part of the cost when one buys or subscribes to a magazine or newspaper. In such cases the forces of the market assure that the products will serve the tastes and interests of the public, or at least the part of the public with the means and disposition to buy.

A third alternative, now become perhaps the most important in our society, is for a third party, involved neither as the originator nor the recipient of the communication, to pay all of the cost (as in broadcasting) or the major part (as in the case of newspapers and most magazines). These are advertisers, who by supporting popular broadcasts or publications seek to draw together a receptive audience that will also receive persuasive information about the products and services they wish to sell. As when recipients pay directly, advertiser support assures that the information flow appeals to the public, but only to that part of the public the advertiser finds attractive as a market. Advertisers seek the affluent, and they generously support publications that appeal to them: prestigious newspapers such as the *New York Times* and magazines like the *New*

Yorker. They are less willing to support tabloid newspapers catering to a blue-collar readership; they would not be willing to give any support to a newspaper or magazine aimed solely at serving the interests and needs of the poor.

Advertisers are also interested in those segments of the public that constitute coherent markets for specific kinds of products. It is easy, for example, to gain advertising support for magazines serving frequent travelers or enthusiasts of tennis or golf or yachting; it is impossible to gain significant advertising support for publications serving the interests of poetry lovers or those concerned with philosophy or mathematics, for they are not in themselves a coherent market for an advertiser to exploit.

Advertising support of communication, for all its faults, has played a tremendously important and useful role. It has made the newspaper as we know it possible. It sustains television, including its news programs as well as entertainment. Magazines, including news magazines and journals of serious discussion, are in varying degrees heavily dependent on it, as are technical and professional journals. Two recent developments in marketing threaten that constructive role, however.

One is the increasing reliance on catalogs and other direct mailings and on point-of-sale displays as marketing instruments in lieu of published or broadcast advertising. This means that hundreds of millions of dollars in annual marketing expenditures no longer serve the additional social function of subsidizing communication through the press and broadcast media. This development has already forced the broadcasting networks to curtail their investments in news programming and is creating major problems for magazines and newspapers.

The shift to direct mail marketing has been brought about in part by favorable third-class mailing rates for catalogs and similar matter. But an even more important factor has been the increasing ability of the computer to identify potential customers for any type of product in highly specific terms, thus enabling the pinpointing of mailings. This same ability has encouraged the development of "niche" magazines, catering to narrowly limited audiences with special characteristics. The expansion of cable systems to 125 or more channels has similarly made possible highly specialized channels catering to specific audiences. Even when marketers continue to use advertising rather than more direct sales approaches, they increasingly find it efficient to place the ads in specialized magazines or cable channels, thus withdrawing support from general news and other programming that links the country together and subsidizing instead information flows serving the particular interests of hobbyists and other special groups.

Clearly, the interests of the consumer of information are best served when the consumer pays and buys just what he or she wants or needs. The problem is that most consumers are unable or unwilling to pay for much of the information and cultural material they need or want. Most broadcasting would disappear from the air if it all had to be paid for on a pay-per-view basis; few, if any, newspapers and popular magazines could be sustained if subscribers had to bear their entire cost.

A remedy, of course, is for government to become a surrogate for the recipients, paying the costs for them by providing free public schools and textbooks, heavily subsidized higher education, free public libraries, and public radio and television. Federal, state, and local governments have generously done so. However, even government payment for communication on behalf of the recipient leans heavily toward aiding those less rather than more in need. Public schools and public libraries are far more adequately supported in affluent than in poor neighborhoods; public broadcasting tends to serve the interests of the culturally sophisticated well-to-do more than those of the poor, partly because it is heavily dependent on corporate support from firms seeking the goodwill of the affluent and from affluent contributors themselves.

The information neediest and hence least empowered in our society are thus thrice penalized in dealing with the problem of who pays for information: they can ill afford to pay themselves, advertisers are reluctant to support media addressed to their needs, and even public subsidies go most to those who need them least.

The twentieth-century revolution in the media may have had other, more subtle effects. We tend to believe that reality is in fact as it is portrayed in the media through which we see it. In preliterate societies the only pictures of the universe were in the flickering memories of individuals, and our forebears believed that reality itself was like that, as changeable and as evanescent. Gods and humans changed form and identity; the boundary was indeterminate and shifting between animate and inanimate worlds, where sun and moon and planets were in some way gods and the mountains and forests were peopled with spirits. The whole universe was embodied in a little matrix of memory of the nearby in space and time. When writing brought a fixity of image, lying unchangeable in its orderly lines, independent of both writer and reader, it brought with it a conception of the universe itself as existing fixedly and unchangeably, obeying laws beyond human reach, and unalterable by human imagining. Printing, by making writing yet more fixed, unchanging through thousands of copies, and by greatly extending the penetration of society by written culture, gave further strength to this conception of a fixed and orderly universe: a universe to be dissected and analyzed by the use of words and arrayed in orderly patterns of meaning like the lines and paragraphs and pages of text. It was this conception of the universe that underlay the great scientific revolution of the seventeenth century and all the science since.

The audiovisual revolution of the present century, with its easy flow of sound and vision, created an image of reality as something to be passively experienced rather than something to be analyzed, described in words, and mastered. As the hours of the day exposed to television multiplied, one can only speculate as to the degree to which the perceptions of an oral society may have been restored and reality perceived again as contingent and unpredictable, beyond rational control.

Not only did immersion in television perhaps change our conception of the fundamental nature of reality, but it also provided perceptions about what day-to-day life is like, in a sort of pattern of linked mirrors. The more relaxed sexual mores of the 1960s and subsequent decades were reflected in television and cinema programming, creating a perception in viewers that this is the way life is, reflected in turn in the patterns of their own behavior. It is impossible to say to what degree the violence on the television screen reflects the violence on the streets and to what degree the slaughter on the streets makes real the images absorbed from the screen. But certainly the young are exposed for many hours a day to vivid pictures that profess to represent what life is like, and this exposure may well override their perceptions of the actual life about them. And we may well deplore that the pictures we may form in our minds from the life seen on television and cinema screens are so dominated by banality, violence, and moral irresponsibility.

George Orwell and others like him feared that before now the power of the new media would have been used to subdue us to an authoritarian will. What tends to have happened is quite different. The worst fear is that, stripped of the matrices of traditional structure in which our individual characters have been formed in the past, we may have been left in an anomic void, surrounded by screens filled with our own aimless reflections.

The autonomy at the precious center of our being may be further threatened by invasions of privacy. The flood of information now captured in the public compendium includes much that is, or ought to be, private: tax returns, medical records, census data, records of credit card and bank transactions, travel reservations, and many others. Efficiency in our complex society requires that these facts be capable of instant recall from the databanks in which they are recorded, and the capacity exists to combine records from various sources to provide an overwhelmingly detailed personal profile of any individual. Partial profiles are already used to pinpoint marketing efforts. Each of us may come to have a parallel disembodied existence as a collection of data assembled from computer memories under a common identification number, subject to manipulation like the digits themselves.

American communications policy was never better stated than in Thomas Jefferson's 1787 letter in which he said that the proper government of the American people must be based on the free flow of information through the "public papers," then the only public medium, and added, "but I should mean than every man should receive those papers and be capable of reading them." That tripartite program could define our goals today: to keep the flow of information free, to make it available to everyone, and to have the citizenry generally capable of using it.

But the problem is far more complex than in Jefferson's day. He could not have foreseen that the flow of communication would not be primarily through "public papers" produced on numerous privately owned printing presses, but through elaborate networks of media owned by large corporations with interests of their own; that agencies of government would be the sources of much of the most important information; that "availability" would mean not so much physical access as the ability to find what is wanted among the daily flood by which we are surrounded; and that mere literacy would be superseded by the possession of more complex skills and the use of expensive equipment as the precondition of access to information. Nor could Jefferson have conceived of our being so immersed in a flow of images that it becomes in many ways more important than the experiences of life itself in forming our perceptions of reality.

The nature of the almost overwhelming structure of communication that surrounds us is, of course, determined primarily by the characteristics of the technology that creates it and by the swirl of competitive economic forces. But public policies can play an important role in helping to assure that society's enormous new powers of communication are guided to serve the public interest. One of our great responsibilities is to determine what public policies are best designed to achieve those original Jeffersonian goals in the light of contemporary reality.

It must be recognized first of all that our communications system operates not under a single "communications policy," but within a matrix of varied policies, often apparently unrelated. These include not only the statutes, judicial decisions, and rulings of the Federal Communications Commission relating to matters within the FCC's jurisdiction but also legal provisions, constitutional, statutory, or regulatory, relating to such matters as freedom of the press, libel, postal rates, import duties on newsprint, antitrust concerns, taxation, employment discrimination, library support, and education.

Since the Carter administration many regulations in the fields of broadcasting and telecommunications have been abandoned, regulations that had been intended to assure the service of the public interest. There has been a return to the concept of the early Republic that the untrammeled operation of private interest, free of governmental censorship and restraint, will effectively serve the public interest in the case of communication as it is believed to do in that of the economy in general.

The deregulatory movement has included an extension of the term of broadcast licenses and a substantial abandonment of their meaningful review at the time of renewal. Licenses are increasingly thought of not as temporary permissions to use part of the public domain in consideration of reviewable commitments to serve the public interest, but rather as the private property of the licensees, which they are now free to buy or sell more or less as they will, subject to only minimal constraints. Limitations on cross-ownership of media, although retained, have been reduced. The fairness doctrine has been abandoned. There has been a marked retreat from efforts to require adequate children's programming and to free it from abuse of commercials. Cable television has been freed to compete as it can with over-the-air television and has been exempted from rate control by local regulatory bodies. (In 1992 legislation was enacted that reversed this trend, in part by allowing local franchising authorities to regain control over rates for "basic" cable, although not for added or premium services, and required cable systems to pay a royalty to licensed television stations for the right to retransmit their broadcasts.) The thrust of these changes is to recognize the great increase in the sources of programming available through television receivers from cable and through VCRs and to respond with reliance on this increased competition as an adequate protector of the public interest. The availability of cultural and other special programming through some cable services has also been used as a justification for efforts to reduce or eliminate federal support for public broadcasting.

There have been similar developments in the telecommunications field. The AT&T's monopoly over long-distance telephone service has been broken up, as has been its near monopoly over the manufacture and provision of equipment to be connected to the telephone network. The monopoly of the seven Bell and other operating companies over local service and their confinement to that service, both decreed in the judicial decision breaking up the AT&T, also seems to be in the process of erosion if not abandonment. The operating companies have been authorized to provide information services over their lines in competition with other information providers. Conversely, cable and other companies are being authorized to provide specialized local telephone and related services, initially primarily to large business users. Further deregulation seems certain.

There is much to commend in these changes. The criteria by which service to the public interest was to be measured in the review of applications for broadcast licenses or for their renewal were always, perhaps necessarily, rather vaguely and subjectively defined, and they were ineptly and inconsistently applied. A burdensome, indeed impossible, load of paperwork was imposed on both broadcasters and the FCC, with little measurable improvement in broadcast performance. The making of judgments as to the quality and appropriateness of programs inevitably pressed toward conflict with the statute forbidding the FCC to censor broadcasts. The power of a politically appointed FCC to make life and death judgments on television stations on relatively subjective bases left broadcasters vulnerable to threatening political pressure, as the Nixon administration used on CBS. The fairness doctrine presented an even more dangerous threat, with a governmental commission reviewing not merely the general performance of a station, as in a license review, but its individual programs, with an authority to determine what was "fair" in the treatment of specific issues or persons. Such a governmental authority with respect to newspapers, magazines, or books would be thought intolerable and would be clearly unconstitutional. The move toward deregulation has come nearer to giving to broadcasts the constitutional freedoms that the press enjoys.

The deregulation of telephone service has lowered the cost of long distance service and enormously increased the variety and quality of services available to telephone users. Without this new freedom the marriage of telecommunications and computer technology that forms the basis of the advanced components of our economy would have been impossible.

On the other hand, the new broadcasting and technology policies, like the economic policies of the Reagan-Bush administrations generally, favor a Benthamite concern for individuals as the only reality, considering the public interest as merely the aggregation of private interests and weakening or dissolving bonds of community. In such a view the "public" interest is best defined and served by the expression in the marketplace of the sum of private interests. This has meant that all the media are freer to serve the specific interests of individuals who are able to enter the marketplace and meet the costs, but are relieved of responsibility to serve a more generally defined public interest or to meet the needs of those unable to enter the marketplace. Cable television, for example, greatly expands the offerings that may be enjoyed by those who are able to subscribe, but it diminishes the programs available on "free" television. The relaxation, indeed, near abandonment, of public service standards for broadcast licenses leaves marketplace decisions as almost the sole determinant of program decisions; inadequate support for public television leaves it responsive primarily to the interests of the affluent. Similarly, the enormous stores of computer-accessible information not otherwise available and the powerful instruments such as LEXIS, NEXUS, and DIALOG for improving access to printed materials are generally available only through subscription to rather expensive on-line services and require sophistication as well as money to use.

Recent public policy has not seriously addressed itself to serving either public interest concerns or individual information needs that are not met by the communications marketplace. In consequence the thirty-five million Americans living in poverty are largely excluded from the benefits of the communications revolution. Tens of millions of others with limited incomes and sophistication participate in them but meagerly. And long-term concerns of society not expressed in immediate individual interests are but glancingly attended.

These needs can be addressed only in part by federal broadcasting and telecommunications policy, but a dispassionate general review of those policies is needed.

It is politically impractical, and in any event it would probably be unwise, to restore a comparative evaluation of service to the public interest as the primary criterion for the granting and renewal of licenses to operate broadcasting stations. Even when such criteria were applied, their use was not successful in assuring a devotion to the public interest. But the use of the radio-frequency spectrum is still a public good of significant, often great, value. Many licenses to use specific wavelengths of that spectrum are valued in the market place at far more than $100 million. Yet they are now given for sole and monopolistic use to private broadcasters with almost no responsibility imposed to use them in the public interest and with no charge. If we had from the beginning offered licenses to the highest bidder for limited terms, renegotiated at current rates upon renewal, a large revenue would have been generated that could have been used to support public radio and television abundantly. Such a course is impractical now, because the sense of outright ownership of licenses has become deeply implanted. Licenses have been purchased at such high prices that now to recover and reissue them would be thought confiscatory. But it is perhaps not beyond the bounds of possibility that in lieu of the now substantially abandoned public interest requirements a modest and gradually increasing spectrum rental might be charged that would not unduly burden licensees and yet would still produce significant revenues for the support of public broadcasting. The auction of newly available spectrum sectors for such uses as cellular telephones has now been initiated, but the proceeds go into the general treasury.

Public broadcasting in turn needs to be more adequately supported and more clearly directed to the needs of the poor and less well educated, who are also the most information needy. The music, drama, dance, and other cultural programs offered on public television are an important national resource and should be enhanced and enlarged, not contracted. But there needs to be more time for children's programming, especially on Saturday mornings and in the early evening, now usually devoted to adult programming, and to instructional television, which now has to rely primarily on the use of tapes made from late-night broadcasts. There is a special need for lower-level adult educational programs addressed to basic literacy and numerical skills but with adult contexts that can be broadcast at hours convenient to the intended audiences. Simple informational programs, in Spanish or other languages when necessary, on civic, health, and employment matters, educational opportunities, tenants' rights, and similar matters important to the informationally needy could serve an especially important purpose. To provide these services without displacing existing important programming may well require, at least in larger cities, an additional, totally publicly supported station.

All consideration of communications technology and policy is now deeply affected, even dominated, by the question of whether the United States should create a universal switched optical-fiber network—an "information highway." The same question confronts or will confront all industrialized nations. The existence of such a network would vastly increase the power of our entire communications system. The quality of voice and musical transmissions would be greatly improved. Enormous masses of digital computer data could be transmitted at far higher speeds and lower costs. An almost unlimited number of cable channels and services, including interactive services, could be made available. The telecommunications basis would have been laid to enable users to call up any desired film, video, acoustical recording, data segment, or digitized book or other publication for display, printout, or downloading to disks at home or office. The entire resources of the whole audiovisual and computer revolutions, of the Gutenberg revolution, and of any future creations could be brought together through a single service.

But before this glorious dream of total communication can be realized, many other questions must be answered. Of what components shall the network be formed? Who will pay for and manage it? Who will have access to the network—will have, in homelier terms, off- and on-ramps to the information highway? What will that access cost and who will pay for it? Who will create and make available to the network the vast resources that are envisioned, and how will the cost of creating and making available those resources be met? A related question is how will the rights of copyright owners be defined and enforced with respect to the dissemination of materials through the network? How will First Amendment rights, freedom of information rights, and rights of privacy (which are sometimes in conflict) be protected? How will a heuristic apparatus be created that will enable a user of the network, standing before this unparalleled mass of information, to find the data or item or performance he or she seeks?

Many components of the envisioned network already exist. The telephone system reaches every office and institution and almost every home in the country with an extremely efficient switched network that has worldwide interconnection with the telephone networks of other countries. The long-distance trunk lines of this network are already largely of optical fiber, complemented by microwave transmission facilities. But the local networks reaching each subscriber are with very few exceptions of copper wire capable of carrying ordinary conversation and music at somewhat low fidelity, but only relatively slow transmission of data streams and very poor carriage of visual images. Even single television programs can be conveyed only by using somewhat difficult data-compression techniques.

Cable television penetrates more than 60 percent of homes and many businesses and institutions with twisted-wire connections capable of carrying up to a hundred or even more simultaneous television programs and, when used for that purpose, fairly rapid and massive data flows. But the cable network as it now exists has no switching capacity. That is, the communications flow is only outward, from a single source to individual recipients, not from the recipients back to the source or among the recipients. And for the most part cable networks are linked with each other and with the sources of their programming only by satellite transmission.

Wireless transmission complements the long-distance telephone cable network and links cable television systems with their sources. Through satellite retransmission it also provides the worldwide dissemination of television programs. It also remains the means of transmission of radio programs to their recipients and of television programs to recipients who are not cable subscribers or who have satellite dishes to enable them to receive cable programs directly. More recently, unwired transmission has been given new importance by its use in cellular telephone service.

A fundamental question is whether there will continue to be two wires into each home, a switched copper-wire line for ordinary telephone service and a high-speed twisted wire or optical cable for television and the promised riches of the information highway. Or will there be a single connection with the capacity of high-speed cable and the switching ability of the telephone network?

The contest to answer these questions has produced intense competition among the owners of the various potential components of the information highway. Almost all of the long-distance telephone, largely optical, network is owned by the three principal long-distance carriers: AT&T, MCI, and Sprint. The great majority of local telephone networks are owned by the seven "Baby Bells" created to take over the local services formerly provided by AT&T but divested by court order. Other local services are owned by such companies as GTE and, in the case of many small-town and rural services, by small local companies. Most cable television companies have now been acquired by one of a few enormous companies, such as Time-Warner, TCI, and Viacom. A few other companies, such as McCaw, have acquired a dominant position in the cellular telephone sector. Further mergers of communications giants are likely.

Legislation and court order have limited the competition of these various groups. The Baby Bells have been forbidden to offer long-distance service or to acquire cable systems in their service areas. AT&T has been forbidden to offer local service. Cable systems have been barred from competing in offering switched telephone service. But insofar as these limitations have been imposed by court order, principally in the cases involving the breakup of the AT&T system, they are being relaxed and will probably ultimately be removed. Congress also seems disposed to make competition freer in its proposals to rewrite the Federal Communications Act, but it has encountered insuperable difficulties over the years in its efforts to restate controversial communications policies by statute.

In the long run, the whole problem is likely to be redefined in unpredictable ways by further technological developments. But for the foreseeable future a good guess would be that homes will continue to have both a traditional telephone service and the option of a more or less traditional cable television connection, probably with a two-way capacity permitting an interactive relation to a perhaps greatly enhanced range of resources available on cable. A fiber-optic connection to the national information highway would be an option for individual homes, but an expensive and probably little used one. Universities, schools, libraries, research institutions, and larger governmental and business offices would probably have fiber-optic links to the information highway that would include among available resources the programming provided by cable television and would probably provide long-distance telephone service and service among heavily used local and internal telephone connections. Continued reliance on the switched copper-wire network is likely for ordinary local telephone service even among such users.

A major question, likely to be hotly debated over the next several years, is the relative roles of governments, federal and state, and of the various competing private interests in the construction and management of the information network. Almost certainly there will not be a single monolithic structure, but rather an assemblage of linked components based on augmented existing networks with some form of integrating superstructure. The component networks, much of which are already in place, will almost certainly be provided by private investment and will be privately owned and managed. Public subsidy, probably largely from state governments, may be necessary to provide the extension of the basic network into rural and other areas in which the volume of traffic is not likely to be large enough to attract unassisted private investment. Some states, such as Iowa and North Carolina, have already begun to address this problem.

The most essential role for the federal government may be to provide the integrating superstructure, as it has in the case of Internet. The connection to the information highway of individual universities, schools, libraries, and similar institutions and of individual businesses—the provision of the off- and on-ramps and of the required internal network—will no doubt remain the responsibility of the participating entities. But the great majority of the libraries and educational institutions are in any case public and will require major public funding in order to participate. Most of this funding, like the institutions themselves, will be state or local, but federal assistance in order to further a national policy of strengthening our educational and research resources will be needed. Public assistance to enable the participation of businesses as well, particularly of smaller businesses, may be sought as a means of enhancing our national economic competitiveness.

To make the benefits of the information highway broadly available to all should be one of the prime objectives of public policy. This does not mean, however, that every home must be fully connected. Few individuals in their personal lives will require individual access to the complete range of resources that could be afforded over a fully optical fiber network and access line. A marriage of existing telephone and cable facilities would provide an adequate structure to call up and receive conventional audio and video recordings and digitized printed material to the extent they are made available for transmission.

What *is* critically important is that all Americans should have access to institutions and services that are strengthened by having at their command the full resources that the information highway can provide. Their children's schools should have available all the educational resources the new technology can create—not merely privileged schools, but all schools. So should all community colleges as well as four-year colleges and universities. The doctors, hospitals, and health centers that serve all Americans, not merely the great research hospitals, should be able to draw on all the latest medical information and to have interactive communication with specialists. Legal aid attorneys, public defenders, and small-town lawyers, like the attorneys in corporate offices and major firms, need to have access to services like LEXIS and WESTLAW. Social service agencies of all kinds should be able to bring to the aid of their clients all the resources that information can provide. But none of this will happen unless there is a major commitment of public funding to assuring the broad availability of the resources provided by the information highway. Otherwise it will be primarily of service to major government agencies, large businesses, and well-funded institutions.

But such major public funding will be required not only to achieve a broad public participation in the benefits of the information highway. Funding is likely to be equally necessary to create and put into digitally transmissible form the vast cultural and informational resources we are promised the information highway will bring us. It has been projected that at least five hundred channels will be available, but what will there be to fill them? The mere availability of the channels will not in itself create the material to flow over them.

There already exists a resource in the many thousands of videotapes of films, including operas, ballets, and drama, and the even larger number of acoustical recordings of both classical and popular music, readings of poetry, and other materials. But even if the complex questions of rights can be resolved, an enormous effort will be required to place these resources in systems from which they can be called up in an interactive network.

The already commercially available videotapes and acoustical recordings are, however, only a fragment of the audiovisual resources that might be made available. These might include, for example, the documentary footage in the National Archives and other institutions, the tapes of network news broadcasts at Vanderbilt University and elsewhere, and the innumerable slides of works of art in museums. It would be an even vaster job to translate these into on-line availability.

The glowing prophecies of the wonders of the new world of the information highway have suggested that it will be possible for users to sit at their computers and call up any book or journal article they may want to consult. This would be within the realm of technological possibility, but only if the material sought has been "digitized" by translation into binary code and fed into the network. So far, this has been done for only a tiny fragment of available printed material. Most of what has been done, like the magazines and newspapers included in NEXUS and the legal material in LEXIS and WESTLAW, has been digitized and put on line not so much to make the texts available (in both these cases the texts are already widely available) as to make them searchable by heuristic techniques that will identify all the documents that contain a specified word or words in a defined relation to each other. Once thus identified, the documents may well then be consulted in their original printed form. A number of encyclopedias and other references works have been digitized and sold as CD-ROMs and placed on line in such services as Prodigy. Some rare research materials, such as the Dead Sea scrolls and their fragments and Greek epigraphs and papyri as well as the entire body of known classic Greek literature and much of Latin literature, have been digitized both to make them available and to facilitate searching them.

But these islands of digitized material emphasize the magnitude of the ocean of other printed material that surrounds them. The Library of Congress has under study an enormous project to digitize a significant portion of its holdings. To "photograph" a page digitally requires the recording of a large mass of "bits" in order to produce a facsimile image, but the labor costs are low because it can be accomplished by a single exposure. This technique is essential for maps and illustrations of all kinds. But it does not permit full-text searching and various kinds of textual analysis. To accomplish this, the text must be recorded letter by letter. Although this process consumes far fewer bits than facsimile reproduction, it is slower and much more expensive because a scanner adapted for the particular typeface must be used or, as is frequently the case, the text must be rekeyboarded.

The present cost of full-text digitizing is estimated to run from $2 to $6 a page, although that figure is likely to be substantially reduced as more efficient scanners come into use. But at best, to digitize a really major part of even the Library of Congress's unique or rare collections could easily run to hundreds of millions of dollars without including the millions of volumes of more recent materials. And even that figure would leave untouched the holdings of other research libraries throughout the country and of the National Archives and state archives.

A basic policy question concerns whether first priority should be given to digitizing actively used current material, primarily journal literature, with the dual objective of making the material more easily searchable and making it possible to obtain a copy of a desired article without awaiting the slow process of mail delivery of photocopies or whether that priority should be given to unique or rare materials not otherwise accessible without a visit to their repository.

The digitizing of current and recent journals does not depend on any particular depository. Progress in this area has come, and no doubt will continue to come, from user disciplines. A substantial part of journal literature has already been made searchable by key words in titles or abstracts, and significant beginnings have been made toward full text recordings. Moreover, because the texts of almost all journals are already digitized at one stage of the printing process, with appropriate administrative arrangements they could be captured for the envisioned journal database accessible through the information highway. A few journals now, and no doubt many more in the future, may be "published" only by having a machine-readable text embodied in such a database. The road to a comprehensive on-line accessibility of journal literature lies through the cooperation of journal publishers and the organizations of the disciplines they serve. To achieve that cooperation will require the development of appropriate copyright standards and procedures that will achieve the replacement of lost subscription revenue. It will also require a strong central planning and directing effort with major federal or foundation support.

The digitizing of manuscripts and other unique materials and of rare books obviously has to be programmed depository by depository. But to the extent that public or foundation funds are used to help meet the cost of such undertakings there will need to be cooperative overall planning to assign priorities to the various bodies of material to be put into the system. In many ways the policy problems resemble those that were faced in earlier projects to microfilm rare and unique materials to provide both for their preservation and availability. As in that case there will be need for a means for an institution to recover charges for the on-line use of its materials to help offset the cost of making them available in that form.

The whole question of copyright and payment for use will present intricate problems, not so much in the determination of rights as in means of recording and collecting payment for use that will not be unduly burdensome. The fundamental principles of copyright should be as applicable to use through the information highway as in the case of use through making printed or other copies: that is that there should be no use without the permission, based on appropriate payment, of the copyright proprietor. The placement of a digitized work in the system will need to be construed as permission to effect the transmission of the material subject to a stipulated payment. In addition there may need to be a recognition of a property right created by the investment in digitizing a document and placing it in the system.

A code embedded in the digitized version of a document could automatically record any transmission and accrue charges and credits, which could be centrally collected and billed as is done for photocopies by the Copyright Clearance Center. The procedures could be much simpler than those of the center because of the possibility of automatic recording of each use and user.

The overflowing abundance of the resources that could be made available through the information highway may create a major problem in finding any desired item. The elaboration of the complex Dewey Decimal classification system and the Library of Congress system was intended to make it possible to find physical objects at a defined place on the shelves, associated with items related in subject matter, but may be adapted to find cataloged items in a database. Library of Congress subject headings provide a blunt means of identifying whole works that relate to broad subject fields but are inadequate compared to the precise heuristic power of on-line searching of texts by key words, a system so powerful that it is likely to defeat itself by overwhelming the user by the volume of response to her or his queries. International standard book numbers (ISBNs) and international standard serial numbers (ISSNs) provide a precise means of identifying a recently published book or serial, and something similar may need to be developed for older material and unpublished documents. A truly major planning effort is needed that will draw on the long experience of the library profession and on experts in the extraordinary recording, encoding and heuristic powers of the new technology.

The questions with respect to a possible national universal fiber-optic network are so complex, and the contending interests so influential and determined, that it is highly likely that no consistent and comprehensive national policy decision will be made and embodied in legislation. The extent to which, and the directions in which, such a network is developed are likely to be determined primarily by market forces and by negotiated agreements among the various contending economic interests. The result is likely to be an economically efficient system avoiding wasted investment in unused or little-used services. It will be a system that serves well those users with the means and power to assert their interests in the marketplace.

But it is also likely to be a partial and select service that only to a limited degree realizes the revolutionary opportunity to open generously to all potential users the riches of the entire public compendium of information and cultural resources. It may in fact further widen the growing gulf between those who have the sophistication and means to benefit by the technological revolution in communications and those who do not.

Although the most dramatic of the policy questions confronting us relate to the telecommunications network, there are others of major importance. Some relate to the postal service, which until recent decades was the dominant communications conduit. The telephone has largely replaced the personal letter, at first locally and then in more distant communication as long-distance telephone service has become cheaper and more efficient. Parcel service has been almost entirely taken over by private carriers. Other private carriers and more recently telephonic facsimile services have essentially replaced special delivery, although the Postal Service has inaugurated its own express mail service. With so much of the profitable "cream" services in private hands, the enormous and expensive infrastructure of the postal service is devoted largely to the carriage of magazines and third-class mail consisting of catalogs and other direct sales material.

A result is that advertising media such as newspapers, magazines, and broadcasts that have supported the cost of more general communication are being replaced by other media, such as direct mail and telemarketing, that do not offer such support. Other nascent services, such as direct marketing via interactive cable, may further threaten the advertising support for newspapers, magazines, radio, and television, our basic media for public communication. Already all the advertising-supported media are suffering from this deprivation, and the drain is continuing. The whole role of the Postal Service will require examination, as electronic services further erode its use in billings, payments, and other financial transactions. Adjusting its rates to favor the editorial content of advertising-supported media and reduce the subsidy of direct mail services that do not contribute to the social cost of conveying information may be in order.

A much more important policy question involves the need for intermediary institutions to make the new technologically supported information realistically available to the general public. Few individuals have the equipment in terms of terminals and modems, the financial means, or the competence to draw from these resources the information that would be useful to them; nor is it practical for citizens generally to achieve those abilities in order to meet what may be only occasional needs. Many specialized intermediary institutions exist to provide that needed assistance. But the only *general* institution able to be the agent of ordinary citizens and enable them to share the new wealth of information is the library.

Most libraries, other than those in schools and smaller public libraries not linked to larger systems, are now linked to the basic bibliographical databases, both for internal purposes and for the benefit of their users. Through OCLC and similar tools they can identify titles and locations and arrange for interlibrary loans. By the use of DIALOG and many similar systems they can assemble lists of articles dealing with defined subjects. Some libraries can go farther and use NEXUS or similar services to make whole-text searches. Library staffs may make searches of these general types for users who lack the competence to make them themselves, although there are usually severe limits on the time given any one user. Or the staff may make a console and terminal available so the user is able to make searches individually. In either case, there is likely to be a line charge for searches of a distant database, although not usually of a CD-ROM in the institution's own collections.

Few libraries, however, other than those of large businesses, subscribe to any of the vast number of statistical and other factual databases or acquire them in the CD-ROM form in which they increasingly appear. The enormous informational resources contained in these materials are realistically available only to those who command the skills, equipment, and means to employ them—in general, only to businesses and professionals. The traditional function of libraries has been to preserve, organize, and make available information-bearing physical artifacts: books, journals, newspapers, and, more recently, films and acoustical recordings. They have been the instrument to unlock for the public the world-transforming resources in the compendium of print. We now need to elevate the function of libraries, and of their related structure of bibliographies, catalogs, and similar tools, so that they can unlock the resources of the now vastly enlarged compendium.

Most important of all is our need to transform education. Schools, at all levels, have always played a dual role in communication. They teach the skills—reading and writing, more effective speech, and the new technologies—by which we communicate. And they are in themselves the principal means by which the lore in the public compendium is communicated from one generation to another. How broadly and equitably the schools convey both communications skills and the substance of information itself is the principal determinant of how broadly and equitably our communications system operates, how broadly and equitably power is distributed in our society, and how inclusive is the cultural community that binds us together.

It was clear to the Founding Fathers of the American republic that a broad popular education opening popular access to knowledge was an essential prerequisite to successful popular government. Their vision outran their ability to provide such an education, and not until the nineteenth-century Industrial Revolution demanded literate skills of its workers and the suffrage was expanded to include all men was there a real commitment to at least elementary education for all, a commitment undertaken by all the Western industrialized nations.

Since that time there has been a continuing movement to raise the level of generally available education, so that in the United States by the 1920s a high school education, which in the nineteenth century was thought useful only for those intending to go on to college, came to be considered the norm and was offered to everyone at public expense. After World War II a college education came to be considered important for full participation in the society and appropriately available to all. The support of public universities was dramatically increased, and scholarships and loans were offered through the G.I. Bill and subsequent legislation to broaden the opportunities for enrollment.

These broader opportunities at all levels of education were, however, qualified by major limitations of class and race. In the southern states, where most American blacks lived, schools and colleges were segregated by race. Although courts had held that the segregated facilities must be equal, they were in fact gravely unequal, and funds per student provided the black schools were a small fraction of those provided the white schools. The differences were even more marked at the level of public colleges and universities. Black institutions did not have faculties or funds or laboratories or libraries at all comparable to those of white state universities in the same states. Even among the prestigious private institutions in the North, only rare and exceptional black students were able to gain entrance. Educational opportunities offered American Indians were, if anything, even poorer than those offered blacks.

Even among white children and youths, educational opportunities differed widely with geography and class. Schools in poor southern states were inferior to those in wealthier northern states. Those in towns and urban areas were generally much better than those in less-well-off rural areas. Well-to-do families, able to live in affluent suburbs with good public schools or to send their children to private schools and universities, could give them a nearly insuperable advantage. The better educated and more sophisticated, regardless of means, could make better choices for their children and send them to school better prepared. The educational system, taken as a whole, perhaps did almost as much to perpetuate class differences and discriminate in opportunities as it did to equalize them.

In the 1960s, during the administration of Lyndon Johnson, a serious effort at equalizing educational opportunity accompanied the civil rights and voting rights legislation intended to give blacks a more nearly equal access to political power. The Elementary and Secondary Education Act of 1965 directed substantial federal funding to poorer school districts and provided for a Head Start Program to help prepare children for school, particularly those who might not have adequate parental support in achieving language and reading-readiness skills. Acting on constitutional grounds, courts in many states ordered legislatures to provide state funding for schools in poorer counties in order more nearly to equalize educational opportunities. Among educational thinkers, more serious attention is being paid to the educational plight of inner-city children, whose usually poor schools mirror the poverty and disorder of their lives outside school. With the passage of the National Literacy Act of 1992, for the first time a concerted focus was achieved on the problem of the tens of millions of adults whose earlier schooling had left them with an inadequate ability to read and who were hence blocked from rewarding employment and effective sharing in political power. There were also large increases in federal and state appropriations for adult literacy training, but as yet there has been no more than a beginning of a solution to the problem.

The goal of educational equality, however, has been but indifferently pursued since the Johnson administration. Vietnam distracted attention, and the communitarian and egalitarian impulses of the earlier years were little felt in the Reagan and Bush administrations. Instead, the Bush administration pursued as its sovereign educational remedy a concept of "choice," which in fact was a subsidy of middle-class parents seeking to escape the public schools, too small to be helpful to the poor, and withdrawing financial and active parental support from the beleaguered public schools.

The enormous enhancement of social power that has come from the new communications technology of the 1990s has benefited primarily the already powerful. The gulf has rapidly widened between the advanced industrial powers and the developing nations. Even better-developed countries, like those of Latin America and Eastern Europe, although progressing slowly, are less and less able to match the powers of the West. Within the United States, the gap in income between the rich and the poor has widened markedly since the early 1980s, paralleling the gap in their participation or inability to participate in the benefits of the high-technology industries employing the new computer and telecommunications resources.

Over the centuries, indeed, the millennia, every new development in communications technology has had the ambivalent capacity to enlarge or diminish the breadth of opportunity to share in the power that knowledge brings. The first of the modern inventions, print, enlarged beyond all prior conception the amount of knowledge that could be embodied in the written word and the number of people who could share it. Particularly was this true after the late nineteenth century revolution in paper-making, typesetting, and printing presses had made printed material for the first time abundantly available to the general population of the advanced countries. The availability of print was associated both with the Enlightenment and the tiered democracy of the eighteenth century and with the mass democracy of the late nineteenth and twentieth centuries. But the granting of so much power to those who could use print diminished those who could not. To be illiterate in the Middle Ages or on the early nineteenth century American frontier did not bar a man or woman from stout equality with his or her fellows. But an illiterate in a contemporary advanced society is enchained by such a disability. The audiovisual revolution, and particularly television, by avoiding the demands of high-literacy skills and of physical access to books and other printed materials and by offering substantially the same fare to all, has done much to equalize access at least to a superficial flow of current information. But it invests great power in those who control access to broadcasting networks; we have seen in some countries how easily it can become an instrument of totalitarian domination.

We now face the same ambivalence in our newest communications revolution. It makes incomparably more information available with almost unbelievable ease and speed. Dramatically lessening cost and a much more general attainment of computer skills have combined greatly to widen the possibility of participation in the benefits of that revolution, but at the cost of a further gap between those who do and those who do not enjoy that possibility. To achieve an equitable flow of benefits from the new technology, it is not necessary that all should become sophisticated computer users. What is essential is that the structure of society should make the products of the new communications skills available to all.

Successive advances in communications technology and skills have given us an almost inconceivable power both to master and shape reality and share that capacity benignly throughout society. How we use that power and how broadly we share it will depend on our wisdom and our will.

Bibliography

Aitchison, Jean. *The Articulate Mammal: An Introduction to Psycholinguistics.* New York: McGraw-Hill, 1978.

Altick, Richard. *The English Common Reader: A Social History of the Mass Reading Public, 1800–1900.* Chicago: University of Chicago Press, 1963.

American Library Association, Commission on Freedom and Equality of Access to Information. *Report.* Chicago: American Library Association, 1986.

Bailyn, Bernard, and John B. Hench, eds. *The Press and the American Revolution.* Boston: Northeastern University Press, 1981.

Barnouw, Erik. *A History of Broadcasting in the United States.* 3 volumes. New York: Oxford University Press, 1966–70.

———. *Mass Communication: Television, Radio, Film, Press: The Media and Their Practice in the United States.* New York: Rinehart Publishing, 1956.

Barron, Jerome A. *Freedom of the Press for Whom? The Right of Access to the Mass Media.* Bloomington: Indiana University Press, 1973.

Berkman, Ronald, and Laura W. Kitch. *Politics in the Media Age.* New York: McGraw-Hill, 1986.

Berlanger, Terry. "Publishers and Writers in Eighteenth Century England." In *Books and Their Readers in Eighteenth-Century England,* ed. Isabel Rivers. Leicester: Leicester University Press, 1982.

Bickerton, Derek. *Language and Species.* Chicago: University of Chicago Press, 1990.

Blondheim, Menaham. *News over the Wires: The Telegraph and the Flow of Public Information in America, 1844–1897.* Cambridge: Harvard University Press, 1994.

Bogart, Leo. *The Age of Television: A Study of Viewing Habits and the Impact of Television on American Life.* New York: Frederick P. Ungar, 1972.

Branscomb, Anne Wells. *Who Owns Information? From Privacy to Public Access.* New York: Basic Books, 1994.

Brown, Richard D. *Knowledge Is Power: The Diffusion of Information in Early America, 1700–1865.* New York: Oxford University Press, 1989.

Cater, Douglass, and Richard Adler, eds. *Television as a Social Force: New Approaches to TV Criticism.* New York: Praeger Publishers, 1975.

———. *Television as a Cultural Force.* New York: Praeger Publishers, 1976.

Censer, Jack R., and Jeremy D. Popkin, eds. *Press and Politics in Pre-Revolutionary France.* Berkeley: University of California Press, 1987.

Choldin, Mariana Tax. *Russian Censorship of Western Ideas under the Tsars.* Durham: Duke University Press, 1985.

Cole, John Y., ed. *Books in Our Future: Perspectives and Programs.* Washington, D.C.: Library of Congress, 1987.

Commission on the Freedom of the Press. *The American Radio: A Report on the Broadcasting Industry in the United States.* Chicago: University of Chicago Press, 1947.

——. *A Free and Responsible Press: A General Report on Mass Communication: Newspapers, Radio, Motion Pictures, Magazines, and Books.* Chicago: University of Chicago Press, 1947.

——. *Freedom of the Movies: A Report on Self-Regulation by Ruth A. Inglis.* Chicago: University of Chicago Press, 1947.

——. *Freedom of the Press: A Framework of Principle by William Ernest Hocking.* Chicago: University of Chicago Press, 1947.

——. *Government and Mass Communication by Zechariah Chafee, Jr.* 2 volumes. Chicago: University of Chicago Press, 1947.

——. *Peoples Speaking to Peoples: A Report on International Mass Communication.* Chicago: University of Chicago Press, 1947.

Conant, Ralph W., ed. *The Public Library and the City.* Cambridge: MIT Press, 1965.

Corballis, Michael C. *The Lopsided Ape: Evolution of the Generative Mind.* New York: Oxford University Press, 1991.

Coser, Lewis A., Charles Kadushin, and Walter W. Powell. *Books: The Culture and Commerce of Publishing.* New York: Basic Books, 1982.

Czitron, Daniel J. *Media and the American Mind: From Morse to McLuhan.* Chapel Hill: University of North Carolina Press, 1982.

Darnton, Robert. *The Forbidden Best-Sellers of Pre-Revolutionary France.* New York: W. W. Norton, 1995.

——. "What Is the History of Books?" *Daedalus* 11 (Summer 1982): 65–85.

Darnton, Robert, and Daniel Roche, eds. *Revolution in Print: The Press in France, 1775–1800.* Berkeley: University of California Press, 1989.

Davidson, Philip. *Propaganda and the American Revolution, 1763–1783.* Chapel Hill: University of North Carolina Press, 1941.

Davis, Richard Beale. *A Colonial Southern Bookshelf: Reading in the Eighteenth Century.* Athens: University of Georgia Press, 1979.

Dennis, Everette E. *Reshaping the Media: Mass Communication in an Information Age.* Sage, 1989.

Dewart, Leslie. *Evolution and Consciousness: The Role of Speech in the Origin and Development of Human Nature.* Toronto: University of Toronto Press, 1989.

Diringer, David. *The Alphabet: A Key to the History of Mankind.* Second edition, revised. New York: Philosophical Library, 1953.

Eisenstein, Elizabeth L. *The Printing Process as an Agent of Change: Communication and Cultural Transformations in Early Modern Europe.* 2 volumes. New York: Cambridge University Press, 1979.

———. *The Printing Revolution in Early Modern Europe.* New York: Cambridge University Press, 1983.

Ernst, Morris Leopold. *The First Freedom.* New York: Macmillan, 1946.

Febvre, Lucien Paul Victor, and Henri-Jean Martin. *The Coming of the Book: The Impact of Printing, 1450–1800.* New edition. London: N.L.B., 1976.

Fielding, Raymond. *The American Newsreel, 1911–1967.* Norman: University of Oklahoma Press, 1972.

Gaur, Albertine. *A History of Writing.* New York: Charles Scribners, 1985.

Goodby, John Rankin, ed. *Literacy in Traditional Societies.* New York: Cambridge University Press, 1968.

Goodby, J., and I. Watt. "The Consequences of Literacy." *Comparative Studies in Society and History* 5 (1963): 305–45.

Graff, Harvey J., ed. *Literacy and Social Development in the West: A Reader.* New York: Cambridge University Press, 1982.

Graubard, Stephen, ed. *Reading in the 1980s.* New York: Bowker, 1983.

Greenberger, Martin, ed. *Electronic Publishing Plus: Media for a Technological Future.* White Plains: Knowledge Industry Publications, 1985.

Hackenberg, Michael, ed. *Getting the Books Out: Papers of the Chicago Conference on the Book in Nineteenth-Century America.* Washington, D.C.: Library of Congress, 1987.

Harris, William V. *Ancient Literacy.* Cambridge: Harvard University Press, 1989.

Havelock, Eric. *The Literate Revolution in Greece and Its Cultural Consequences.* Princeton: Princeton University Press, 1982.

———. *Preface to Plato.* Cambridge: Harvard University Press, 1963.

Homet, Roland S., Jr. *Politics, Cultures, and Communication: European vs. American Approaches to Communications Policymaking.* Aspen: Aspen Institute for Humanistic Studies, 1979.

Horowitz, Irving Louis. *Communicating Ideas: The Politics of Scholarly Publishing.* Second edition, expanded. New Brunswick: Transaction Publishers, 1991.

Joyce, William L., David D. Hall, Richard D. Brown, and John B. Hench, eds. *Printing and Society in Early America.* Worcester: American Antiquarian Society, 1983.

Kaestle, Carl, et al. *Literacy in the United States: Readers and Reading since 1880.* New Haven: Yale University Press, 1991.

Katsh, M. Ethan. *The Electronic Media and the Transformation of Law.* New York: Oxford University Press, 1989.

Kernan, Alvin. *Printing Technology, Letters, and Samuel Johnson.* Princeton: Princeton University Press, 1987.

Knight, Arthur. *The Liveliest Art: A Panoramic History of the Movies.* Revised edition. New York: Macmillan, 1978.

Lacy, Dan. "The Dissemination of Print." In *The Public Library and the City,* ed. Ralph W. Conant, 114–28. Cambridge: MIT Press, 1965.

———. *Freedom and Communications.* Urbana: University of Illinois Press, 1965.

———. "Liberty and Knowledge—Then and Now: 1776–1876–1976." In *Milestones to the Present,* ed. Harold Goldstein. Syracuse: Gaylord Professional Publications, 1978.

———. "Print, Television, Computers, and English." *ADE Bulletin,* no. 72 (Summer 1982): 34–38.

———. "Reading in an Audiovisual and Electronic Era." *Daedalus* 112 (Winter 1983): 117–28.

Lasswell, Harold D., Daniel Lerner, and Hans Speier, eds. *Propaganda and Communication in World History.* Honolulu: University of Hawaii Press, 1980.

Lehmann-Haupt, Hellmut. *The Book in America: A History of the Making and Selling of Books in the United States.* Second edition. New York: W. W. Bowker, 1951.

Levy, Leonard W., ed. *Freedom of the Press from Zenger to Jefferson: Early American Libertarian Theories.* Indianapolis: Bobbs-Merrill, 1966.

Madison, Charles A. *Book Publishing in America.* New York: McGraw-Hill, 1966.

Marker, Gary. *Publishing, Printing, and the Origins of Intellectual Life in Russia, 1700–1800.* Princeton: Princeton University Press, 1985.

Martin, Henri-Jean. *The History and Power of Writing.* Translated by Lydia G. Cochrane. Chicago: University of Chicago Press, 1994.

May, Lary. *Screening Out the Past: The Birth of Mass Culture and the Motion Picture Industry.* New York: Oxford University Press, 1980.

McCormick, John, and Mairi MacInnes, eds. *Versions of Censorship: An Anthology.* New York: Doubleday, 1962.

McLuhan, Marshall. *The Gutenberg Galaxy: The Making of Typographic Man.* Toronto: University of Toronto Press, 1962.

———. *Understanding Media: The Extensions of Man.* New York: McGraw-Hill, 1964.

McMurtrie, Douglas Crawford. *The Book: The Story of Printing and Bookmaking.* New York: Oxford University Press, 1943.

Meyers, Marvin, ed. *The Mind of the Founder: Sources of the Political Thought of James Madison.* Revised edition. Hanover: University Press of New England for Brandeis University Press, 1981.

Miller, Mark Crispin. *Boxed In: The Culture of TV.* Evanston: Northwestern University Press, 1988.

Milton, John. *Areopagitica.* In *Versions of Censorship: An Anthology,* ed. John McCormick and Marie MacInness, 8–34. New York: Doubleday, 1962.

Moran, James. *Printing Presses: History and Development from the Fifteenth Century to Modern Times.* Berkeley: University of California Press, 1973.

Mott, Frank Luther. *American Journalism: A History, 1690–1960.* Third edition. New York: Macmillan, 1962.

————. *A History of American Magazines*. 5 volumes. Cambridge: Harvard University Press, 1938–68.

Newberg, Paula R., ed. *New Directions in Telecommunications Policy*. 2 volumes. Durham: Duke University Press, 1989.

Nye, Russel Blaine. *The Cultural Life of the New Nation, 1776–1830*. New York: Harper, 1960.

Olson, David R., Nancy Torrance, and Angela Hilyard, eds. *Literacy, Language, and Learning: The Nature and Consequences of Reading and Writing*. New York: Cambridge University Press, 1985.

Ong, Walter J. *Interfaces of the Word: Studies in the Evolution of Consciousness and Culture*. Ithaca: Cornell University Press, 1977.

————. *Orality and Literacy: The Technologizing of the Word*. London: Methuen, 1982.

Pattison, Robert. *On Literacy: The Politics of the Word from Homer to the Age of Rock*. New York: Oxford University Press, 1982.

Pearce, W. Barnett. *Communication and the Human Condition*. Carbondale: Southern Illinois University Press, 1989.

Peterson, Theodore. *Magazines in the Twentieth Century*. Urbana: University of Illinois Press, 1964.

Pinker, Steven. *The Language Instinct*. New York: William Morrow, 1994.

Pool, Ithiel da Sola. *Technologies of Freedom*. Cambridge: Harvard University Press, 1983.

Read, William H. *America's Mass Media Merchants: A Study of the Export of American Mass Media and Their Impact Abroad*. Baltimore: Johns Hopkins University Press, 1976.

Resnick, Daniel P. *Literacy in Historical Perspective*. Washington, D.C.: Library of Congress, 1983.

Schlesinger, Arthur M. *Prelude to Independence: The Newspaper War on Britain, 1764–1776*. New York: Knopf, 1958.

Schramm, Wilbur Lang. *The Process and Effects of Mass Communication*. Urbana: University of Illinois Press, 1955.

Schudson, Michael. *Discovering the News: A Social History of American Newspapers*. New York: Basic Books, 1978.

Sklar, Robert. *Movie-made America: A Cultural History of the American Movies*. New York: Random House, 1975.

Smith, Anthony. *Goodbye, Gutenberg: The Newspaper Revolution of the 1980s*. New York: Oxford University Press, 1980.

Smith, Jeffery A. *Printers and Press Freedom: The Ideology of Early American Journalism*. New York: Oxford University Press, 1988.

Steinberg, Sigfrid Henry. *Five Hundred Years of Printing*. New York: Penguin, 1974.

Tebbel, John William. *The American Magazine: A Compact History*. New York: Hawthorne, 1960.

————. *A History of Book Publishing in the United States*. 4 volumes. New York: W. W. Bowker, 1971–82.

Tebbel, John, and Sarah Miles Watts. *The Press and the Presidency: From George Washington to Ronald Reagan.* New York: Oxford University Press, 1985.

Warner, Michael. *Letters of the Republic: Publication and the Public Sphere in Eighteenth-Century America.* Cambridge: Harvard University Press, 1990.

Winterowd, W. Ross. *The Culture and Politics of Literacy.* New York: Oxford University Press, 1989.

Index

abolition movement, 61–62
Adams, John, 50, 52, 59
Adams, Samuel, 50
advertising: as a source of income for media, 68, 70, 140–41, 159–61
Alien Act, 54
alphabet, origins of, 10
American Anti-Slavery Society, 62
American Book Company, 67
American Broadcasting Company, 102, 146
American Economic Association, 74
American Economic Review, 69
American Historical Association, 74
American Historical Review, 69
American Library Association, 75
American Magazine, 140
American News Company, 67–68
American Revolution, 32, 46, 49–50, 55, 59
American Telephone and Telegraph Company, 80, 88, 106, 164, 169
Anderson, John, 100
Annapolis, Md., 48
Appleton publishing house, 66
Aquinas, Thomas, 20
Archimedes, 14
Areopagitica, 41–42
Aristotle, 14
Associated Press, 79, 191
Atheneum Books, 145
Atlantic Monthly, 62
audiovisual media: technology, 79–86; regulation of, 87–108; social consequences of, 109–24; and politics, 115–20; and religion, 121–22

Augsburg, Germany, 22
Aurignacian culture, 2

"Baby Bells," 169
Baker and Taylor, 67
Baltimore, Md., 63
Bamberg, Germany, 22
Bantam Books, 146
Barry, William T., 46
Basel, Switzerland, 22
Battle of Lexington, 50
Bell, Alexander Graham, 80, 88
Bellamy, Edward, 72
Beromunster, Switzerland, 22
Bertelsmann publishing house, 146
Bill of Right (British, 1689), 43
Bill of Rights, 51–52. *See also* First Amendment
Blackstone, William, 43, 51, 59
Blue Book, Federal Communications Commission, 95–96
Boccaccio, Giovanni, 20
Bok, Edward, 68
Book of Mormon, 77, 122, 156
Book-of-the-Month Club, 139–44
book publishing: in eighteenth century, 31, 33, 35; in nineteenth century, 66–68; in the audiovisual and electronic era, 139–40, 142–49
Boston, Mass., 47, 48, 50, 63
Boston Public Library, 75
Boston Tea Party, 49
Brady, Mathew, 81
British Broadcasting Corporation, 87
broadcasting networks, 83–84, 90, 101–2

Bryan, William Jennings, 77
Bush, George, 165, 178

Cable News Network, 152
cable television: 84–85; regulation of, 103–5
cable (transatlantic), 61, 79
Calvin, John, 20, 24, 37
Cambridge, Mass., 47
Cambridge University Press, 146
Canfield, Cass, 147
Carnegie, Andrew, 70
Carrington, Edward, 46
Carter, James Earl, Jr. (Jimmy), 164
censorship, 37–45, 53–55, 92–94, 97, 100
Charlemagne, 19
Charles I, 40
Charles II, 38, 42
Charleston, S.C., 48
Chaucer, Geoffrey, 20, 26
Chem Abstracts, 128, 137
Chemical Society of America, 74
Chicago, Ill., 63
Civil War (1642–49, England), 32, 40, 41
Civil War (1861–65, U.S.), 110
Coke, Edward, 59
Collier Publishing Company, 68
Collier's, 140
Cologne, Germany, 22
Columbia Broadcasting System, 90, 144, 146
Columbia University Library School, 75
Columbus, Christopher, 24
Commentaries on the Laws of England, 43
Common Sense, 49, 50, 59
The Commonwealth (1649–60), 8, 40, 42
comparative hearings, for broadcast licenses, 95–96
COMPUSTAT, 137
computer-assisted photocomposition, 127
computers, 125–38; and cataloging, 128; and indexing, 128; and power of societies, 130–31; and distribution of power, 132–33; and perception of re-
ality, 133–34; and access to information, 136–38; and book distribution, 149; and science, 153; and on-line information, 172–74
Comstock Act, 88
Comstock, Anthony, 72–92
Concord, battle of, 50
Congress of the Confederation, 56–58
Congress, power of, 51
Constitution of the United States, 51, 53–54, 58–59
Constitutional Convention, 51, 59
Continental Congress, 49, 56
Cooper, James Fenimore, 62
Copyright: Act of Anne (1709), 34; Act of 1870, 56; lack of protection for foreign authors, 67; Act of 1891, 72; and Library of Congress, 75; and cable television, 103–4; and videocassette recorders, 105; and information highway, 173–74
Copyright Clearance Center, 174
Copyright Tribunal, 104
Corporation for Public Broadcasting, 108
Coughlin, Fr. Charles Edward, 117
Council of Trent, 37
Crerar Library (Chicago), 75
cross-ownership of media, 101
Curtis Publishing Company, 68

Daily News (New York), 146
Dante Alighieri, 20, 26, 27
Daye, Stephen, 47
Debow's Review, 62, 69
Declaration of Independence, 49–50
Defoe, Daniel, 44
Delaware, 47, 48, 52
Delineator, 68
Dell Books, 144, 146
Dewey, Melville, 75
DIALOG, 137, 166, 176
Dickinson, John, 49, 50, 59
Diderot, Denis, 33
dime novels, 68
Dodd Mead publishing house, 66
Doubleday Publishing Company, 67, 146
Douglass, Frederick, 62
Dutton publishing house, 66

Edison, Thomas, 81
education: in ancient Greece, 12; under
   Charlemagne, 19; in early United
   States, 55–58; in industrial age, 73–
   74; use of audiovisual materials in,
   107–8; and information highway, 171;
   contemporary expansion, 177–78
educational television. *See* public broadcasting
Eisenhower, Dwight, 117
election of 1896, 76–77
electrical industries, 63–64
Elementary and Secondary Education
   Act of 1965, 143, 150, 178
Elizabeth I, 27, 38
Encyclopedie, 33

factory production, 63
fairness doctrine (FCC), 96, 97, 107
Farrar-Straus publishing house, 147
Federal Communications Act of 1934,
   100, 101, 106, 119, 169
Federal Communications Commission,
   84, 94–95, 99–107 passim, 163, 165
Federal Radio Act of 1927, 94–95, 100–
   101
Federal Radio Commission, 94–95, 97,
   100–103
Federalists, 52
The Federalist Papers, 51
Filigno, Italy, 22
First Amendment, 52–54, 91–92
FM radio, 90, 102, 106
foreign acquisition of American publish-
   ers, 145
Foreign Affairs, 148
Fourdrinier paper-making machines, 69
Fourteenth Amendment, 52
Franklin, Benjamin, 49
freedom of the press, 43, 52–55. *See also*
   censorship; First Amendment
French Revolution, 32, 38

Galileo Galilei, 24, 38
Garrison, William Lloyd, 62
General Electric Company, 144–45
Genesis, 1, 16
Geological Society of America, 74
George, Henry, 72

G.I. Bill of Rights, 123, 177
Glorious Revolution (1688), 32, 43, 44
Good Housekeeping, 141
Gospel of St. John, 1
Grotius, Hugo, 58, 59
GTE, 169
Gutenberg, Johannes, 21–22

Hamilton, Alexander, 59
Hanna, Mark, 76
Harcourt Brace Jovanovich, 146
Harper and Brothers, 62, 66, 67
Harper-Collins publishing house, 146
Harrington, James, 48, 51, 58
Hartford, Conn., 48
Harvey, William, 24
Head Start program, 178
Hearst, William Randolph, 70
Hemingway, Ernest, 80
Herodotus, 14
Henry VIII, 38,39
hieroglyphics, 9–10
Hill Publishing Company, 69
Hippocrates, 14
Hobbes, Thomas, 48
Hoe Press, 65
Holmes, Justice Oliver Wendell, 4
Holt, Henry, 147
Holt publishing house, 67
Home Box Office, 105
Homer, 16
Horton, Willie, 119
Houghton-Mifflin publishing house, 66
Hume, David, 51, 58

The Iliad, 7
indecent language, 104
indecent words in broadcasting, 97
Index of Prohibited Books, 37, 39, 45,
   88
information highway, 167–72
Innis, Harold, 11
Institute of Electrical Engineers, 74
International Business Machines Company, 144
Irving, Washington, 62

Jacksonianism, 61
Jay, John, 59

Jefferson, Thomas, 46–47, 52, 55, 57,
  59, 163
Johnson, Eldridge, 81
Johnson, Lyndon, 150, 178
Johnson, Nicholas, 96
Johnson, Samuel, 33–34
John Wiley and Sons, 62, 145

Kennedy-Nixon debates, 98
King, Martin Luther, Jr., 119
Kipling, Rudyard, 124
Knopf, Alfred A., 147
Knopf publishing house, 140
Knox, John, 37

Ladies Home Journal, 68, 141
law: effect of media on, 12, 15–16, 27
League of Women Voters, 98
Legion of Decency, 95
Leibniz, Gottfried Wilhelm von, 24
Leslie, Frank, 68
Letters of a Pennsylvania Farmer, 49
LEXIS, 128, 137, 166, 171–72
Liberator, 62
Liberty, 140
libraries: growth in late nineteenth cen-
  tury, 74–76; and encouragement of
  reading, 122; as providers of access to
  databases, 137–38, 175–76; and federal funding, 143, 149–51; as surrogates
  for public in the marketplace, 161;
  and digitizing of collections, 172–73
Library Journal, 75
Library of Congress: and Copyright Act
  of 1870, 75; as provider of catalog
  cards, 75, 128; digitizing of collections, 172
Library Service Act of 1958, 143, 150–
  51
Life, 140
Lincoln-Douglas debates, 98
linotype machines, 65
Lippincott publishing house, 66
literacy, 17–18, 28, 33, 72, 76, 178–79;
  in ancient Egypt, 11; in ancient
  Greece, 12–14; in ancient Rome, 13
Literary Guild, 139
literature: effect of media on, 7, 16–17,
  33–34, 68, 77–78, 146–48

Little Brown publishing house, 66, 144
Locke, John, 51, 58
Lollard movement, 19
Long, Huey, 117
Look, 140
Looking Backward, 72
Lorimer, George Horace, 68
Louis XIV, 27
Luther, Martin, 20, 25, 27, 37

Macmillan Publishing Co., 145, 146
Madison, James, 46, 54, 55, 58, 59
magazines, 66, 68–69, 140–41, 144, 149
Mainz, Germany, 21, 22
MARC tapes, 128
Marx, Karl, 67
Mary (Queen of England), 38, 39
Mason, George, 59
Massachusetts, 47, 57
Maxwell, Robert, 146
"McAndrew's Hymn," 124
McCall, James, 68
McCall Publishing Company, 68
McCarthy, Joseph, 88, 117
McClure, Sam, 68
McClurg company (book wholesalers),
  67
McGraw-Hill, 144, 145, 146
McGraw Publishing Co., 69
MCI, 169
McKinley, William, 77
MEDLINE, 128, 137
Metropolitan Opera, 113
Milton, John, 41–42, 48
Minow, Newton, 96
monotheism, 16, 25–26
monotype machine, 65
Montesquieu, Baron de, 51, 58
Morgan, J. P., 70
Morse, Jedidiah, 57
Morse, Samuel F. B., 79
motion picture industry code, 91–94
Motion Picture Producers and Distribu-
  tors Association, 45, 89, 92–94, 100
motion picture theaters, 83, 93, 140
motion pictures: technology of, 82–83,
  85; control and censorship of, 87–89,
  91–94, 104, 105; social consequences
  of, 114, 120

Murdoch, Rupert, 145
music: effect of media on, 34–35, 112–13, 123
Music Corporation of America, 145, 146
Mussolini, Benito, 117

National Advisory Commission on Libraries, 150–51
National Association of Broadcasters, 45, 96, 98, 100
National Broadcasting Company, 90, 101–2
National Commission for Libraries and Information Science, 150–51
National Defense Education Act of 1957, 107, 143
National Geographic, 114
National Literacy Act of 1992, 178
National Technical Information Service, 126
NBC Symphony, 113
Neanderthal man, 2
Neolithic cultures, 5
New Bern, N.C., 48
Newberry Library (Chicago), 75
New Haven, Conn., 48
Newhouse newspaper chain, 145
Newport, R.I., 48
newspapers: in late eighteenth century, 31, 36, 44; in seventeenth century, 40, 41; Jefferson on importance of, 46–47; in American colonial and Revolutionary period, 48–51; and abolitionist movement, 62; in late nineteenth century, 65–66, 69–71; and computers, 127; impact of television on, 141–42
Newton, Isaac, 24
New York City, 47, 48, 50, 63
New York (colony and state), 52, 57
New York Daily News, 70
New Yorker, 145, 159
New York Public Library, 75
New York Times, 141, 142, '149, 159
New York World, 55, 70
NEXUS, 128, 137, 156, 172, 176
Nixon, Richard, 117, 151
North American Review, 62, 68
North Carolina, 48, 170

North Star, 62
Northwest Ordinance, 56
Norton publishing house, 147
novels, 33–34, 67–68, 77
Nuremburg, Germany, 22

obscenity, 72, 92–94
OCLC, 128, 137, 151, 176
The Odyssey, 7
Office of Facts and Figures, 99
Office of War Information, 99
Otis, James, 50, 59
Ovid, 15
Oxford, England, 41
Oxford University Press, 146

Paine, Thomas, 49, 50, 59
Pantheon Books, 145
paper manufacturing, 65
papyrus, 12
Paramount Company, 145, 146
Paris, France, 22
Pennsylvania, 47, 52
Pennsylvania Evening Post, 48
Pergamon Press, 146
Petrarch, Francesco, 26
Philadelphia, Pa., 47, 48, 50, 63
phonographs, 81–82
photography: technology of, 81; social consequences of, 113–14
pictographic writing, 10
Plato, 14
poetry: in oral societies, 5, 7, 16; in early print societies, 33; in era of print dominance, 77–78
political conventions, 115–16
political sequences of media: in oral societies, 6–7; of writing, 10; of print, 26–28, 36, 50–51; of mass print, 76–77; of audiovisual media, 88; of television, 97–98, 117–20, 157; of radio, 117; of print and audiovisual media contrasted, 123–24, 161–62
Polynesian culture, 6
Portsmouth, N.H., 48
Post (New York), 146
Postal Telegraph Company, 88
power: in oral societies, 6; in scribal societies, 11, 13–14; in early days of print,

19, 29; in eighteenth century, 32; in
early American republic, 58–60; in era
of print dominance, 61–62; with audiovisual media, 118; in the computer
age, 131–33; at present and in the future, 154, 179–80
power of societies and media: in oral societies, 6–7; in scribal societies, 10–11,
13; in early days of print, 19, 29; in
era of mass printing, 78; in the computer age, 130–31; at present and in
future, 153
Prentice-Hall, 145
printing: invention and early development of, 21–30; in eighteenth century,
31–36; control and censorship of, 37–
45, 51–55; and founding of the United
States, 46–51; in era of mass printing,
61–78; and social structure, 122–24;
and computers, 127–29; and audiovisual ad electronic media, 139–51
progress: concept of, 6, 14, 19, 30
Progress and Poverty, 72
Providence, R.I., 48
public broadcasting, 102, 108, 166–67
public compendium: in oral societies, 5;
in scribal society, 14; with print, 22;
with the computer, 135–36
Pulitzer, Joseph, 54
Putnam's publishing house, 66, 145
Pythagoras, 14

radio: technology of, 83–84; regulation
of, 87–90, 94–102; social consequences of, 110–12
Radio Corporation of America, 144, 145
railroads, 62–63
Random House, 139, 145
Reagan, Ronald, 106, 107, 117, 178
reality, perceptions of: in oral societies,
3–4, 6; in scribal societies, 15; in print
societies, 109, 114–15; with audiovisual media, 109, 114–16; and computers, 133–34, 153
religion: in oral and early scribal societies, 16, 19–20; and printing, 25–27;
and mass printing, 77; and television,
121–22
Renaissance, 19, 23

Republicans (Jeffersonian), 52, 59
Rome, 22
Roosevelt, Franklin, 117
Roosevelt, Theodore, 55
rotary presses, 65

Saturday Evening Post, 140
Savage, J. W., 34
Savannah, Ga., 48
*Science and Health, with Key to the
Scriptures,* 77, 122, 156
Scribner's publishing house, 66, 145
Sedition Act, 53–54
seditious libel, 52–53, 55
Seville, Spain, 22
Sharpton, Al, 119
Shay's Rebellion, 46
Simon and Schuster, 139, 145
Southern Literary Messenger, 62, 68
Soviet Union, 131, 155
speech, 2–3, 4–5
Sprint (telephone company), 169
Stamp Act, 49
Star Chamber Court, 41
Stationers' Company, 39, 45, 93
Stevenson, Adlai, 117
St. Louis, Mo., 63
Strasbourg, Germany, 22
Subiaco, Italy, 22
Sun (New York), 70

Tea Act, 50
telecommunications: and computers,
127
telegraph: importance of to newspapers,
61; technology, 79; regulation of, 87–
88; social consequences of, 110
telephone: technology, 80; social consequences, 110–11
telephone systems: regulation, 87–89,
106
television: technology, 84–85; regulation
of, 87–90, 92, 94–108; social consequences, 114–23; and publishing,
140–42; and violence, 121
Television Code of the National Association of Broadcasters, 98–99
Thirty Years War, 40
Thucydides, 14, 15

Thurmond, Strom, 100
Time, 139
Time, Inc., 144–45
Time-Warner Company, 145–46, 169
Times-Mirror (Los Angeles), 141
Turner, Ted, 146
Two Treatises on Government, 58

UHF television, 90, 102, 106
Union List of Serials, 128
University of Georgia, 57
University of North Carolina, 57
University of Paris, 19
University of South Carolina, 57
University of Virginia, 57
urban growth, 63
USA Today, 148
U.S. postal service, 49, 56, 72, 175

Vail, Alfred, 79
Vail, Theodore, 80, 88
Van Nostrand publishing house, 66
Vattel, Emerich de, 59
Venice, Italy, 22
Vesalius, Andreas, 24
Viacom, 146, 169
videocassettes, 85, 105, 106
Viking Publishing Company, 139
Villon, Francois, 20
Virginia, 54, 57

Voltaire, 33
Vulgate Bible, 23

Waldo, Peter, 19
Wallace, Henry, 100
Wall Street Journal, 148
Washington, George, 57
Washington Post, 141
Webster, Noah, 51
Western Electric Company, 89
Western Union, 79, 88, 101
Westinghouse company, 146
WESTLAW, 171, 172
William and Mary (King and Queen of
   England), 43
William and Mary College, 57
Williams, Roger, 42
Williamsburg, Va., 48
Wilmington, N.C., 48
Wisconsin, 56
Women's Home Companion, 141
women's rights movement, 61
Wycliffe, John, 19

Xerox company, 144

Yugoslavia, 155

Zenger, Peter, 52
Zola, Emile, 67

D<small>AN</small> L<small>ACY</small> has had a long career embracing almost every aspect of communications and relevant public policy. He has been an instructor in history at the University of North Carolina, assistant national director of the Historical Records Survey, assistant archivist of the United States, deputy chief assistant Librarian of Congress, director of the Information Center Service in the Department of State responsible for overseas libraries and publishing, managing director of the American Book Publishers Council, and senior vice president of McGraw-Hill, Inc., with responsibilities relating to book and magazine publishing, broadcasting, computer information services, and copyright.

He was appointed by Lyndon Johnson to the National Advisory Commission on Libraries and Information Science and by Gerald Ford to the National Commission on New Technological Uses of Copyrighted Works. He served as chair of the American Library Association's Commission on Freedom and Equality of Access to Information. He has been an adjunct professor in the Graduate School of Library Service of Columbia University and served as founder and co-chair of Columbia's University Seminar on Communications and Society.

He has been a member of the boards of visitors of the Rutgers University Press, the Duke University Library, and the Duke University Press and is a member of the board of visitors of the School of Information and Library Science of the University of North Carolina. He was a founding director and vice president of the Business Council for Effective Literacy. He holds the Superior Service Medal of the Department of State and an honorary Litt.D. degree from the University of North Carolina.

Dan Lacy is the author of several books, including *Freedom of Communications, The Meaning of the American Revolution,* and *The White Use of Blacks in America.*